# TRANSFORMING RELIGIOUS EDUCATION

# TRANSFORMING RELIGIOUS EDUCATION

## Beliefs and Values under Scrutiny

*Brian Gates*

continuum

**Continuum International Publishing Group**

The Tower Building
11 York Road
SE1 7NX
London

80 Maiden Lane, Suite 704
New York,
NY 10038

www.continuumbooks.com

**British Library Cataloguing-in-Publication Data**
A catalogue record for this book is available from the British Library.

ISBN: 0826496830 (hardcover)

**Library of Congress Cataloging-in-Publication Data**
Gates, Brian.
Transforming religious education: beliefs and values under scrutiny / Brian Gates.
    p.cm,
ISBN–13: 978-0-8264-9683-6 (hardcover)
ISBN–10: 0-8264-9683-0 (hardcover)
1. Religious education. 2. Moral education. I. Title.

LC331. G35 2007
371.07- - dc22

Typeset by Fakenham Photosetting Limited, Fakenham, Norfolk
Printed and bound in Great Britain by Athenaeum Press Ltd., Gateshead, Tyne & Wear

# Contents

# Introduction

It was once a biblical prophet's hope that there would come a time when there would be no further need for Religious Education. Irrespective of social status everyone would know God in their hearts and respond accordingly (Jeremiah 31: 31–4). Whether in Israel or the wider world, the challenges facing citizens in the twenty-first century are scarcely evidence that this moment has yet been realized. On the contrary, the scale of estrangement which exists across societies has never been greater. Neither has the need for transformation, both personal and collective.

Religious Education can take many forms, but it is the thesis of this book that an approach which is exclusively cast in terms of one particular faith perspective is inadequate. No less inadequate is an approach which remains only as distanced observation looking at any and all religions externally. The logic of religion requires inter-religious encounter. It also requires internal and well as external human conversation An effective RE recognizes this. And it then takes on the capacity to be universally transformative.

Such judgements may strike some as exaggerated, or others as trite. Far better to concentrate on learning the basic skills of oral and written communication, as also now of information technology. Without these, people will lack the confidence and competence to function effectively in a global environment marked by heightened competition. Without such qualifications and expertise to generate significant income, there will be greater challenges ahead.

What puts a different complexion on the whole matter is the newly perceived realization of the potency of religion for division and hurt. In its name there is not only permission for, but incentive towards violence. This impression of religion has come even to be more predominant than its potency for revelation, personal illumination and social reconciliation. All too evidently its transforming powers can work for evil and not necessarily for the good.

Imagine a small child who does not yet understand the capacity of a ceramic hob to scald and burn as well as to warm and boil. That ignorance is potentially debilitating. The dangers in the first respect are no reason to justify inattention regarding the second. Children can learn to be discerning in the realms of kitchen or road safety and this enabling is far preferable to avoidance of modern culinary technology and transport.

Though greater complexities and intimacies are involved, it is no less true of religion. Avoidance and evasion are counter-productive, both in school and in lifelong learning. What is needed is understanding and discernment as characterized by becoming 'religiate'. There is a modest engine here with transformative energies for personal, moral and spiritual vitality, individual and global health.

Regarding their sources, this collection of articles and papers spans a thirty-year period. They reflect a professional lifetime of involvement with Religious Education. The inspiration for that involvement has derived from many quarters and continues to do so: from positive experiences of RE as a pupil in primary and secondary schools and as a student at universities in England and the US; from teacher colleagues in schools and higher education; from boys and girls interviewed, and students taught; and, since its inception, from colleagues on the RE Council of England and Wales and its Executive. Delightfully, there is always more to understand and be challenged by.

*Note.* The date at the end of each chapter is the year the article or paper was published or presented. It was deemed unnecessary to update the material, although a few essential minor amendments have been made, either for factual amplification or to comply with the present publisher's house style.

# PART ONE

# Rationale and curriculum content

Religious Education has been a priority throughout the history of human civilizations. It has taken a variety of forms. There has been informal exposure to parental beliefs and values in the home, as well as to those of the wider village, town and national community. This is still the case. There has also been more explicit teaching, again sometimes in the home, but also in the more formal educational context of school.

Until the latter part of the nineteenth century, this latter institutional provision of education was itself directly linked with a sponsoring religious tradition, so that the whole of education for most children was set within the frame of one particular belief system. Since then, there has been increasing diversity as individual nation states have taken on the responsibility of making public provision for education for all.

Some national education systems are still exclusively associated with one religious tradition (e.g. Pakistan), and the provision which they make for Religious Education is focused singularly within that one faith. In the light of religious diversity and the fact that religious belief is itself open to challenge, other nations (e.g. France) have insisted that public education should not be linked with religion and that there is no place for any teaching of religion in its own right in the school curriculum.

The chapters which follow consider the different options that can be advanced for giving attention to religion in the context of public education. They identify the relevant educational arguments, such as are philosophically grounded, regarding its provision. They also explore the emergence of a form of RE which is not owned by one particular faith community and how that might still be compatible with the interests of faith communities. While reference is made to patterns of provision in the USA, continental Europe and elsewhere, special attention is given to the 'agreed syllabus' model of England and Wales.

The first three chapters were written at the time when the new educational model was being formulated and put into practice. The interweaving of the relevant conceptual and contextual complexities is set out in Chapter 1, with its detailed notes (see Notes pp. 209–22). Many of the issues which have subsequently remained contentious were already in evidence. For instance, the question of how susceptible religion is to rational understanding is addressed in Chapter 2, and this is the sustained focus of Michael Hand's recent book

(Hand 2006). Similarly, in Chapter 3 the issue is opened up of the importance of themes and motifs in personal and social identity which recur within and between cultures. This is presently pursued in the media culture approach to RE advanced by Jan Pieterse (2004) and Manfred Pirner (2006).

The 'more' of potential shifts in content from a biblical core to something more are analysed in the first chapter and exemplified in practice in the fourth. Thus, the extension to Christianity as a living religion and the further thrust to the inclusion of other world religions is promoted, but not in such a way as to be careless of the tradition which remains fundamental to the fabric of the UK (Thompson 2003).

Chapters 3 and 5 point up the direct correspondence between, on the one hand, the deepest concerns and most powerful vehicles of human identity, and, on the other, the intrinsic ingredients of diverse religious traditions. Any superficial reduction of religion to its exterior manifestations that has occurred in intervening years owes more to underqualified and overused teachers (Gates 1993) than to inherent limitations in conceptual intent. Chapter 6 picks up the prompt from the Millennium to affirm that religion and religious education is concerned with the ends and purposes of humanity.

Throughout all these chapters reference is made to the global context. The others in this section take that further. Picking up the cue from the first chapter, they argue that it is in the interests of thriving democracies that religion is taken seriously in every system of public education. The argument is pursued with particular reference to the US in Chapter 7. In Chapter 8, using the same principle it is extended to Commonwealth countries.

Within this last chapter, specific acknowledgement is given to the role of the Shap Working Party on World Religions in Education, founded in 1969 (see website: www.shap.org), in the transitional process towards a universal education enriched at every level by attention to world religions. This includes an affirmation of the complementarity between deeply held Christian convictions and a desire to understand the religious experience of others. By implication, the same complementarity may be explored from within and between all the world's religions.

# Chapter 1

# Varieties of Religious Education: a survey of curriculum content in schools

Controversy surrounds the future of religious education (RE) in English and American schools.[1] In the discussions and debates which abound, it is all too easy for polarization to take place – for or against – without any discrimination between one form of content and another. It is as though RE is Religious Instruction, whether it is referred to as RI, or as Divinity, Bible Teaching, Religious Studies, Scripture, Religious Knowledge, or Learning for Living. Such different labels may represent distinct alternatives, carefully made and insisted upon by those responsible for religious education. Or, they may reflect much less logic than local lore. Yet these labels do not necessarily stand for the same thing, any more than RE generally must be cast in monumental monochrome.

Without an appreciation of the varieties of RE, it is all the easier for prejudice to prevail among friends and foes alike. Abolitionists can tilt against compulsory Christian catechizing as just another example of latter-day ecclesiastical imperialism. Apologists can invoke the shielding authority of Christian revelation and fight the good fight of children's right to religious insight. But whatever justification there may be for either of these positions, their clash will remain blinkered so long as they operate in terms which are mutually exclusive and make little or no reference to details of content, both in the one that they are presupposing and in alternatives to it.

As a means of preliminary clarification, this article examines the content of RE as a separate subject in the school curriculum. The examination is rooted in the English situation with a sideward glance towards North America. It has seemed wise not to attempt systematically to catalogue all the known variations of content currently existing, but rather to sketch some general characterizations based on surveys and personal observation. The result is six summary types. The first three seem fairly to represent the status quo, and the others realistic alternatives.

Religious Education has been on the timetable of English schools since state education began over a century ago.[2] For fifty years Local Education Authorities have been setting out a basic syllabus for use in their areas.[3] In the main the older schemes tended to be 'Bible-based' and the newer ones 'Life-centred'. These Agreed Syllabus schemes provide examples of the first two types of RE.

# 1. Biblical type

Since the 1870s RE has meant Bible teaching.[4] Within the limited time made available for RE during the 8 to 10 years of compulsory schooling, there has been deliberate concentration on the history of Israel and the text of the Old and New Testaments, with occasional forays into Church history.[5] Most public examinations in religion have been entitled 'Scripture', without further quali-fication, and concerned with pupils' knowledge of the text.[6] Books, pamphlets and visual aids from school publishers have had the same emphasis.[7]

Historically it is not difficult to see how the type came to predominate. The Cowper-Temple clause ruled out theology from the classroom[8] and a 'theology-free' Bible became the Highest Common Factor of English religion. Even in universities and colleges of education where the teachers were trained, a classical Oxbridge pattern of Bible text and history has lasted through the 1960s.[9] The precise consequences are disputed. A bishop claims the spirit of ecumenical understanding between churches as first fruits of this type of RE,[10] whereas a sociologist ascribes to it the instant appeal of the proof-text, and the success of bible sects and fundamentalist groups. Certainly it provides no evidence that G. M. Trevelyan's reference to the previous century's 'Bible religion of the English' is not still apt.[11]

Among the most significant of the critical weaknesses of this variety of RE would seem to be the following:

(a) Granted that the Bible contains the charter documents of the Christian churches, their full tradition of faith is even richer. This is not to denigrate the crucial importance of the scriptures for Christians or to devalue the school of biblical theology popular for much of this century.[12] Rather it is to insist that these be set back in the context of the larger whole.

(b) The Bible is thoroughly theological. By its very nature it calls for interpretation and response.[13]

(c) Even if many of the difficulties which children seem to find in understanding the Bible[14] can be overcome by better teaching, it remains disputable how much of this learning would be transferred by them to relate to the present day.[15]

(d) There is an implicit devaluation of the scriptures of other religious traditions.[16]

The *Biblical* type then is something of an erratic boulder on the landscape of contemporary curriculum development.

## 2. Life and Living Type

Where as the first type of RE concentrates on teaching the Bible, with the intention of laying firm foundations on which (hopefully) the individual pupil might base his or her life, the *Life and Living* type starts 'at the other end'.[17] That is to say, it begins with the world of today and seeks to deal with the pupils 'where they are' and to meet their 'felt needs'. In many of the older Agreed Syllabuses there had been occasional sections for older pupils on ethical questions and social problems. But increasingly during the last decade there has been a tendency to make these the basis of the entire syllabus, and to bring in biblical material only where 'relevant'. Several schoolbooks have been produced which follow the lead of Loukes' 'problem syllabus'.[18] Many of the pamphlets, charts and study kits produced by the Christian Education Movement for use in schools have taken just this form.[19] Even the most recent rash of Agreed Syllabuses[20] have followed the Life-Theme approach as advocated by Goldman's *Readiness for Religion.*[21] In many schools this type of approach to RE has also been extended to include local community service.[22]

The appeal of this second type coincides with a reaction against Bible teaching: how much more invigorating to plunge directly into the river of life.[23] It is far too early to assess any long-term effects. Teachers' reactions are evidently mixed. A comment often forthcoming from pupils who have experienced this approach goes something like this: 'Please Sir, why don't we do RE any more?' For some teachers this is a moment of triumph. But for others the sense of failure is as great as it was when they were not communicating biblical insights very well either.

Among the most significant of the critical weaknesses of this type would seem to be the following:

(a) The straight leap from contemporary problem to biblical passage underestimates the major hermeneutical difficulties which are inevitably involved. It usually means doing less than justice to the Bible.[24]
(b) Many of the characteristic themes and questions dealt with would be found in the course of general teaching in infant and junior schools anyway.[25] In the secondary school they can occur in English, Social or General or Integrated Studies, and depending on the time available they may be handled there just as effectively, if not more so.[26]
(c) Some kind of theology of correlation is attempted, but the categories of natural theology preselected are rarely specified and the interpretative key is still invariably biblical.[27]
(d) Although RE has everything to do with life, the substance of religion cannot be exhausted in terms of social gospel. 'Oxfam RE' is not enough.

Doubtless there are a great many variations within the general framework of *Biblical* and *Life and Living* types. The *reductio ad absurdum* of the first is the 'Bible cake-mix'[28] and reading verses from the Bible in turn round the class;

and of the second, a general trading of opinions in which the teacher is blown by the class 'where it listeth' – which after a time means doldrums.

Religious Education of the predominantly *Biblical* type has the potential advantage of focusing attention on material which is expressly theological in intent. But in a society which also includes believers of other faiths and atheists, it is difficult to see how RE whose content is exclusively concerned with Christian scriptures can be justified. Just as the Christian tradition includes more than its scriptures, so the human phenomenon of religion includes a diversity of traditions besides the Christian one.

Religious Educaion of the *Life and Living* type on the other hand excels in pointing up that religion divorced from life is a contradiction in terms. Religion is mummified without an existential dimension. But in so far as there are other occasions in the school curriculum that deal with life, the onus is on the RE teacher to demonstrate the distinctive contribution which s/he can make. RE is redundant if it has nothing but gaps in the curriculum to rely upon.

If the preceding two types were the only possible varieties of RE, then the logic of the situation might well be to exterminate the subject from schools. The North American version of this final solution has been on the statute books for just over 100 years.[29] It has been more generally enforced since the Supreme Court's ruling on school prayers in 1962, but even now there are pockets of dissidence.[30] Strictly speaking the 1962 ruling finally closed the door to sectarian RE in public schools, but opened another to 'teaching about religion'. In the furore which followed the ruling this opening was largely ignored.[31] America's agreed silence can therefore provide the third type of RE.

## 3. Vacuum type

This *vacuum* of RE (i.e. its absence) seeks consistency with the constitutional separation of Church and State. In its favour therefore is its refusal to give imperial preference to any one religious tradition or group. The actual plurality of beliefs and life styles within society is in principle acknowledged and the onus of parent religious communities for confessional RE very clearly underlined.[32]

Many limitations are apparent in its working, however, some of which are intrinsic to the type:

(a) If RE disappears as a separate subject, it is none the less manifest elsewhere in the school curriculum, e.g. in History, Geography, English, Social Studies, not to mention pupils' questions and teachers' personal beliefs.[33]

(b) The school is prey to functional, even nationalist, substitutes for religion, e.g. in the daily ceremonial pledge of allegiance.[34]

(c) By implication the rationality of religion is denied (to call this a limitation is not to suggest that religion is demonstrably true, but that there is a logic to the truth claims of any particular religious community).[35]

(d) In effect religion is privatized and thereby made more subject to individual whim than public scrutiny – a feature of American religious life remarked by sociologists.[36]

These very limitations at once serve to demonstrate, albeit negatively, that a deliberate vacuum where RE is concerned is yet a distinctive variety of RE and an inadequate one. The variety is not confined to America. It might for instance arise in English primary schools where individual teachers, for whatever reason, let it go by default, or in a secondary school where the RE periods are absorbed into some joint humanities scheme and conveniently forgotten.[37] There is also a similarity in the position of parents who attempt to avoid all reference to religion in order that the child 'may decide for himself when old enough'. Neither school nor family can in practice preserve a *tabula rasa* in respect of religion.

What emerges from the analysis of these three varieties of R E is the existence of a blatant muddle about the place of religion in the curriculum on educational grounds, and about the nature of religion itself as a curriculum subject. The first makes RE depend upon some extracurricular authority, the second puts RE on the open market of the humanities but as an amateur without the discipline and resources of what become its competitors, and the third accepts an uncritical ignorance as a form of respectful silence. Fortunately the fate of RE does not rest with any of these propositions.

Instead, work in the philosophy of religion and of education has cleared the ground on which alternative varieties of RE can legitimately be constructed. Of particular importance in this connection is the work of Philip Phenix, Paul Hirst, and Ninian Smart. Phenix has explicated the nature of religion as a synoptic realm of meaning, 'the most comprehensive, profound and unified of meanings obtainable', permeating the whole curriculum.[38] Hirst has dealt with religion in relation to other forms of knowledge, e.g. mathematic, scientific, moral; religions provide distinctive ways of seeing the world.[39] And Smart has shown by phenomenological analysis the multidimensional forms of religious tradition and the logic of their interdependence.[40] Here are firm foundations for RE in a secular school curriculum.

The following three alternative types of RE presuppose this philosophical groundwork. They take for granted the personal nature of the educational process and religious traditions; the necessary interplay of pupils' needs and interests with knowledge and understanding of the universe; and the wrongness of attempting to induct boys and girls unquestioningly into a set of beliefs, without encouragement to think and feel them through for themselves. None of the three is yet fully fledged, but each has already taken recognizable shape.

## 4. Ethics type

The *Ethics* type focuses on the moral component of man's religion and on secular versions of morality. Thus, issues of personal and social ethics are explored: telling the truth; care for the neighbour; respect for persons; property rights, keeping contracts and promises; sexual mores; international relations; medical ethics; stewardship of resources; punishment. This can be done as much by reference to plays, stories, and films, as to particular situations as they are actually happening, and all exegeted in the light of social customs, criminal law, natural law, and the commands of scripture or conscience. The validity of the ethical teachings of a particular religious tradition would not be taken for granted, any more than those of a non-religious tradition or ideology; but they would all be taken seriously. Also the disputability of much ethical teaching would be acknowledged, but not so as to produce an unthinking relativism.

There is no assumption that religion can be reduced to morality; indeed that no more is involved in Christianity than commitment to an agapeistic way of life. Regardless of what looks like an element of faith in the decision to adopt any ethical position[41] it is appreciated that for many persons there seems to be little connection between religion and ethics.[42] Yet since it is clear that the religious experience of mankind includes a moral dimension that informs whole cultures and civilizations, the juxtaposition of religion and morality in an Ethics type of RE is considered fair.

The task of programming the constituent elements of ethical experience and moral education has been attempted by the Farmington Trust Research Unit under its first director John Wilson.[43] Much of the work has been deliberately analytical, but its potential for practical application is evident.[44] The production of age-related school materials is being tackled by the Schools Council Projects on Moral Education in the Primary and Secondary Schools directed by Peter McPhail.[45] They utilize a social interactionist model of learning, with motivation rooted in a situational interplay of sympathy and self-interest.[46] Attention is also directed at the impact of school structures, assemblies, and teacher–pupil relationships on moral understanding.

In the same way that much of this material is relevant to work in other subjects,[47] so there are materials from elsewhere that are relevant to this Ethics type. Most influential of these are those emerging from the work of Lawrence Stenhouse.[48] They deal directly with value-controversial questions (e.g. family, war, education, race) by the distinctive method of a neutral teacher armed with collections of primary sources pack-full of partiality.[49] There are relevant materials also from the General Studies Project at York,[50] the Keele Integrated Studies Project,[51] or in the abundant crop of learning games.[52]

A major limitation of this Ethics type as a variety of RE is its deliberate concentration on the moral aspects of religion. Nor has it thereby automatically become a stronger contender for a place in the curriculum than the following two types: moral knowledge, autonomous or otherwise, is disputatious as is religious knowledge.

On the other hand certain educational philosophers have in the past been more ready to recognize the claims of ethics on the curriculum than those of religion.[53] Support from outside the school for ethics in the curriculum is considerable. Much of the popularity of RE with parents may have reflected an everyday understanding that being Christian means 'helping lame dogs';[54] recent polls on moral education as a separate subject show widespread support.[55] The Social Morality Council, incorporating the Campaign for Moral Education, is another strong advocate.[56] It represents the different religious traditions found in England, and through its Humanist chairman Harold Blackham can fairly call its own the new *Journal of Moral Education*.[57] The stage is therefore set for the *Ethics* type to play a distinctive part in the school curriculum.

# 5. Christian type

The *Christian* type is concerned with initiation into the cumulative religious tradition that has brought the churches to where they are today. As such it entails exploration of: the beliefs of Christians, as set forth in scriptures, creeds and systematic theologies; their worship, hymns and prayers, sacraments and festivals and the places where they meet; the influence of faith on individuals' lives and on social action, and as expressed in art and learning.

Its substance could be approached from two different perspectives. It would be possible to concentrate on a contemporary encounter with Christianity, beginning with local communities and then ranging worldwide over Christendom. Or the approach could be historical, in which case it would be a matter of getting inside the communal reality of the tradition as it has changed and developed over 2,000 years. But since it is the logic of the past (and the future) which for Christians gives them their present, it would seem unsatisfactory only to look at the present day. And it would seem equally unsatisfactory to look only to the past, because that past would not be done until it were present.

Providentially for Christians, interdenominational strife no longer makes it necessary to pretend that by concentrating on the Bible, major theological questions can be avoided. Their Ecumenical Movement presages the importance of exploring the tradition in all its different forms – Eastern and Pentecostalist, as well as Protestant and Catholic. Moreover, Christianity as the nearest religious tradition to hand, and the one that has predominated in the West, must be central to an appreciation of mankind's religious experience for most people living there.

Resources and field experience should not therefore be a problem for this variety. Syllabus materials can be adapted from the long tradition of confessional Christian education; at best this is alive to its multidimensional character. For instance, there are the newer catechetical materials associated with the liturgical movement.[58] In America where the onus for confessional

RE is more clearly placed with the parent religious community the supply of such materials from the churches abounds.[59] But in England the Christian Education Movement is already greatly experienced at servicing state schools and could well give greater priority to providing materials which enable pupils to glimpse what it might mean to be Christian than to their reduced kind already referred to in *Learning and Life*.

The *Christian* type, in its secular rather than its confessional form, would leave open the question of the truth claims of the faith, but insist that no decision were possible on this issue without first having fathomed its fullness. Theology would be used to demonstrate the process of belief continually explaining itself to unbelief. The objective would be sympathetic grounding in Christianity and at the same time the kind of sensitivity with which any other religious believer or tradition could be approached. Indeed, some reference to other religious traditions would be inevitable in so far as the logic of the Christian faith has to do with both Church and World. In that spirit the Anglican Report, *The Fourth R*, commends this openness of learning about the faith of other folk even within the context of church schools;[60] *Learning for Living* (A Journal of Christian Education) devoted an entire number to articles on Islam;[61] and the Bloxham Project whose brief it was to examine Christian education in boarding schools has produced materials drawing on the religious experience of mankind.[62] Thus whether on Christian or open educational grounds this variety of RE has much in its favour.

# 6. World Religions type

Here the concern is initiation into the religious experience of mankind and an appreciation of what it might mean to be *religious*. This would entail consideration of 'primitive religion', the development of world religions and the contemporary religious situation. Again, belief systems, patterns of worship, and ways of life are involved; the rich store of myth and ritual, and the immense range of cultural expressions are there to be explored. The choice of historical or contemporary perspective of approach is also again open. But there would be no blurring of differences which bespeak the vitality of religion, rather care to get the distinctive 'feel' and knowledge of particular traditions.

The dialogue between different religions has increased as people have become more aware of each others' beliefs, past and present.[63] Religion in the future is bound to be influenced by this interchange. To a certain extent it will be going on in any school or local community in which there are children from different religious backgrounds or none. Therefore as well as showing sensitivity to children of all sorts and conditions, this *World Religions* type would seek to deepen understanding between nations and cultures. In these respects it would be serving the interests of both parents and religious communities, and need not cause offence to traditional supporters of RE.[64]

The major problem remains, however, and it rests largely with the teachers. It is that of selection and of how to begin to do justice to the vastness of religion and at the same time avoid superficiality, stereotypes, and distortions. One consideration might be contrast with prevailing religious life styles, for instance, extra-careful attention to the teachings of the Buddha in Northern Ireland.[65] In addition some preparation in the basic skills for handling religious concepts, symbols and gestures would be a helpful start.[66] Conceivably the diversity of expertise required of the teacher could come from greater use of team teaching.

During the last five years prospects for this *World Religions* variety of RE have taken a tremendous leap forward, as a direct result of continuing work by the Schools Council Projects on RE[67] and the Shap Working Party on World Religions in Education.[68] An effective rationale for this kind of RE is provided by the Secondary Project's Working Paper, and its practical accompaniment – units of work for use in school are emerging, first for secondary, then primary.[69] Doubts as to the availability of supporting visual aids, cultic objects, recordings, practising consultants for every faith, etc., will be largely dispelled by even a cursory glance at the Shap Handbook.[70] A mark of this achievement is its acknowledgement by the examinations system; two GCE Boards are now offering papers in World Religions.[71] Similar developments in Canada,[72] Sweden,[73] and the United States,[74] though not yet as comprehensive in school ages covered, suggest that this variety of RE is gaining international recognition.

Christianity itself as a world religion has an obvious place in this variety of RE. So too has ethics in the form of distinctive life styles and values of the different religious traditions.[75] In a sense therefore the *World Religions* type can claim to include the emphases of both the preceding types, now placed within a larger framework, at once religious and secular. As such it could claim to be the most authentic version of RE for publicly funded schools.

Any shift from the first type towards the last depends upon a generous supply of competent teachers. Those already teaching may demand 'remedial' courses in religion to enhance their previous qualifications. Student teachers will need every opportunity at college or university for a training richer in religion than hitherto available.[76] Danger that this will not be provided persists. Yesterday's philological-historical exercise in departments of Divinity or Theology can easily be exchanged for today's sociological-historical exercise in departments of Religious Studies. Religion as a subject is well served by second-order disciplines in literary criticism, sociology, psychology, and philosophy.[77] But perhaps it is only properly entertained by fully fashioned phenomenological study.[78] At an everyday level sympathetic imagination that seeks to enter another's world is the most direct route to discovery of what it means to be religious. Such engagement with religion puts an end to any inert appearance it might have had. What seemed to be the terminal moraine of institutional religion can quickly become an adventure playground.

Teacher and pupil alike will be on the common ground of the shared experiences of mankind. The teacher's commitment will be great in terms of wanting to take these experiences seriously; but s/he will be able to do this as, e.g. Atheist, Congregationalist, or Jew. The pupil's autonomy of religious understanding will be striven for, but relative to the faith of other folk.

## Constitutional conclusion

Constitutionally the difference between English and American provisions for RE is great. This article has opposed both as they are normally understood. There is little place in an open educational system for exclusive induction into one particular religious tradition, however hallowed its relation with the state. But every person has as much right to religious understanding as he has to be numerate or literate. In fear of fascism the 1944 Education Act affirmed that right and sought thereby to confirm the individual conscience and centre of values; but its means to that end were unduly constricted. In the name of freedom the Supreme Court's ruling does seek to preserve the interests of religious minorities; but those who interpret its ruling to entail the way of silence in public schools put the very sources of values beyond the bounds of human rationality. Neither constitutional solution matches its declared intentions. It is left therefore to the constitution of the subject of religion itself to provide the foundation for a variety of RE which matches the intent of an open society.

(1973)

Chapter 2

# Religious Education: a proper humanism

## Educational grounds?

Religion like education is at once a prompt for learned dispute among philosophers and instant opinion from anyone else. Put education and religion together, and the potential for ambiguity is enormous. To a certain extent, then, it is gratifying to see an increasingly common affirmation that any place which religion has in the school curriculum must be 'based on educational grounds'. What this means in positive terms remains subject to a variety of interpretations, but its negative message is clear: RE stands or falls independently of ecclesiastical authority or government decree (Martell 1972, Jones 1973), and grounds for including it in the curriculum must be sought elsewhere. Attention now focuses on the *nature* of religious belief and understanding. Here, alas, any apparent unanimity dissolves: on the one hand, there are those curriculum philosophers for whom religion is meaningless and religious language no more than nonsense; for them religion has no place in rational education. On the other hand, there are those for whom education and religion are about the same process of human becoming to such an extent that they are virtually synonymous.

What follows is an attempt to typify three different approaches to religion that fairly represent the current range of views. Each reflects a developed philosophy of education and a matching counterpart in theology and philosophy of religion. The first emphasizes the limits of the relation between reason and faith; the second is prepared to affirm the logic of religion; the third asserts the inevitability of religious questions and concerns for Everyman.

# Religion in the philosophy of education

## Religion as non-rational

The proponents of this first approach maintain that religious language is either meaningless or so private a kind of 'language game' as to be incomprehensible to all but a believer. The most abrasive dispute the meaning of any statement that is not immediately verifiable by means of the senses. Classically the approach finds expression in the 'flat-earth metaphysic' of Ayer's claim (Ayer 1936) that 'all utterances about the nature of God are nonsensical', but it persists in some recent pronouncements about RE. It may have been behind the Plowden minority Note of Reservation on RE (DES 1967), of which Ayer himself was a signatory, and it is quite explicit in the educational philosophy of O'Connor and Dearden. According to O'Connor (1957), 'we have no right to ask such questions' as 'What is the purpose of man?' or 'What is the meaning of life?' They are but 'pseudo-questions'; religious beliefs are non-rational. Although he believes that morality has an essential link with education, he denies that religion is relevant at all. Similarly Dearden (1968) suggests that if the notion of God were stripped of images and analogies, it would disappear altogether as an object of belief. He considers RE to be indoctrination, attempting 'to deform the growth of rationality', and therefore concludes that for epistemological and moral reasons primary schools ought to 'lead the way' by abandoning it. Clive Jones' position (Jones 1973), representing the views of the British Humanist Association, is substantially similar: 'Religious understanding', he says, 'is … only possible as a concomitant to existing faith, and we regard the aim of inculcating religious faith as neither educational nor honest.' Thus, in his view too, RE disqualifies itself from the state maintained school.

There appears to be some deference contained in these views to the distinctiveness of religion; but this is apparent only. In practice, the lip-service paid to the special operation of religious language remains within the confines of an earlier positivist tradition that found it philosophically respectable to deride religion for its irrationality, just as once it was popular to caricature African religion as Mumbo-Jumbo. The logic of much religious belief or the reasons given by believers themselves for their professions of faith still get overlooked. To be sure, such reasons may be compressed in the form of myth, ritual and symbolic image, but they are still open to rational scrutiny. Before dismissing religion as senseless or penetrable only by a process involving 'corruption of innocence' the philosopher or the educationist would do well to examine the entire web of meaning of a religious tradition.

One religious view, however, does doubt the relevance of reason to faith, judging reason to be too much man-made or else considering religion more an affective than a cognitive matter. Were this the believer's typical view, it might indeed be difficult to justify RE in state schools. But since it is not, it remains important for the philosopher of education no less than for children and young people to 'grapple with the grammar of theological concepts'.

**Religion as a form of knowledge**

In this approach philosophers of both education and religion talk specifically of the logic of religion. The position is most clearly represented in
terms of curriculum philosophy by Hirst (1967). Having rejected any easy
confusion of morals and religion, and any attempt to justify the inclusion of
RE in the curriculum by appeal to revelation alone, he affirms that religion
is a form of knowledge into which pupils may legitimately be initiated: 'It
demands enabling pupils to see how believers look at the world and at human
experience … It means getting a glimpse of the world "through religious
glasses". After all, religions are claimed to be ways of seeing things and not
just cultural objects to be observed, say, historically.' The contrast with Jones'
position when he advocates studying religions merely as cultural background
is evident. Both writers, however, emphatically agree that it is not the school's
place to determine which, if any, of the alternative sets of glasses its pupils shall
wear.

Hirst clearly recognizes the difficulties entailed in RE, not least in the view of
the plural form of religion in the world. In our own society an understanding
of religious beliefs must include the predominant Christian tradition, but also
other world religions, 'pseudo-religions' and humanism. So long as no attempt
is made to indoctrinate or to disguise the fact that claims to truth in religion
are disputable, RE, in his view, is no less important than moral education
(ME).

Here, then, is a very different point of view from the first. It corresponds
with Ninian Smart's philosophy of religion. Smart (1968b) maintains that to
understand man or religion a 'sensitive and artistic heart' is required. 'Since
the study of man is in an important sense participatory – for one has to enter
into people's intentions, beliefs, myths and desires in order to understand
why they act as they do – it is fatal if cultures including our own are described
merely externally.' His is a sure way to an appreciation of the religious form
of knowledge, in which Hirst's emphasis on concepts and propositions is set
within the richer context of a manifold tradition of faith.

Smart offers his sixfold (later seven) model of religion (summarized in
tabular form – see p. 16) as a heuristic device to disclose the multidimensional
reality of religion, tangible, though diversified, throughout the experience
of mankind. Since the moral dimension of religion is clearly specified, the
question of the relation between ethics and religion is raised. Even apart
from the interest which different lifestyles and social patterns create, religious
ethics have an additional contribution – serving to highlight, by contrast, the
motivating basis of rationalist and humanistic ethics. Too often the polarization of ME versus RE conceals that common root in an individual intention
which it is their prime concern to educate.

According to the view represented by Hirst and Smart, RE involves initiation
into an understanding of religion as a human, self-transcending phenomenon.

**Table 2.1**　Ninian Smart's dimensional model of Religion (for exposition, see Smart 1968b: 15–18; Smart 1969a: Ch. 1; Smart 1983: 1–11; Smart 1989: 9–25; and Smart 1996 *passim*. The seventh dimension was adumbrated in 1983 and had become formalized by 1989).

| DIMENSION | DEFINING CHARACTERISTICS | EXAMPLES |
|---|---|---|
| DOCTRINAL + PHILOSOPHICAL (systematic theology) | Attempt to give clear, rational order to the faith so as to form coherent and consistent whole. | Christian doctrine of Trinity, Original Sin; creeds Buddhist *dharma* – Four Noble Truths. |
| MYTHIC and NARRATIVE (traditional stories and imagery) | Stories of God/gods and invisible world, and of relation with human beings. History of salvation. | Genesis Creation and Fall stories; Exodus; Olympians gods of Iliad.  Buddha's career. |
| ETHICAL and LEGAL (individual behaviour) | Consequences of faith for individual way of life. Codes defining how this is to be ordered. | Passion of Christ and *Imitatio Christi* care of the neighbour. Buddhist compassion. Muslim *jihad.* |
| RITUAL and PRACTICAL (worship, prayer and offering). | Outer behaviour coordinated with inner intention as expression of deeper meaning. | Christian sacraments, liturgy and private prayer. Meditation and yoga. |
| EXPERIENTIAL and EMOTIONAL | Personal experience of God; sense of presence, or of other world. Inner awareness. | Buddha's enlightenment. Inaugural visions of biblical prophets. Revelation of Krishna to Arjuna in *Bhagavadgītā.* |
| SOCIAL and INSTITUTIONAL (group life) | Communal organization of believers. Social roots and effects of religion. | Christian Churches, Buddhist Sangha. Priesthood, castes and monasteries. |
| MATERIAL (external symbols) | Buildings, works of art and environmental features expressing religious meaning. | Cathedrals and mosques. Icons and statues. Sacred rivers & mountains. |

Neither the conscience of the individual pupil nor the vitality of the religious tradition under scrutiny is violated. Both stand their ground in a personally engaging process.

## Religion as 'locus of ultimacy'

This third approach raises the question whether religion is inevitable across the curriculum, and for teacher and pupil alike. Something along these lines was implied by Hemming's affirmation (1973) that RE and ME have to do with 'the values at the centre of the school' and giving 'a credible and if possible inspiring understanding of the universe'.

Alongside Hemming and Loukes (1965) (who invented the expression 'locus of ultimacy') the curriculum philosopher who has developed the position most systematically is Philip Phenix. Writing expressly to counter the devaluation of religion by some American philosophers, Phenix proclaims religion as the most inclusive of all the realms of meaning into which the content of the curriculum can be analysed. 'Regardless of the result of the search, religious enquiry is directed towards ultimacy in the sense of the most comprehensive, most profound, most unified meanings obtainable. At very least faith refers to an ideal and a hope for maximum completeness, depth and integrity of vision' (Phenix 1964: 251–2).

Religion can be studied as a separate subject, or as an explicit aspect of another subject; but, he says, it is implicit in questions anywhere in the curriculum about the whence and whither of life, suffering and failure, freedom and creativity. RE, then, involves helping pupils to understand and articulate 'the really profound questions of life, death and destiny' (Phenix 1958: 93).

Phenix's counterpart in the philosophy of religion is Paul Tillich. Tillich's definition of religion as the dimension of depth in existence, and the realm of ultimate concern shared by all people everywhere, is well known. Formally, everyone has faith, although its content varies. There is no 'unfaith' even if there are faiths with unworthy contents, even subject to momentary whim. 'They invest something preliminary, finite and conditioned with the dignity of the ultimate, infinite and unconditional. The continuing struggle through all history is waged between a faith directed to ultimate reality and a faith directed towards preliminary realities claiming ultimacy (Tillich 1963a: 130–1).

According to Phenix and Tillich, therefore, the universal involvement of man in religion is a simple expression of the contingency of life. How he responds or interprets this condition varies greatly. But atheism, agnosticism and apathy qualify (as do theisms and deisms) as different, albeit negative, forms of religious understanding.

Here, then, the grounds for recognizing the place of religion in school are that the whole curriculum is laden with potential for doubt or faith; teacher and pupil alike are in an arena where religious understanding is crucial to their identity as persons. On this road which Hemming (Humanist) calls the 'continuing search', it would not be surprising to find a signpost which reads: 'Here be dragons.'

## In search of a humanist religious education

During the last century the usage 'humanist versus Christian' has come to predominate over the once-popular (Christian) humanist. Similarly one particular philosophical stance has driven a wedge between education and religion. This is the weakness of the first approach described. Although it provides a healthy warning against assuming the indisputable truth of religious belief, it fails to understand the nature of religion and unnecessarily constricts the horizons of the human condition. Contestable assumptions about 'reality' are employed to foreclose an issue which is open. Thus its humanism is careless of any distinctive insights generated by religious experience.

The humanism of the second approach is more circumspect. Instead of deciding that reason is as superfluous to religion as to any superstitious belief, the approach takes seriously the logic of the believer's world-view. For inter-subjective checks on the internal coherence of a faith are as important to a religious tradition as to any group of natural scientists. Without them any common identity or claim to truth would be impossible. From an educational point of view, opportunity to check these credentials against personal experience is a very proper activity. RE along these lines would distinguish between encouraging children to become religious and enabling them to discover for themselves what it might mean to be a believer or an atheist – enabling them to become *religiate*, to coin a term. Ignorance, like blinkered bigotry, in this respect can be more crippling for a person's humanity, and not only in Northern Ireland, than if s/he could not read or write.

If there were any doubt that the term 'humanist' might yet reclaim its more original inclusiveness, the identification of James Hemming with the third approach must dispel it. Here the place of human beings in the cosmos occasions both wonder and doubt. They look for rhyme or reason for being. Their search is not solitary, however, for they see it as a continuing response to the universal human predicament, always a major preoccupation of religion.

This emphasis is a necessary complement to talk of religion as a form of knowledge, which at worst could mean just frozen, foreign facts, about religion. Likewise it enriches the notion of becoming religiate, which could be reduced to the maximum of intellectual aloofness along with the minimum of personal engagement. On the other hand, familiarity with the general characteristics of religion may at times be useful for distinguishing genuine faith from arbitrary wish-fulfilment.

Religious Education properly deals with how people focus their concerns for meaning in life. Teacher – let alone pupil – can never be entirely neutral in the process: their own frame of reference – whether Christian, Marxist or Jewish

– will determine who they are in the classroom. Tillich (1959), from a Christian viewpoint, stressed the importance of 'theologies of education', spelling out the implications of any personal faith for the entire curriculum. Others have taken up the term and used it without qualification, as if supposing that the only possible theology were the Christian one. In principle, it is possible to construct theologies of education in terms of any of the world's religions, beliefs and atheisms. An embryonic example of the last might be found in O'Connor's *Introduction to the Philosophy of Education*. The outlines of Christian theologies of education are noticeable in the works of Loukes (Quaker) and Phenix (Episcopalian), and Hindu, Jewish and Muslim equivalents are in the making. In an increasingly pluralistic society such as ours, any such theology raises questions for every other. Dialogue in school at this level would be a sure way of enlarging the horizons of our common humanity and of allowing a child to become his/her own humanist, relative to others.

## Framed by tradition

It might be right, following fashion, to scorn the support of RE by church and law; but once the educational grounds for RE have been established, these former aids can be judged afresh.

The Christian churches' support for RE is all of a piece with their general support for education – the association of godliness and good learning stems from the Christian belief that all truth resides in God. By implication the churches plead for a deepened religious understanding among all people, for a sustained dialogue between those of different faiths, including secular humanism; and education is one means to this end. Their support for RE now has the broader base of the other religious communities that have come to enrich our society. They have a common cause in wanting children and young people to understand what it might mean to be religious.

Government decree is a different matter. The 1944 Act is an outdated promulgation, but it was not an arbitrary one. Major economic and political considerations were involved, including the problem of meeting the costs of education, and the then relations of church and state. Equally important was the nation's plight in fighting the war against Nazism. As a result it was believed that the projected post-war reconstruction would be incomplete without some explicit affirmation of the importance of 'personal and spiritual values' such as those enshrined in the Judaeo-Christian tradition. Hence the RI clauses in the Act. But these clauses were not deemed to *create* the value of religion or to introduce it to the school for the first time, any more than a wedding ceremony provides the sources of value for a marriage or marks the moment when love first comes into the relation between a man and a woman. Rather, they under-lined a liaison already considered valuable. The legislation of RE has ironically come to present religion with a position of weakness not of strength. To repeal the law and remove the 'millstone' might indeed have salutary effect; but the actual result might satisfy only the literalist. On the other hand, the symbol of the RI clauses might with a little imagination be interpreted to safeguard the springs of action and belief in every child. To enable a person to become religiate is a proper educational objective for a participating democracy.

(1974)

# Chapter 3

# Groundwork for the future: curriculum innovation in Religious Education

If tracts for the times are to be believed, both Education and Religion are under final sentence. In the 1960s, talk of the Death of God reached the cover of *Time* magazine and eager disciples proclaimed the Non-Church identity of their new movement (Billington 1966; Ogletree 1966). Now in the 1970s, proclamation that school is dead is also paperbacked and popular; 'free schools' abound (Richmond 1973; Kozol 1972; Reimer 1971). Predictably, *The Times Educational Supplement* has carried the headline that conjoins the two – 'Religious Education: the Death of a Subject' (Loukes 1968).

Such talk of the end of RE might be seen as a simple reflection of its reduced status at the 'butt-end' of the school curriculum, held in being only by legal inertia and a well-meaning minority of qualified staff.[1] But the language of prophetic hyperbole is not exclusively negative in its implications. The de-schoolers affirm that education proper is more than the years of compulsory schooling, that the child's world is bigger than a scholastic institution. The Death of God theologians affirm that the question of God is bigger than any single individual or institutional representation (containment) of it. So, too, in writing the epitaph for one restricted version of RE the birth of a richer alternative is pending.

In fact the crisis that has goaded some of today's educationists and social scientists to become prophets[2] is of peculiar concern to RE. For in part at least it is a crisis of beliefs and values, of the bases of social and political order in the Western world. The patterns inherited from the past have had *religious* roots in Athens, Jerusalem and Rome. Any attempt to construct new order for mankind may yet find relevant meanings compacted into these former terms of reference; there will certainly be additional sources to be fathomed in the traditional hinterlands of Delhi, Peking and Cairo. Whether collectively or individually, the process of ordering life, of making sense of being in the universe at all, is an adventure of religious proportions. RE therefore, in so far as it begins and ends with groundwork in the religious experience of mankind, is preoccupied with questions of human order. It is on this account that RE affords such great potential for curriculum innovation.

## Multicultural horizons

Even without living in London, Birmingham, or Huddersfield, a child born in England in the second half of the twentieth century is born into a multicultural society. Jews from Eastern Europe, Catholics from Poland, Sikhs and Hindus from India (via Kenya or Uganda), Muslims from Bangladesh, Cyprus, or Pakistan, are but the latest additions to the social and ethnic mixture that has made the English (Bridger 1974). Whites, Anglo-Saxons and Protestants may be disguised as one, but children can see that at home or abroad the world is manifold.

A recent report jointly sponsored by the Schools Council and the National Foundation for Educational Research (Townsend and Brittan 1973) has estimated the extent to which English primary and secondary schools are alive to this reality. To the apparent surprise of the authors, RE is specially mentioned by primary headteachers as an area of the curriculum where at the moment much is being done to prepare children for life in a multicultural society. Similarly, in secondary schools the RE syllabus is demonstrated to have more direct concern with this than any other single subject, more even than the other humanities grouped together; moreover, if heads of departments are to be believed, there is evidence that this will become even truer for RE in the future than for any other subject.

To a certain extent, however, this positive finding for RE is a reflection of yesterday's presuppositions. Board school RE since 1870 and the Agreed Syllabuses underwritten by the 1944 Education Act have set out to be comprehensively Christian in a way that bypasses interdenominational strife. Whatever further initiation were to take place in the parent religious community outside school, the English educational system was structured to introduce children to the personal and spiritual values common to the Christian tradition at large, especially as enshrined in the charter documents of the Bible. Churches, teachers' unions and political parties have concurred with this. Not surprisingly therefore, some teachers quoted in the report refer to the Christian notion of the brotherhood of all in Christ as the justification for multicultural education and RE's part in it.[3]

This may have been acceptable enough in 1944; T. S. Eliot could still be having ideas of England as a Christian Society (Eliot 1939). But thirty years on the situation is dramatically changed. Then there were many churches. Today there are still many churches, but there are also many religions, and many alternative ideologies all represented within the one society. The temptation may be real to try to fall back on the compromise of yesterday's uniformity; alternatively to put up with sharply segregated groupings. But the challenge of the English political tradition is to begin to force a social understanding which is a creative synthesis of distinctive social and cultural strands.[4]

This would entail the transformation of the 1944 politico-religious settlement to include the other religious communities as well as the churches and humanistic alternatives. The first steps towards this have already been taken at local and national levels. Locally, two education authorities (Birmingham 1974 and Bradford 1974) have taken the initiative of involving representatives of minority religious communities in drawing up new agreed syllabuses suggesting the lines along which RE might best be approached. As well as seeking to explore the major world religions, there is a strong recommendation that avowed atheistic lifestyles, including communism, be also examined in the course of RE. Nationally, a Religious Education Council of England and Wales has been established on which all religious communities and teacher associations with an interest in RE are represented.[5] It has the task of balancing proper professional educational interests with the confessional aspirations of individual religious loyalties. Both elements are indispensable to an effective RE for the future.

Communal dimensions are intrinsic to this RE. Already by involving voluntary associations from outside schools in consultations about the substance of the curriculum, acknowledgement is made of the larger community context in which schools operate. But in addition, any religion is in itself a cumulative tradition involving myriad individual believing men and women, in diverse times and places; together they have created its organic and communal reality. RE by definition therefore is an exercise in community understanding, but with several different communities to look at. Though the process begins with the local parish church, synagogue, or gurdwara, it will also move to cross national boundaries and centuries of change. A child's social horizons are stretched to come to terms with these.

A child's social horizons will be partially established in the home. Indeed in a matter so intimate as RE parental influence and interest cannot be avoided. But if the following three statements are in any way typical, a multiculturally grounded RE would come closest to satisfying the expectations of many parents:

### Anglican

As a C. of E. parent I'd like our Michael to be given a glimpse of the riches of the Christian heritage from its beginnings till now. I'd like him to see how it's helped to make England, and Europe and America; something too about the local churches – their history and things they do now.

I suppose he ought to learn about other religions, too. We never got the chance when we were young. He should be able to understand how it is that different people believe different things (and stick up for himself!). It wouldn't be right to expect the school to teach him to say his prayers, or get him ready for Communion. I know we aren't as good at it as we should be ourselves, but that's why we've sent him to Sunday School and Confirmation class. But school can show him something about the people who have done good by being true to their faith.

### Humanist

As a member of the British Humanist Association, I'd like our Margaret to be given every opportunity to love all that is good and beautiful in human life and history. I think it's important for her to appreciate how people in different cultures used to believe in God and built great buildings, painted, and told wonderful tales about their beliefs. She should see that some people still think this way.

But I'd like her to think through for herself why people have outgrown much of this, what I call, childishness; I don't want anyone trying to persuade her that people don't have to stand on their own feet, or that they're always in need of supernatural help. Don't offend her conscience by asking her to put her hands together and close her eyes and pray. By all means let her look at some of the social justice that's come from Religion, as well as the injustice and oppression. But teach her too that not all good deeds are done by people who are religious.

### Sikh

As a Sikh I am happy for my children to be in English school and to learn about the British way of life. My religion teaches me to believe in the brotherhood of all and I don't like nasty feelings between people. Religion should bring people together and not make them enemies.

Our children like to hear about the Bible and Jesus; they were even a bit envious that they hadn't heard of so many miracles by the Gurus. But do you not think that the English children would like to hear something of our religion? I can understand why some of the older men have been talking about the idea of separate schools for Sikhs. At times it's as though you want to keep us separate and apart like the Jews. But I hope this doesn't happen. Maybe our children's children will have easier time.

On any such parental reckoning RE. is crucial preparation for life in a multicultural society.

## Personal horizons

So far, the contribution of RE to curriculum innovation has been dealt with tangentially by reference to the interdependence of school and communities – local, national and religious. But much of the curriculum potential of RE depends upon the extent to which it succeeds in enabling a child to explore the grounds of his or her own religious identity.

The personal identity of the religious believer, as also the 'unbeliever', is cumulative and on the move. Any shared matrix of meaning into which a child is born will be tried out from within, and expanded, contracted or transformed by new experiences and encounters. Any focusing that takes place around particular cores of experience and which leads one to say 'I'm a Catholic', another 'I'm a Muslim', or another 'I'm an atheist', is individually achieved.

From the very earliest years every child is growing a coherent world-view at once highly individual and highly complex. Religion figures doubly in this process. Firstly it figures institutionally as a child forms concepts (first- or second-hand) which represent the ongoing presence of religious practice and belief in the neighbourhood. Secondly, it is found unlabelled in feelings and sensations that are basic to being human: a sense of wonder, of trust, or even of contingency ('a *floor* is so you won't fall into the hole your house stands on'). In these respects every person, parents, teachers and children alike, is privy to a religious identity that is their own.

Given that the formation of religious identity is a lifelong process, its beginning and end are beyond (empirically and theologically speaking) the school. But the school curriculum might still be one means of enabling an individual to come more into their own thoughts and feelings in the realm of religion. Whether they leave as a believing Methodist, devout Parsee, or doubting atheist, what matters is that they are this for themselves and not in a blinkered or half-digested sort of way. Can the school perhaps help them become 'religiate', whether or not they would go on to call themselves religious?

There is evidence that this personal groundwork is not entirely *new* to RE. Harold Loukes in his 1960s review of the effectiveness of the subject in the classroom showed convincingly how secondary school pupils were appreciative of the 'personal dialogue' in the classroom that characterized the subject at its best (Loukes 1965 and 1973; for primary equivalent: Madge 1965; Mogford 1968). Independent corroboration of this comes also from the Writing Research Unit at the University of London Institute of Education. Samples of children's writing collected over a number of years from many different schools and from all subject departments have been analysed to see what kind of writing is done right 'across the curriculum' (Schools Council Writing Research Unit 1974). It was discovered that the only other place where personal and expressive writing was to be found to any significant extent, apart from in English work, was in RE.

But the full extent of the contribution which RE could make to a curriculum concerned with personal identity is far from fully realized. In fact the self-same vehicles which are well tried by tradition for building religious identity are equally central to any kind of self-understanding. Three formal illustrations can be given: stories; ritual actions; and example. Each of them can appeal to the imagination in a way that minimizes any split between heart and mind, reason and emotion – a split that can be crippling for both education and religion.

*Story*

Several years ago Huw Wheldon of the BBC was quoted by the *Observer* newspaper on the theme of storytelling. He began:

Of all the instruments of communication, the story is the most important.

It is by stories that people learn to look at themselves and discover what the world is like. It is no accident that religion, and indeed civilization itself, is based on parable and myth. And a story lies behind every television programme: the news consists of stories, a documentary is a story. There are stories in even the most unstorylike programmes: Take a general election results programme: behind it lies the story of two kings who fought at sunset and all the world knew that only one of them would live to see the dawn. *Softly Softly* is the archetypal story of the pursuer and the pursued. There's no doubt that what we all like best are stories. (Wheldon 1972)

Stories from books, stories from TV, from daily papers or women's magazines, or even from the hairdresser's or barber's shop, continue even for adults to be a major part of our life world. Somehow in stories and in gossipy conversations which are akin to them, we try out, confirm, or transform each other's expectations in life, our views of the world. Story is a vehicle for exploring what it means to be human for children and adults alike.

Children are doing this when they produce stories of their own; the books of J. Britton (1970) and D. Holbrook (1964) abound with examples. Children are also doing this when they listen to stories and play with them in their minds. The so-called dirty story may have its limitations as an art form, but the dawn of sexual sense could be humourless without them.

Now as Wheldon following Cassirer 1953 and Langer 1957; the point is well established) remarks, it is no accident that religion and civilization are based on stories in the form of parable and myth. What better way then for initiating children into the religious experience of mankind than by letting them work and play with stories from the myths and parables stored up in humankind's historical identity chest? Admittedly there is some danger in stories being misunderstood, as Plato and Rousseau were at pains to point out. But adults too can watch or hear the same story and end up with very different understandings. Carefully handled by the storytelling teacher, the story can be a vital vehicle throughout the process of education.

A bigger problem perhaps is the selection of stories in the first place. Once upon a time it was possible to pretend that there was only one set of stories that really mattered. Now we are faced with diverse sets of stories. The broadcaster meets with the same problem:

You could say that the business of broadcasting is choosing what stories to tell. Now if the audience is united there is no difficulty. The story of the nineteenth century was Stanley's meeting with Livingstone: it had everything: Christianity, the empire, exploration. The audience was united. There was no difficulty broadcasting during the last war: the nation was united and everyone wanted to hear the same story. But when the nation is divided as it is now then broadcasting becomes very, very difficult ... the only thing to do is let all the singers sing. And as we grope our way ahead, we may sometimes tell a story so good that it transcends all divisions. (Wheldon 1972)

Letting all the singers sing in the course of RE will entail sensitive selection of stories from different religious and cultural traditions.[6] Fortunately, as well as the obvious diversities which will emerge, there is no dearth of stories here that can both celebrate differences and transcend boundaries.


## Ritual

If stories are verbal ways of learning to look at ourselves and of discovering what the world is like, ritual action and gestures are ways of physically representing meanings in our lives, both trivial and profound. They too are significant for enabling anyone to order their world.

One thinks of an old person patting or stroking the arms of the chair in which he or she is sitting, indicating perhaps a state of gentled security. Or maybe, of an alcoholic friend who finds in tidiness and care for detail an order which is missing elsewhere in his life. In children one thinks of 'Ring a ring of roses' in which all fall down, but all get up again (unlike Humpty Dumpty) and get back to the security of the rhythmic circle; or of the gesture of touching a sailor's collar for luck (Opie and Opie 1959: 219). Ritual holds us in being for much in our lives – in our jobs, in our family relationships; and it holds children at their desks, or in their classrooms or working areas at school from start to finish.

A child going to bed may well perform certain ritual actions before settling down – putting Teddy in the right place, looking under the bed, climbing the stairs on one leg, saying prayers (Newson 1968: ch. 10). An explicit religious ritual such as this last is not of an entirely different order from the other rituals mentioned. But certainly they abound in 'hello–goodbye' situations: getting up–going to bed; being born–dying; *Gruß Gott*–God be with you. Religion and rites of passage are closely intertwined.

Not all ritual (one thinks of school assemblies) will necessarily be meaningful: some may be empty and dead, some gathering up deep layers of hidden signifi-cance and association. But life-enhancing or life-denying, ritual expression is a vital vehicle for sensing meaning with our bodies.

Not surprisingly ritual is rife in religion, whether in the rites of passage already mentioned, or in liturgy and sacred dance. The human resonance of religious ritual can easily be missed, however. Erich Fromm elaborates its importance in the following way:

What was the function of Greek drama? Fundamental problems of human existence were presented in an artistic and dramatic form, and participating in the dramatic performance, the spectator – though not as a spectator in our modern sense of consumer – was carried away from the sphere of daily routine and brought in touch with himself as a human being, with the roots of his existence. He touched the ground with his feet, and in this process gained strength by which he was brought back to himself. Whether we think of Greek drama, the medieval passion play, or an Indian choice, whether we think of Hindu, Jewish or Christian religious rituals, we are dealing with various forms of dramatization of the fundamental problems of human existence, with an *acting out* of the very same problems which are *thought out* in philosophy and theology. (Fromm 1956: 145)

It would not be misleading to make similar claims for the Theatre of the Absurd today (Esslin 1968: ch. 7).

Children and adults learn from ritual. By making their own or watching the gestures of others, pupils can be taken into the heart of a religious tradition. The breaking of the bread in Eucharist, the family celebration of Pesach, can disclose in a bodily way much more of what it means to be a Christian or a Jew than much talk. The level of understanding may be primitive in early years, but a sense of the significance of the occasion will certainly be communicated to be filled out in more elaborated reflection at a later age (Smart and Smart 1967: 297–9). Ritual joins hands with story as a fundamental means for exploring identity.

### Example

This is the third formal vehicle of human and religious understanding to be dealt with. It arises from the fact that *imitation* is a basic means of learning in life. This is visible in the adult phenomenon of 'keeping up with the Joneses', or in adolescent 'pashes' on pop or soccer stars, or again in the daughter's or son's wish to be like mum or dad, and do as they do. We all of us, consciously or unconsciously have models and heroes to emulate, and perhaps to avoid too. In school especially there is the opportunity to size ourselves up, and to find out more about who we are or who we would like to be, in relation to the example of others ... classmates, teachers, older children.

Indeed lifestyles may well tell us more about a person's real identity than any number of things that he or she may claim for themselves. This at least is a commonplace of Adlerian psychology: watch what they do rather than what they say they do.

If this is true generally of human behaviour, then it is also true in respect of religious behaviour. 'By their fruits you shall know them' is fair comment on the way in which the religions of the world teach that religious faith and understanding have consequences for individual and social action. Exemplary action is therefore another important vehicle for getting at the heart of what a religious tradition is all about.

Martin Luther King, or a Buddhist monk perishing in petrol flames may be dramatic examples of what a religious faith has meant for certain individual believers. Sometimes the examples will be as dramatic as this in disclosing the heart of a faith. They may even be totally alien ('the vision that thou dost see is my greatest enemy'), such as the following from India: at daybreak, a young man lies in the gutter with his face down, gulping down handful after handful of the thick, black, stinking filth that is being swept to the river. Why? He wishes to prove by this behaviour that literally everything is Brahman (Klostermeier 1969: 46–7). But more often they will be everyday examples of ordinary folk living out their lives in a faith received from their parents and parents' parents. These ordinary examples are less startling to communicate, but no less important for that. In any of these different kinds of examples, people, and of course teachers, can be as living parables.

Story, Ritual and Example then, three vehicles that can so conjure with the imagination and thought of the individual at any age that their world is enlarged and the religious experience of mankind can come alive for them. Here is firm ground for the teacher to stand on, even when times are a-changing. Without that ground, there can be little exploration of identity or education for being.

## Afterword

An RE that is deeply personal and world-embracing in its horizons must have far-reaching curriculum consequences. For instance, it may lay claim to special time of its own in which the distinctive features of religion can be scrutinized, but it will frequently appear as an element in other subject areas. It will also lend itself to attempts at curriculum integration (RE as 'curriculum cement') and in its dissatisfaction with penultimate answers will encourage thorough-going enquiry methods of work. Further, it will be impatient about the traditional act of worship in school, but in its place seek to generate class, year, or whole-school rituals that authentically explore and express the human and, dare it be said, religious identity of a community of learning. Groundwork for the future is a powerful force for curriculum innovation.

(1974)

# Chapter 4

# Teaching world religions

Less than ten years ago the place of world religions in education was marginal. At the time of writing the situation has dramatically changed to such an extent that a 'world religions approach' to religious education has apparently become accepted as normative.

This change can most easily be illustrated by reference to two Agreed Syllabuses drawn up by Local Education Authorities as guidelines for all those responsible for religious education in the schools of their areas.[1] The first is from Yorkshire (West Riding 1966). It can be summarized as follows:

*Early Childhood: 4–7 Years*
Introduction to God's care through an exploration of the natural environment and relationships; biblical associations to arise from living experiences connected with the following themes: Homes and Families; Autumn and Harvest; Winter and Christmas; Spring and Easter; Summer and Whitsun; Friends and Followers of Jesus.

*Middle and Late Childhood, Pre-Adolescence: 7–11 Years*
Religion is the essence of all life, illustrated by material from everyday experience, the Bible and other sources in such themes as: Caring, Thankfulness, Courage, Forgiveness; Sheep and Shepherds, Wells and Water, Corn and Bread, Highways and Journeys; Discovering the Bible; Life in Bible Times; and Christian Festivals.

*Early Adolescence: 11–13 Years*
Discovering Jesus: highlights in Jesus' life based on Mark's gospel. Discovering Christianity today: the New Testament Church; Church History; the Church in the twentieth century.

*Middle Adolescence: 13–16 Years*
Christian worship and practice: in Old and New Testaments and today. Personal relationships: Love and Responsibility with reference to the New Testament and contemporary problems. Christianity in the modern world: questions about the Bible, Jesus, God, Sin, Suffering, Prayer, the Church, Science and Religion. World Problems: media; hunger; work and leisure; gambling; refugees; illiteracy; world religions.

*Late Adolescence: 16–18 Years*
Religion and life in contemporary society: religious faith; unity of the Bible; Christian doctrine; Christian morality; Alternatives to Christianity; Comparative Study of Religions; Christian Deviations; Christianity and the Arts; Science and Religion; the Ecumenical Movement; the Liturgical Movement.

The influence of this syllabus was not confined to the north-east of England, and similar emphases are to be found in subsequent syllabuses produced in Hampshire, Kent, Lancashire, London and Wiltshire. Its most noticeable characteristic is an attempt to relate the biblical concerns that had predominated in previous syllabuses to the present world of pupils. In this, the contemporary Christian theological concern with 'finding God in the midst of life' had conspired with warnings of developmental psychologists about 'unreadiness' for handling religious concepts in junior years.[2] As in all previous syllabuses, however, world religions is confined to a minor role even in late adolescence.

The second syllabus has recently emerged from the city of Birmingham. Its contents can be summarized as follows:

*Infancy and Early Childhood: 3–8 Years*
A selection from each of the following topics: Festivals – Christian, Hindu, Jewish, Muslim and Sikh; Rituals and Customs – in family and religious community; Stories from World Religions; Wonder and Mystery in the Natural World; Relationships with Others – illustrated by examples from world religions.

*Later Childhood: 8–12 Years*
Religious ideals and aspirations expressed in family and community life. Religious faith as represented by festivals and customs. Religious faith as represented by sacred places and the observances associated with them. Sacred writings preserving and inspiring traditions of religious faith; their distinctive language and literary form. Ways of living illustrated by stories of founders and great exemplars of world faiths and humanism.

*Adolescence: 12–16 Years*
Direct study of religion: Christianity and choice of up to three other religious traditions, including a non-religious stance for living. Indirect study of religion: religious beliefs, values and attitudes as relating to select topics in personal and social ethics.

*Sixth Form: 16–18 Years*
Further study of Adolescent topics. Study in depth of such topics as: Buddhism; philosophy of religion; religion and arts; mysticism; etc. (Birmingham 1974).

This and the accompanying Handbook (Birmingham 1974) represent five years of collaboration between teachers from schools, colleges and universities, with representatives of all the local religious communities. The thoroughgoing concern with all manner of religious and non-religious life-stances, as well as Christianity, is evident even in the approach to the infant classroom. Initial anxieties on the part of certain local politicians about the inclusion of Communism, even as the negation of religion, did delay the publication by some months, and the controversy persists. But the syllabus now carries official status in accord with the 1944 Education Act. If the importance of world religions in the curriculum has been given this degree of public recognition, no one familiar with the pressures of institutional inertia within local government and educational administration can deny that a revolution has occurred.

## Ignorance unchanged and unchallenged

However compelling these signs of revolution, their impact is as yet limited. Extensive ignorance persists in the community at large about the variety of religious belongings to be found in England and the world. Even the simplest features of different religious identities are apparently beyond the ken of many pupils and their parents (Gates 1975). Instead, prejudice-ridden images of a few religious allegiances are still rife. Among Christians, Catholics may be described as 'worshipping Mary', Protestants as 'not believing very much', and Jews as 'mean'. Jews and Muslims may speak bluntly of Hindus as idolaters; or Sikhs tell tales of Muslim murderings. To a Humanist, religious belief may mean 'anti-intellectual oppression'; in turn, he may be regarded by the religious believer as an 'agent of Lucifer'. The negative attitudes implicit in such views can easily interfere with attempts to provide more sympathetic perspectives.

Even if all teachers were free from any such distortions, they might yet define their own position about religious education – positive, negative or indifferent – in terms of the presuppositions of the older Agreed Syllabuses. Indeed, the persistence of the legal requirement for a daily act of worship,[3] invariably understood as Christian, in all schools may encourage them to do so. The pressures involved are illustrated by the following statistic on the personal beliefs of staff, given in a recent report on religious education in primary (Schools Council 1972: 27–8 and Appendix C). Of teachers in selected schools, 1.9 per cent described themselves as atheists, 7.2 per cent as agnostics, 16.7 per cent as Humanists, 31.1 per cent as nominal Christians, and 43.1 per cent as committed Christians; of headteachers in the same schools, three described themselves as non-committed Christians, 47 as convinced. The leap in the extent of conviction can be variously interpreted, but it is difficult to avoid reading it as other than evidence of continuing institutional bias towards Christianity.

On the other hand, however willing individual teachers and headteachers might be to introduce world religions to their schools, professional reticence may in fact discourage many of them from the attempt. Less than 40 per cent of the RE teachers in secondary schools have specialist qualifications, and of these only a minority have had world religions courses in colleges or universities. Primary school teachers are generally responsible for the religious education of their class, but the amount of religious education built into their own initial training as teachers has only exceptionally included world religions (Marratt 1971, Rainbow 1975).

The competence and motivation of those who have sought to introduce world religions in their schools is not always above reproach. It is not unknown for a teacher to set about teaching world religions with no more background understanding than that acquired from an introductory school text intended for 12 to 15 year olds. The risk of superficiality and distortion is enormous anyway – even for the specialist – but in such instances as this 'good intentions' are almost bound to be counter-productive. Unfortunately publishers sensing the commercial possibilities of an expanding world religions market have sometimes been so eager to join in that they have failed to realize the shoddiness of what they were offering.

As for wrong motivation, there are instances where teachers have made references to different religious traditions only then to go on and compare them unfavourably with the true religion – Christianity. Rather differently, others have come into world religions 'on the rebound' from personal engagement with 'religionless Christianity' and 'death of God' theologies; here the risk may be a naive exaltation of any faith other than the one in which they have ceased themselves to believe.

The 'world religions revolution', therefore, may have begun but can hardly be described as complete. The size of the task, together with counter-revolutionary elements, could threaten the whole movement. Much depends on efforts presently being made within the religious communities and professional academic centres and associations to consolidate the changes already achieved.

## Parent religious communities

The provision for religious education has traditionally been by agreement between churches and local education authorities. The Agreed Syllabuses from the 1920s to the late 1960s were successive local attempts to arrive at a common-denominator version of Christianity which could unobjectionably be taught in a public educational system. However diverse the range of belief and unbelief in English society during this period, the Christian community was institutionally established as the nation's norm.

Thus, the Jewish community, settled in the country for over 300 years, now numbering 400,000 to 500,000, and no longer confined to two or three ghetto areas, could yet be effectively ignored by the syllabus-makers. Indeed, the Old Testament treated only as a prolegomenon to the Christian tradition, and

Pharisaic piety presented in imprisoning contrast to the gospel of liberation added insult to the injury of nigh total silence about the Jewish story beyond 70 CE.

Neither was there much recognition of the position of the unchurched majority of the population.[4] To be sure, there is negative acknowledgement of the possibility of conscientious objection to Christian-based teaching in schools, in the withdrawal rights guaranteed to pupils' parents by Act of Parliament (guaranteed since the beginning of state education in England (Cruickshank 1963: ch. 2). But there was no deliberate representation of non-theistic philosophies of life. This is not made any easier by the fact that only a small proportion of the 'unchurched' are avowed secularists, Marxists or members of the British Humanist Association (Campbell 1969), but with or without such institutional labelling their respective allegiances function in their lives in a fashion comparable with religion.

Ironically, legislation that sought to stem the flow of immigration from the Commonwealth and overseas in 1962 affected the entire situation of minority and majority groups in this country. Many of the folk from India and Pakistan, Cyprus or the West Indies found they could no longer return to their homelands without loss of right to re-entry. Thus, migrants became settlers; wives and families were nurtured over here, and the schools by the late 1960s received increasing numbers of children of different complexions, and of which religion was a major distinguishing feature (Morrish 1973, Krausz 1971).

The religious pluralism of English society became so obvious that, in certain areas at least, Christian allegiance was revealed as one among many. A local authority conference of Bradford teachers in consultation with minority groups produced a supplement to the West Riding Agreed Syllabus entitled *Guide to Religious Education in a Multi-Faith Community* (1973), in which Christianity was set as equal alongside Hinduism, Islam, Judaism and Sikhism (Cole 1973). This, and the even more inclusive Birmingham Syllabus, indicates the potential support available from the parent religious communities, including the British Humanist Association, for a broadly based religious education.

Risk to this potential is considerable, both from the professional limitations already mentioned and from inter-faith suspicions. Of particular importance, therefore, are two national bodies that have been established in the last three years.

The first is the Standing Conference on Inter-Faith Dialogue in Education.[5] It provides a forum in which the communities of faith can informally discuss any matters of common educational concern. At a recent gathering (1975), which was devoted to the process of initiation in education and religion, the following recommendations were agreed:

1.  *County schools and local authorities* to recognize fully the needs (including factors affecting diet, dress and festivals) for all minority communities, and to provide opportunities for them to make their unique contribution to the religious and cultural life of the school.

2. *Minority communities* to make known their felt needs and aspirations to schools and local authorities, and to encourage their own people to be trained as teachers so that they may play their full part in the county school and in the production of suitable material concerning their own faith for teachers of RE in the county schools.

3. *Parents and families* of all communities to examine (and perhaps to redefine) their own situation in a pluralist society, to encourage their children who are students in schools and colleges to contribute to the exchange of views with their peers in the fields of morality and religion, and to support the school as well as their own children by participating in its extracurricular life.

4. *Support for religious education* conceived 'as a developmental process by which every child, wherever he lives, will have the opportunity of learning about the ideals and insights, religious and non-religious, which inspire mankind' (1974 Inter-Faith Conference Statement) in the belief that religious education so conceived would provide a climate congenial for the participation of all communities.

5. *Members of Parliament, the Department of Education and Science, local education authorities and the Community Relations Commission and its local councils* to take note of the above recommendations and to seek ways of implementing them.

Translations were made for publication in the several ethnic newspapers.

The second is the Religious Education Council of England and Wales. Like the Standing Conference this includes representatives from every major religious community in the country, along with the British Humanist Association, but all professional organizations (school-, college- and university-oriented) associated with religious education are also officially involved. Representation is formally agreed and the constitution carefully balanced for professional and confessional interests. Where once the government's Ministry of Education primarily consulted the churches about matters pertaining to religious education, this council is now the most authoritative advisory body, and tacitly recognized as such.

Parent religious communities, therefore, are making a significant contribution to the cause of teaching of world religions. There is a domestic consequence for them, however. In addition to provision for study of their own faith, they are faced with an urgent theological priority – that of coming to terms with the plurality of religious truth claims. The logic of the Christian faith, for instance, requires that some positive sense be made of this world and of all that is in it, including other religions (Hocking 1940, Tillich 1963b and 1966, Christian 1972, Hick 1974). A Christian education would in itself be incomplete without direct dealing with the faith of other folk ((Smart 1968b, Church of England Commission on Religious Education in Schools 1970: 61–3, 102–3). This is true of the other communities too. Thus the mutual involvement of schools and communities, which is an important feature of the

English scene, has in this way become a spur to theological explorations. In turn, any one tradition drawing on its own theology of education may throw up questions about prevalent educational assumptions (Ferré 1967b, Broudy 1971, Tibawi 1972).

## Professional academic concerns

The long-term strength of the movement towards teaching world religions needs also to be guaranteed by professional academic developments. The revolution was philosophically propelled, almost independently of the recognition of religious pluralism in the country. A professional consensus emerged that religion's place in any curriculum had to be justified 'on educational grounds', and seen to be so (Schools Council 1971, Hull 1975a).

The consensus in part reflected the concern with the philosophy of education that burgeoned in the mid-1960s. Curriculum philosophers focused attention on the different forms of knowledge, and thus questions about the logical status and distinctiveness of religion were raised. The more abrasive took the priority given to the Bible throughout English education as indication of covert assumptions about special revelation, predicated on faith rather than on reason. The school of reason should not be confused with any stable of revelation! Others recognized an alternative perspective in the philosophy of religion.

For, simultaneously with these concerns in the philosophy of education, the pattern for the study of religion in universities was changing. Theology, however scientifically studied, had in university usage meant predominantly the Old and New Testaments, church history and doctrine. The now generally accepted change of nomenclature to departments of religious studies which has taken place since 1966 (when the first was established at the University of Lancaster) represents an acknowledgement that these elements form part of the larger Christian tradition, which in turn is part of the larger religious experience of mankind. University theological horizons are expected to be comprehensive (Smart 1970a, Galloway 1975, Parrinder 1975); even as a result of historical accident the study of religion in a public educational system should not remain 'sectarian'. Acceptance of this point provides the second ingredient of the professional consensus.

These academic concerns are effectively conjoined with those of the parent religious communities on the Religious Education Council of England and Wales. Immediately, criteria are operative in the selection of priorities for religious education which are not dependent on the present composition of English society and local variations. Otherwise, the fact that there are as many followers of the Baha'i faith in England as there are Buddhists might be made to justify giving these two traditions equal weight. Or, again, distinctive dress and numerical strength of the Sikh community might be a distraction from the claims for due attention of the Hindu tradition, slightly smaller in its English representation. Similarly, the relative absence of immigrants from such parts of the country as Cornwall or Hereford or Cumbria might be presented as a reason for ignoring there any faith other than Christianity. Against these kinds of danger, the disciplines of religious studies and the larger context of the religious experience of humanity at large provide a necessary guard. The task of selection from within such inclusive horizons remains daunting, however, and definitional disputes among scholars compound the difficulty (Smith 1962, Spiro 1966, Baird 1971, Smart 1973a and 1973b, Streng 1973). The most systematic attempt to deal with this question of criteria in religious education has been by a group of philosophers and educationists appointed by the Schools Council to produce a taxonomy of religious education. Their 'ground-plan' for the subject, with its selection of salient concepts, skills and attitudes from respective religious traditions, is greatly needed (Schools Council 1977a, in consultation with faith communities, via the newly formed RE Council).

This Schools Council report should serve as further theoretical consolidation for the revolution. But arguably the most urgent consolidation is with teacher education. In this field much pioneering has been done by the Shap Working Party on World Religions in Education. Established in 1969, and consisting of teachers and lecturers from all levels of education, it sponsors regular in-service courses all over the country on world religions. The courses have been designed to give intensive introductions to a particular religious tradition and to give guidance about classroom application. Response in Wales and Northern Ireland has been limited, less so in Scotland, but in England their success has been such that many local education authorities and teachers' centres are now offering similar courses. In addition to the courses, the Shap Working Party provides a general information service on world religions, and has a series of regionally based working groups, which concentrate on such priorities as world religions in the infant school and in public examinations (www.shap.org). Independently, the two national resource centres for religious education, government-financed, and a similar Church of England centre, carry most of the available world religions 'teaching aids', and actively encourage this approach to the subject.[6]

Such provisions for in-service re-education, together with those presently being trained in universities and colleges, may eventually mean that the world religions revolution is practically as well as theoretically reinforced.


## The hermeneutics of teaching

During the transition period, and probably beyond, there are likely to be different ways of teaching world religions. In history teaching, there is continuing dispute as to whether it is more effective to take a 'grand survey' approach or to concentrate on a much more specific time and place. Is it misleading to build a year's work around a few key figures? Would it be more instructive to focus on social and economic conditions? Is it possible to single out some central concern which can be said to be the prime objective of history teaching – for example, 'sense of time perspective' – and to work consistently for that? (Burston and Green 1972). Comparable questions are asked about teaching world religions, with no immediate prospect of final solution.

The ambiguity of suggesting that a *historical approach* should be employed is already clear. But psychological considerations further complicate the matter. Some who have taken the historical tack have ignored the findings of developmental psychology about children's capacities for chronological understanding (Godin 1971). Others sadly report the lack of interest of their pupils when faced with the Indus Valley civilization – a response previously familiar in dealing with the history and archaeology of Israel.

A *phenomenological approach* has appeared to some to provide a more effective alternative. But in school versions this has sometimes meant little more than visits (audio-visually arranged, if local resources were otherwise limited) to temples and synagogues, and tales of 'founders' and festivals. By these means, familiarity with external trappings may have been achieved, but not necessarily appreciation of what it means to be a Sikh or a Jew.

A more personal emphasis has been present in an *archetypal approach*. Especially in the primary school, this has involved the selection of certain themes, such as trust, light, wonder, helping, representing basic elements in religion. Personal engagement may have been created as a result, but often variations between religions have been blurred. Common denominators of what it means to be religious are not so easily available, and the Humanists in particular are wary of the 'conversion by definition' which they fear might follow from presenting everyday human concerns as religious.

To a certain extent, assessment of the limitations and relative merits of such different ways of teaching world religions depends upon the resolution of methodological issues in the academic study of religion. An educationally balanced procedure will probably include each of the main emphases here represented as separate approaches. As in the historical approach, there will be the priority of factual detail and perspective; as in the phenomenological, the priority of structures of meaning and distanced understanding; and, as in the archetypal, that of locating common human concerns. But a major responsibility must lie with individual teachers. They have a double loyalty – to the religious experience of humankind in all its diversity, and to the individual experience of children. This entails hermeneutical skills in both directions at once.

The child-centredness characteristic of primary school education, if consistently applied to the teaching of world religions, can be a guard against 'inert' learning. But, more important, it can also mean that teachers are sensitive to the range of individual understandings in any group of children. A teacher is their interpreter.

At the same time, teachers must have interpreted and understood at their own level the aspects of religion which they wish to share with the children. Such sensitive hermeneutics should prevent superficiality or syncretistic distortion. Thus, by this double commitment to the children in their own right and religion in its own terms, the dialectic of reason and revelation in religious understanding can itself be respected.

Something of this dialectic may have been lost in too simplistic applications of Ninian Smart's six- (later seven-) dimensional model of religion to religious education. So widely has this been disseminated through the Schools Council Projects on Religious Education and other literature[7] that in the space of five years it has become for some, as it were, a new 'hexateuch'. This typology of the major constituent elements of religion – doctrinal, mythical, ritual, ethical, social, experiential – has served to highlight the multidimensional character of religion, an invaluable reminder in a situation where even 'Christian man' was cast in syllabus terms as 'one-dimensional'. The danger is real, however, that the dynamic intent of the scheme, essentially dependent on the distinctive expressions of any one tradition of faith, may be obscured. Religion may once again be conveniently packaged – and lifeless.

This risk will be all the greater unless the correspondence between the components of being religious and those of being human is appreciated. For each religious component is reflective of elemental aspects of human being, as can be illustrated most easily by the accompanying chart (Figure 4.1).

In seeking to further a child's religious understanding, their general/secular understanding is also inevitably involved.

| | |
|---|---|
| Formal reasoning in science, maths or history | DOCTRINAL |
| Storytelling and gossip | MYTHOLOGICAL |
| Ordering of personal interests, priorities and ambitions | ETHICAL |
| Playground games and gestures of friendship | RITUAL |
| Intimate feelings of self-awareness | EXPERIENTIAL |
| Social and political belonging in family and school | SOCIAL |
| Houses and shopping arcades | MATERIAL |

**Figure 4.1** 'Secular' counterparts to Smart's constituent elements of being 'religious'

The objective of a religious education defined in such terms would not necessarily be to make a child 'religious'. The logic of a plural religious situation in society entails recognition that there are many different ways of being religious and irreligious, and in a public system of education the truth claims of none can be taken for granted at the expense of the others. It would be entirely proper, by contrast, for a school to seek to enable a child to become 'religiate', in other words, to enable him to understand what it might mean to be religious – in, for example, Catholic or Protestant, Buddhist or Muslim terms – or what it might mean to reject religion in the name of Marx, or Freud or Sartre.

Understanding of this kind would complement any personal religious identity or questing, bequeathed by the home or parent religious community.

By providing the human checkpoints for different religious and atheistic viewpoints, it would challenge blinkered attitudes and encourage careful pondering about their respective beliefs and values, both as separate symbolic constellations and as impinging on each other.

## Teaching world religions: religious education

In the 'early days' of the movement towards teaching world religions, the possibility was discussed of treating them separately from (Christian) religious education (Hinnells 1970: ch. 3). This would have preserved the traditional provision of induction into the Christian tradition while allowing world religions to be taught in a manner free from any evangelistic aims. But, as well as proving unrealistic in terms of the overcrowded school timetable its division of labour was too simple. As already indicated, Christian education in itself requires reference to the faith of other folk and their alternative claims to truth; openness in this regard can be a model for educators in any religious community. Moreover, it is a mistake to suppose that it were educational to ignore the vitality of other faiths.

Instead, therefore, of speaking about 'teaching world religions' the term 'RE' itself can now fairly be used to include this orientation. The time for artificial polarization between Bible teaching and life-concerns, between teaching Christianity or teaching world religions, is passing. An authentic religious education for the future involves wholehearted initiation into the manifold structures of religious experience worldwide and the rich diversity of human being (Holm 1975).

(1977)

Chapter 5

# Understanding the real context for world religions in education

## The real world?

What is the reality which provides the context for considering the place of world religions in education? What strikes me forcefully is that there is much in the world that is disturbing, even shocking for any religious believer.

Three different forms of this disturbance are as follows:

Religion is *diverse* – there are very many different ways of being religious. To be Buddhist or Baha'i is very different from being either Jewish, Druze or a follower of Rajneesh. The history of religions shows us that the quest for a common essence of all religions is even more illusory than the quest to identify the essence of Christianity. Then there are important variations within religions, almost from one believer to another, just as there are *between* religions. Consider some leading politicians all of whom claim to be active in their Christian faith: President Nyerere of Tanzania, Prime Minister Margaret Thatcher and President Ronald Reagan. No doubt we could all think of others. By their own claim they are authentic in their faith, but with manifestly different results. Moreover, other Christians would be variously positive or negative in their evaluation of them. Comparable differences are there between and within denominations, as also among theologians. Christianity is incredibly diverse and so too is religion generally.

Not surprisingly therefore, religion is evidently *divisive*. It may not be the only factor in the explosive social mix of humanity but it's certainly a powerful one. We have only to look at the current struggle between Buddhists and Hindus in Sri Lanka, Sikhs and Hindus in the Punjab or Christian and Muslims in the Lebanon. These are all examples of tensions *between* religions but we also find tension between those of the same faith allegiance as in Iran versus Iraq, Northern Ireland or Nicaragua. Human beings are in turn aggressive or defensive in relation to their deepest convictions. In this they may be fairly sophisticated or crudely blunt. The Bible is the Word of God, not the Gita, Granth or Qur'ān! The Pope was right to hold audience with Kurt Waldheim because Christianity teaches forgiveness whereas Judaism preaches the *lex talionis*. But that's not how I see it *if* I'm a Hindu, a Sikh, a Muslim or a Jew. 'Out, out, out' chant the National Front against Pakistani Muslims in the East End of London, 'Aus, aus, aus' chant the Neo-Nazis against Turkish Muslims in Hanover – all on a Saturday night.

Would that modern Europe had found it easy to be more accommodating to Jews and Muslims than our Medieval Christian inheritance inclines us to be.

Religion is also **disputed**. On *psychological* grounds, religion is rejected as an illusory projection: a hangover from the childhood of the human race or early infancy, lingering like parentally induced inhibitions on a young couple's honeymoon, or, a mindless mystic drive for the bliss of the unborn baby safe and warm in a black hole of security.

Similarly, *literary critical* investigations can be sceptical of the documentary evidence to support the historicity of claims associated with Moses or Muhammad; Gautama, Jesus or Nanak.

Yet again, leading *physicists and astronomers* repudiate the claim that there ever was a time when the universe did not exist – so much the worse for theologians' talk of creation.

We are all familiar with such arguments as these – sometimes expressed in elaborately reasoned language, other times blurted out with gut-felt conviction: 'rubbish!'. Either way, religious language/god talk is rejected as phoney currency, 'funny money'.

If these three points are not shocking enough, when we continue to look around, we observe two further contemporary facts of life.

For many, **life is unjust**. Although we may blot them from consciousness, they or their equivalents are there everyday:

- the victims of Sudanese, Ethiopian or Indian famines;
- those infected by Aids – not just because as a young woman I've left my village in rural Rwanda to earn money from Western tourists in the big city and have caught it; but because I'm a six-year-old boy who has been unwittingly given a transfusion of contaminated blood;
- those born deformed or mentally defective;
- and what of the aborted foetus?

For all, there's the **nuclear threat**. Hiroshima and Nagasaki were more powerful than all the previous explosive power used in human history. Yet they are as a single letter on this page in comparison with current stockpiles of nuclear weaponry represented by all the print on ten complete pages. There is an aweful mixture of dangerous risk and calculated security here.

The Real World is shocking for both education and religion.

## So what's new?

Surprising though it may be on first reaction, it should not be since religion has always been diverse, divisive and disputed. *Diverse*: look at the Ancient Near East, Ancient India or the Medieval western world. *Divisive*: look at the struggle between Elijah and the prophets of Baal in the Jewish and Christian scriptures, at events in first-century Jerusalem or Rome or in sixteenth and seventeenth-century Europe. *Disputed*: remember the ancient Latin tag from the poet Statius 2000 years ago: *primus in orbe deos fecit Timor* – 'in the beginning fear created the Gods' – not, after all, a Freudian discovery. Philosophical atheism was not invented by the European Enlghtenment; it is well documented throughout the ancient world, in Greece, India as well as China. Historical scepticism is there in first-century Palestine in the inscription that forbids any tampering with graves; or the excision from first- and second-century Jewish writings of any positive references to Jesus. And as for the clash between scientists and theologians over creation, there is an abundance of creation stories from all over the world sufficient to match virtually anything a physicist or astronomer can come up with. Already these stories were at odds with each other.

That *life is unjust* for many has been widely commented on in 'Job stories' from ancient Babylon, Israel or West Africa. Poverty and plague aren't new; indeed as Max Weber pointed out, religions the world over are direct responses to the problem of innocent suffering. They provide a *theodicy*; they make reality bearable.

Finally the *unpredictability of life and death* was evident long before Hiroshima and Nagasaki. Learning to live with the fact that I'm also dying has been a common counsel of religious traditions.

## Is there anything which is really new/different in our contemporary situation?

It is important to recognize as least three of the main novelties.

The first of these relates to our *demographic context*.

At over five billion and still expanding, there are more people alive now than ever before. More surprisingly perhaps, there are more Christians alive now than the sum total of all those who lived between AD 30 and 1920. This is also comparably true of many other faiths/world-views but not for all. Some are static in numbers or have declined or even become extinct.

There is no doubt that the scale of religious traditions is enormous, but one consequence is that the question of what should be seen as normative in each religion is greatly magnified. By implication also I cannot claim to understand the world at large unless I get to know the different world-views that shape it, not as static entities, but as in process of organic development.

The second relates to our capacity for a *global perspective*

The history of humankind has now reached the point at which *global* self-consciousness is possible, i.e. not just national, or regional, but *worldwide* awareness of being human. This potential is typified by the view from Apollo of our own globe. At the same time we have discovered that this world is but an atom in a universe that is immeasurably beyond our imaginations in size. One implication of this is that a sense of the collective oneness of the human race may be that much easier to develop.

My third novelty arises from the **communications revolution**. Once upon a time the domestic hearth was largely closed off to the outside world. The words and deeds which were shared there were produced and controlled by the family unit and folks present. Now more often than not the flickering fire at the centre of the home has been replaced by the TV screen and children are tuned into it with their mother's milk. It is possible to speak disparagingly of the dulling effect of *Dallas* in 65 countries. I want instead to stress the eye-opening, horizon-stretching impact of TV. Like it or not human beings are now increasingly privy to other people's lives because their own homes have this extra window on the world.

## Reality for world religions in education

It is important to consider this with the main participants in turn in mind.

### The parental religious traditions and the logic of religion

Although some would wish that it were otherwise, *no single religion has an incontrovertible claim to truth.* No one world-view can prove itself true and all the others false. If the attempt is made to do this by appeal to Revelation alone, then another community may in turn appeal to another Revelation. Both can have the satisfaction of being safe within a self-contained theological framework but this will be at the expense of communication with each other or the wider human community in terms of any public language. The world might be a poorer place in the absence of fundamentalists or sects of this kind, but by definition they are not responsible for public education.

Alternatively a religious tradition may endeavour to explain and justify itself by use of rational argument. If so, it will be persuaded of its own truth but at the same time must allow that others may come to a different conclusion. That conclusion or alternative world-view may be seen as a comparable equal or judged inferior. Either way rational argument, public evidence, and 'inter-subjective' criteria will have been used. On such a basis there need be nothing to fear from a public approach to treatment of world religion in education.

Although some religions are more missionary-minded than others, it is usually the case that whatever someone's faith they are likely to want to share it. If they do not, that suggests that they think very little of the worth of other human beings, or that they do not care that much about their faith. Whether formally or informally, religious traditions will usually want to make special arrangements to perpetuate and extend themselves. That will of necessity require extra initiative and provision beyond that available in the context of public education.

## The logic of public education

Schools and colleges have often been founded to further a particular faith or ideal. This might be a church school, a Hasidic school, a Qur'ānic school, even a Montessori or Rudolf Steiner school. National education systems may also be tied in with a particular religious tradition, or equivalent world-view as in say Pakistan with Islam, our own two countries (Germany and the UK) with Christianity, and the USSR with Marxist-Leninist ideology. In any of these the degree of openness that is shown to other world religions will depend on how the issue of truth claims, first mentioned, is resolved. In some contexts the system will be single-mindedly closed.

However, in a participant democracy, the logic of education requires explicit recognition of the validity of alternative viewpoints – hence the invocation in this respect of what is referred to as the 'Thomas Jefferson principle'. Unfortunately, in the American model the total separation of church and state is often interpreted to mean no RE at all in public schools.

Thinking pictorially; there are two extreme positions on a spectrum of **open** ←——→ **closed**. Examples of the more closed approach would be Pakistan or the USSR; in neither setting is critical questioning of the established faith/ideology actively encouraged. Nor is sympathetic appreciation of other religions actively promoted. At the opposite end of the spectrum the USA is so open in its acceptance of the validity of alternative religions that none of them is actively explored or interrogated in school.

What about England? Where does that fit? I would say substantially more open than closed. True as here the church is still established, but there are no obligatory church taxes. Moreover, although RE is required by law in all schools, this does not have to be exclusively Christian. In the church schools, which are 85 per cent state funded, and which educate about a quarter of all children, the syllabuses are within the control of local school governors or dioceses. Here we see again the different degrees of openness to other faiths. In the county schools, which provide for all the other pupils, the RE syllabus is agreed locally between teachers and the local faith communities. Until 1975 these were predominantly and in some cases exclusively Christian; since then they have become affirmative of other faiths as well. The mechanism for these syllabuses is quite distinctive since it entails collaboration between not just the Church of England, Roman Catholicss and the Reformed Churches, but in principle also Jews, Muslims, Sikhs and Hindus as well as teachers and education advisers.

A reference point nationally is the RE Council of England and Wales which has represented on it all the different teacher associations for schools, colleges and universities, advisory resource centres, together with each of the parental faith communities – the Christian spectrum from Catholics to Quakers, Baha'is, Buddhists, Jews, Hindus, Muslims, Sikhs and the British Humanist Association. There is a balance here, a healthy tension, between professional and confessional interests as they apply to public education. While I might firmly believe that this is a model worth imitating elsewhere, it is for others to decide and implement.

## Pupil prerogatives

This is where I believe the heart of the discussion ought to lie. RE will not succeed unless it starts with the child. Our attention has been drawn to the way we and they always bring our presuppositions to bear on anything they or we want to understand and interpret. In Germany it seems that most boys and girls are given a religious label – Protestant or Catholic (or emergent Muslim) – when they go to school, even if beforehand their actual qualification for this might be judged to be in breach of a 'trade description Act'. It is worth remembering also that children have other sources of information in addition to parents and teachers, especially the TV as already mentioned, but also *peer group learning*. Even in infant school there is a significant playground culture which is a vital source of beliefs and values to the young child that we often overlook. They also do their own share of *personal wondering*. In some respects children, and not just older students, may already know more than we their teachers of some aspects of life and death, and indeed religion. They will certainly have questions to ask if we are present and receptive enough to hear them.

It seems likely that at different ages boys and girls will be more or less able to understand and express themselves in different modes of thinking. Without becoming too mechanical in applying the conclusions of developmental psychology, we do well to recognize the different power and potential of language. It may be full of fairy tale and fantasy, more concrete and circumstantial, or more fully elaborated in its patterns of reasoning. There is much that can be said and done in each mode that can deepen and extend an understanding of religion.

Finally what of you and me in relation to children, in relation to our students?

## Professional teacher response

For effective RE in public education, I do not think there should be a private beliefs test. This is a lesson we have learned gradually but well in England. A certain asceticism over display of my individual beliefs may actually be quite healthy. Far better that as teacher I can be passionate and impartial in seeking to bring to life with and for the pupils this aspect of Islam or Hinduism or Christianity. Far better that I can stand with a particular child in their beliefs and move with them in an act of further understanding.

But as a teacher, I must also have much to share that will take boys and girls below the surface and into the heartlands of religions. I cannot know everything, but that will not matter; it is not my job simply to churn out a massive array of intellectual data which they could instead be encouraged to find out for themselves in reference books. However, I should be familiar with more than the tradition of my own private faith; how impoverished will be my own European Christianity if I've never met with a different world-view. I should also be growing a repertoire of resources that can be deployed as occasion arises. There will not just be learned texts that tax the intellect but stories and myths, play and ritual, pictures and images that form the fabric of everyday human life and meaning as well as religious tradition.

## In conclusion

Understanding reality for world religions in education is quite a challenge. It is evident that anyone who is professionally involved must be ready to grow and change in the process.

(1987)

Chapter 6

# The end of religion in the UK and beyond

## Humanity is waving farewell to religion

There is a dominant myth that religion is in decline in the UK and that in so far as it thrives elsewhere in the world, this is a sign of social backwardness. For instance, Richard Dawkins (1997: 64–9), the public advocate for better understanding of science, wastes few opportunities to belittle religion as inheritor of pre-scientific beliefs which will not bear sustained rational scrutiny. Or again, commentators on world development attribute to Hinduism a major responsibility for slow economic growth in India (see Siegel 1986: ch. 8). Such judgements are commonplace in the western world-view which inducts us into Marxist and Freudian ways of thinking. Religion belongs in our childhood, both as individuals and, more collectively, as the human race. Whether in the form of some all-powerful, parent-like, protective power, or a back-to-the-womb mysticism, it is there as consolation in the face of misfortune and as promise of alternative compensation in some future world beyond the present. Accordingly, how can it be other than patently false? It has no more credibility than the self-projected belief in Father Christmas, or the fleeting internal glow induced by one or other of the socially accepted drugs, contemporary opiates of the people.

## The evidence of decay

### The numerical decline of organized religion

The evidence on which the myth is based is of two kinds. Firstly, there are the annual inventories of churchgoing, conducted by the churches themselves, such as the Church of England's returns on Easter communicants, or the Marc Europe/Christian Research surveys of all the Christian churches (see *Church of England Yearbook 1997*, Brierley 1997). They reveal that only 10 to 12 per cent of the population are in active membership, as measured by regular and frequent churchgoing, of whom more are under 15 years of age or over 50.

By all accounts, the other established religions show similar seepage. In the case of the Jewish community, the statistics are scarcely more encouraging and a special initiative entitled Jewish Continuity has been launched to attempt to reverse the trend.[1] For a variety of reasons, comparable figures for the other faith communities are difficult to obtain. Complications include debate over who should 'count' as a Hindu, Muslim, or Sikh. Ethnicity may be a guide, but only partially so. The reintroduction of a question about religious identity in the next census might therefore in this regard be very revealing.[2] In the meantime, however, there is extensive concern expressed from within these communities regarding the perceived trends towards 'fall-out'.[3] Similarly, Buddhist societies and meditation centres are popular, but the scale of active membership remains quite modest.[4]

In hard-edged institutional terms, traditional religious belonging no longer has the strength it once did. Even the pattern of preferred arrangements for marriage and the ceremonies associated with it confirm that this is so.[5]


## The dubious worth of religion

This impression of religion as a minority activity is further reinforced by the impression advertised in the media that religion fuels extreme fanaticism and conflict on the one hand and quaint superstition, if not endemic corruption, on the other. Thus, a Rabin or a Gandhi is killed by a fellow Jew or Hindu. There are riots between Hindus and Muslims in India over the site of the Ayodhya mosque, or between Buddhists and Hindus in Sri Lanka, Shi'ite Muslims in Iran and Shi'ite Muslims in Iraq, and remnants of mistrust between Protestants and Roman Catholics in Ireland. In Japan the determination of the Aum Shinrikyo cult to engage in large-scale extermination of the general public is as grim as that of the Hale-Bop enthusiasts to take their own lives and so hasten transition to another planet. And still the Millennium is yet to arrive. Religion on this evidence is a destructive force and we are to be thankful that the majority are not touched by it.

At the same time, there are reports of church statues which weep tears of blood, or of stone figures which drink milk in Hindu temples. The faith which is shown may be touching, but in the eyes of an independent observer it is gullible and naive. The fantastic history of relics in medieval Christendom or of self-serving gurus in India today expose very clearly how vulnerable individuals can be abused and exploited in the name of religion (see Duffy 1992: chs 5 and 8; Mehta 1980). With such track records as these, the sooner religion is dispensed with the better. It is perhaps no great surprise that Dawkins compares it to a genetic disease which warrants urgent eradication.[6]

# Counter evidence

Such data of religious decline give only a partial picture. There is a wider context and there are other perspectives.

## Any established institution is vulnerable to the effects of rapid change

The context is one of extraordinary social and technical change, along with the unsettling of familiar social forms; all this impacts on religion. World-wide urbanization, air travel, electronic media, artificial birth control, longer life expectancy, transplant surgery and all such new phenomena together entail that human life today is a different experience from when we were born. Moreover, because the process is continuous, this is true whatever our age. Alcopops, Aids, Attention Deficit Syndrome, and computer-animated pets will give way to, or be joined by, other striking developments within the year.

In the midst of such dramatic change, it is no surprise that all established institutions, social and economic, religious and political, are experiencing some turbulence and disaffection. The family is a typical example. In the UK, the rate of family breakdown has never been higher. This is evident in the figures for divorce, the incidence of pregnancies outside of marriage and of child abuse.[7] In each case there are qualifications to be made. For instance, in spite of the high divorce rate, remarriage is very popular. Unmarried mothers may be more numerous, but a higher proportion of them have their babies also registered with their father's name, suggesting a continuing relationship. And the known extent of child abuse may be more a reflection of our greater sensitivity to its likelihood, than any sudden growth. The overall effects, however, are unsettling and there is crisis talk about the family's future (see Berger and Berger 1983, Davies 1993).

Similarly, there is talk of alienation from the political process, exemplified by the numbers, including young people, not voting in elections. Accordingly, political parties and trade unions are restructuring their operations; but so too are banks, hospitals, law courts and schools. Change is evident on every institutional front. In some respects this is indicative of decay, but just as frequently it is a sign of rethinking and new growth. Arguably, therefore, it would be surprising if the same mixture of elements were not also at work in the sphere of institutional religious life.

## The persistence of religion in personal experience

Many other perspectives on religion are less jaundiced. The sociologist of religion like the opinion pollster may well point out that religion is more organically present in the interstices of family life and personal conviction than church attendance figures by themselves would suggest (see Davie 1994, cf. Greeley 1992). They may go on to draw attention to the reported incidence of individual religious experience as far more widespread, even in modern western societies, than might ever easily have been guessed. This indeed has been remarked by a range of investigators, with and without any 'religious axe' to grind. In this vein Alister Hardy (1979), Edward Robinson (1977) and David Hay (1982), successively directors of the Religious Experience Research Unit, remarked on the widespread incidence of the wider population's readiness to acknowledge such experiences as their own. Marghanita Laski (1980) independently came to the same conclusion, as did Andrew Greeley in North America (1974). Yet others, associated with the Impicit Religion Network coordinated by Edward Bailey, have drawn attention to the vitality of religion, living as it were unassumingly in the plain clothes of everyday life. Thus, they point to functional alternatives to traditional religion, not only in the labelled form of cults, but also in the less obvious ways in which a particular company, leisure enthusiasm, or even television can take over the role of providence and direction in life.[8] To the list might well be added the incidence of religious motifs in fantasy forms of Hollywood sci-fi and horror movies, or of computer adventure games.

### Religion as a continuing feature of national and international constitutional debate

It is significant too to observe the persistence of the religious ingredients in fundamental debates about national and international constitutions. Whenever the identity and future of a nation is 'up for review', it seems that religious considerations are commonly called into play. This has been evident in the UK throughout its history with respect to the monarchy, or, more particularly but perhaps less noticed, in England and Wales whenever, since 1870, there has been debate about a national curriculum. In Parliament, the shape of provision for education has invariably been associated with lengthy and acrimonious debate in which religion has loomed much larger than might have been anticipated by the politicians of the day. This happened in the 1987–8 debates about the Education Reform Bill, and it will happen again. Further afield, religion has featured directly in the constitutional reviews that have been taking place over the last decade in Eastern Europe, as for instance in Bulgaria, Hungary, Poland or Russia.[9] Similarly, it has warranted deliberate attention in the peace talks in Bosnia and the Middle East, as again in the Punjab and Tibet. Indeed, at least one observer speaks dramatically of religious nationalism as a challenge worldwide to western secular assumptions (Jurgensmeyer 1993).

At one level this might be interpreted as a lingering hangover of the unfortunate influence of institutional religion among people who have yet to come to terms fully with the sober realities of living in a free society. At another it would be recognized as sensing that in any discussion of human boundaries, far-reaching questions will arise which have to do with the bases for believing and valuing within which that humanity is rooted (see Bowker 1997: xvi–xxiv).

## Cosmic wonderings

Another area of evidence which provokes scepticism regarding the myth of religion on its last legs comes from reaction to scientific and technological achievements. One effect of these is that awareness of mortality and of the cosmic dimensions of life has been magnified. In a curious way, the very technology, which in other ways is associated more with mechanical control and technical mastery, serves to highlight precariousness and contingency in our existence. Accordingly, consciousness that we are mortal, or that the universe is of mind-boggling proportions, still arouses in human beings sensations and wonderings that put more immediate and functional preoccupations in the broader setting of concern over what we are to make of living in the first place. After all, we might never have been, either as the individuals who we are, or in more collective and organic connectedness.

Dependence is not a state of being which autonomy usually celebrates, but in so far as we might ever be moved to acknowledge the giftedness of life, we may find ourselves individually admitting there is that which is beyond us, on which we do depend. This might be a parent, the sunshine, or perhaps even the internet. Whichever it may be, these in turn may point beyond themselves. And therein lies the stuff of religion (cf. 'theistic evidences' in Richmond 1970).

## Alternative sources of salvation

In one sense it is too easy to invoke religion. Whenever that is done, proper scrutiny is called for, lest indeed it serves to confine and constrain the human spirit. One example of over-easy religious embrace may be seen in a general reaction to the experience of change and uncertainty, or of contingency as just described. Unnerved by one or more of these experiences, there is a rush to find immediate certainty. This simple and appropriate observation is all too quickly turned into dismissive explanation, heard alike from secularist social commentators and from defenders of established religions against more authoritarian versions of their faith or to counter the rise of the cults (see Evans 1973: 'Introduction', Marty and Scott Appleby 1991–5: *passim*).

The distinction needs to be made between shrewd comment and reductive explaining away. Another example of how the one can elide into the other is apparent in the magnetic attraction which the national lottery so evidently has for a substantial majority of the British population. It is certainly true that human beings enjoy gratification. It is also true that the mood of the moment is to prefer that this gratification is more granted in the present than delayed. What is more contentious is whether, when presented with the opportunity to engage more subtly with questions of longer-term meaning in their own lives, people will be driven by whatever instant scratch card solutions they can find in charisms, cults or casinos. 'Playing the final meaning game' may be an aspect of what is involved in both institutional religious behaviour and seeking salvation by lottery, but it begs the question to explain away either as only to do with materialistic intent, or alternatively with yearning for spiritual release.

Arguably, it is in the interests of any society in its provisions for public education to want to challenge unthinking credulity as demeaning of the human propensity for freedom and truth. By a similar line of argument, religious traditions of any standing in the world arena will be no less enthusiastic in encouraging their inheritors to use their hearts and minds fully in making the faith their own. There is a coincidence of potential opposites here: if closed-mindedness is the enemy of participational democracy, then it is no less the enemy of truth in religion.

## The public credibility of religions

The established religions owe it to the world, as to their present followers and patrons from of old, to represent themselves in ways that are compelling of good sense. This is true of every faith. It is the reverse of any flight from reason, as represented by some cults and closed-minded forms of fundamentalism, but it is more easily pointed out than acted on. In each religious tradition there are those who are more preoccupied with maintaining the purity of the inheritance than with translating it into contemporary expression. This is their prerogative, as it often was for the followers of what we now remark as the dead religions which litter the past of human civilization (see Bowker 1978: ch. 1). It might be argued that the future of contemporary living religions may actually be better preserved by the path of separate conservation than by the one of engagement. However, if that were the typical response then their opportunity to enrich present and future generations would be considerably reduced and the dominant myth, with which we began, might after all come more closely to match reality.

It is perfectly possible to present each of the traditions, identified since 1988 as the principal religions of England and Wales,[10] in ways that demonstrate their internal coherence and consistency. In terms of their own theological (or Buddhalogical) circle, they have their own credentials which deserve to be understood. What is trickier, yet no less crucial, is the degree of mutual questioning which is seen as a proper part of the process. In so far as each tradition makes claims to truth that go beyond the confines of its immediate followers, that is of double interest. Firstly, the followers themselves will wish to demonstrate that their claim will stand close scrutiny, and, secondly, those outside the faith might, for their own sake, reasonably wish to check that this is so (see Christian 1987).

The common human discourse for such exchanges is reason. Again, some parts of some traditions will find it more, or less, acceptable to trade in these terms. Depending on how Revelation or illumination is understood and appropriated within the tradition, open, rational enquiry may be welcomed or avoided. For instance, if Biblical or Qur'ānic Revelation were seen as only to be heard and never argued with for fear of offending God, that would reduce the degree of engagement with either or both religious traditions which could be effected within the sphere of publicly funded education. In fact, this is not the only view which is found in either community (see Barr 1993, Hourani 1985).

In highlighting the importance of reason, there is always the risk of becoming so rationalistic as to ignore the depth of human logic that is conveyed in other forms than verbal formulae. Fortunately, those studying religion from the outside are increasingly as sensitive to this point as those practising the religion from within. In good faith, and in the interests of mutual understanding, religions need to demonstrate a readiness to be subject to exploration and experiment that test the claims to truth which they advance. From their own heartlands they may then find they stand on common ground in asserting the wider, even universal, importance of humanity (Green 1988).

## Partnership in groundwork on beliefs and values

Religious Education, as developed within the public educational provision of England and Wales introduced in 1870, can itself help with this process. Its potential to do so is there, in principle, throughout the tradition of Agreed Syllabuses, as also in the dual system. The syllabuses are envisaged as controlling the content of RE teaching in such a way as to avoid religious strife, and to be acceptable within a legal framework which expressly rules out denominationally specific teaching.[11] The dual system was a constitutional commitment to a national educational system provided by a partnership of church and state.[12] Both of these aspects of the provision are in process of being extended, but they are faced with two foes.

### Agreeing the syllabus

LEA Agreed Syllabuses emerged in the 1920s and 1930s, as a means of managing the religious diversity which was already apparent. They applied in both county maintained schools and those church schools which were designated 'controlled' rather than 'voluntary aided'. They avoided denominationally specific catechisms and formularies, as legally proscribed, for divergent priorities and emphases were evident between the different Christian denominations, as well as with the still largely self-contained Jewish community, and the growing secularist movement. Instead, the biblical common denominator found in all these syllabuses until the late 1960s was set out as common ground and may have contributed to a prevailing sense of national cohesion and identity.[13]

Since 1975 the extension on the syllabus front has gone beyond the bounds of agreement being primarily between the different Christian churches, and a sideward look to the Jewish community. It has extended to other religious communities that are part of modern Britain, and this inclusiveness was reinforced by the wording of the 1988 Education Reform Act, which makes it illegal for any syllabus not to give due regard to any of the principal religious traditions which now form part of the national community (see Hull 1989, Marratt 1989). In place of the biblical core that was normative for the older Agreed Syllabuses, there are new agreed cores for each of Buddhism, Christianity, Hinduism, Islam, Judaism and Sikhism. These are intended as norms, for each of the traditions, which local syllabus conferences can work to (SCAA 1994).

Considering the decades and even centuries that can pass before agreement may be reached in efforts to define the beliefs and values of a particular religious tradition, it is remarkable that these cores, and national model RE syllabuses based on them, were produced within a two-year period. They are the fruit of collaboration between representatives of the different faith communities and professional educators who met sectionally, according to faith, as well as all together. It is not clear that the cores have yet been validated by the authoritative councils of the respective faith communities or indeed by the specialist academic networks (Everington 1996). There are issues of 'ownership' in which the self-definition of any one faith community may be challenged by an independent scholarship which might find more fluidity in the tradition and individual sense of religious identity than 'official' versions would immediately acknowledge (see Jackson 1997). Nevertheless, until there is further revision, the realm of public education is promoting the understanding of individual religions as determined at least in part from within the self-definition of each of them.

## Extending the partnership of churches and state

Enlargement of the dual system of partnership between the churches and the state, in together providing for the nation's educational needs, has moved more slowly. In part, that may reflect some confusion within the thinking of the two churches (Anglican and Roman Catholic) most involved in partnership provision with the state. Are the church schools for the whole community or for boys and girls from the one denominational background? In general, the Roman Catholic emphasis has been more on education for families from that denominational background, whereas the Churches of England and Wales have usually served the wider neighbourhood (Church of England Commission 1970: ch. 7). Admissions policies vary, however, from school to school, with some Catholic ones having more open access and some Anglican ones, most especially secondary, becoming more selective (O'Keeffe 1986: chs 2 and 3, Catholic Commission for Racial Justice 1984, Chadwick 1994: ch. 2). That said, both churches accept that their receipt of public funding depends upon their willingness to deliver the agreed national curriculum in all the other subjects, even if they choose to do their RE differently.[14]

The number of other Christian denominational schools is small,[15] as is that of any other religious community. Among those schools which are Jewish, there are the same variations in admissions policies, but at least they do exist.[16] By contrast, the development of state-funded Buddhist, Hindu, Muslim and Sikh voluntary aided schools has been scandalously slow.[17]

The implication must be that schools with non-Christian religious affiliation are perceived as politically suspect and likely to encourage divisiveness. This is all too reminiscent of the religious intolerance of 1902, when people campaigned against 'Rome on the rates'. The lack of financial support from the public purse, to help the different faith communities to develop at least a few schools of their own, is in sharp contrast to what happened in the early decades of public education. Then large numbers of church schools were judged to be making only poor quality of provision which could only be improved by the injection of public funds; accordingly, these were provided (Evans 1985: 69, 76, 94). In the interests of community relations and good education, it remains a disappointment to many that the historical generosity of this dual partnership has yet to be extended to a more plural one, encompassing other faith communities. Their members pay the same taxes as Christians, or any other citizens of the UK.

## Further opposition to open collaboration

The foes of such extension continue to mount a rearguard action. On the one hand, latter-day Christian imperialism still seeks to reassert a more exclusively closed establishment position. This has been evident in the wholesale resistance to public endowment of any Muslim schools, but also in the triumph of the lobby which engineered the notorious Circular 1/94 (DfE 1994; for fuller discussion, see Gates 1995, Robson 1997). At a stroke this Circular interpreted the law as requiring schools, as never before, to conduct confessional Christian worship. Such interpretations which already appeared in the draft version of the Circular had been expressly castigated by representatives of the churches, other faith communities and educationists, but their advice was overruled.

Narrowness of these kinds only serves to reinforce the impression that religion is self-seeking and out to achieve its own sectional superiority. When it appears in the name of Christianity, it displays a curious lack of theological imagination in respect of the biblical God of creation, who is more comprehensive in cover and care than any localized boundary, whether national, racial or indeed religious.

On the other hand, persistent secularism also acts in opposition to any collaboration involving religion. Thus, there is a tendency within the educational system wilfully to play down the religious ingredients in school assembly, as also in moral, personal and social education.[18] To some extent this is made into a more justifiable position as a consequence of the infelicitously presumptuous wording of Circular 1/94. That apart, there are creative opportunities waiting to be opened up that would find focus in school 'collective worship'.

Of course, if such school assemblies have the connotation of corporate worship in church, mosque or other faith community, then it is the more intelligible that they should succumb not only to secularist critique, but also to an educational one. By contrast the tradition maintained in primary school assemblies, as also in a minority of secondary schools, is one that explores and affirms practical expressions of basic beliefs and values. With appropriate investment of resources and professional energies there is scope for these integral gatherings to be redeveloped. They would serve very well as centre points for highlighting the moral, social, spiritual and cultural dimensions of the school curriculum and community. And, without presumptions as to any particular religious belief on the part of those present, they would include overt reference to the resources of religions.[19]

## Threats to confidence in the future

Whether such optimism is realistic, however, is another matter. Looking to the future, outside of school, it is difficult to avoid a sense of foreboding. Television and related revolutions in electronic communications magnify the extent of social and moral disorder. It is abundantly visible on every front: in family violence and breakdown, disparities of poverty and wealth that appear obscene, impending environmental disasters, and persistent prejudice and strife that defies reconciliation. Teachers and children bring these concerns with them into school every day, from wider society if not also from their own homes. From within school itself, there may be struggles arising of a different kind, as from such as new curricular expectations, record-keeping arrangements and inspection preparations. Putting all this together the prospect is daunting.

In response, the actual need for resilience in personal and professional terms is great. The sources for that resilience lie largely within the individuals concerned. Their inner springs have to do with senses of purpose and meaning, sensitivity to human delight and sorrow, and visions of what might be, combined with a determination to bring it to fruition. In principle, every one of these aspects can be fed creatively from the combined institutional strengths of religion and education. In practice, either or both of these can also be drudging and draining. Accordingly, if either is intellectually enfeebled, or they fail to collaborate effectively, the worst foreboding will materialize.

## Shared values and a global ethic

To anyone who is at all sensitive to the ambiguities of religion in human experience, the suggestion that religion might actually have some direct relevance for addressing the position we find ourselves in might seem almost risible. How and why should we look with any positive expectation to resources associated with religion, when it is religion itself which is claimed often to be at the root of the problems themselves?

The answer to this challenge lies in the nature of humanity. Intrinsic to being human is a preoccupation with meaning. It has arisen continually from a universal experience of life bounded by death. It has worked itself out from earliest times in the fabrication of cave paintings, carved figurines and stone circles, or in the more developed cultural forms, both religious and scientific, in subsequent civilizations. These forms have served to bond and unite, but also to estrange and divide.

Men and women have created and articulated a communal sense of order, as in the varnas and the doing of dharmic duty, the sangha and eightfold path, the priesthood of all believers and the pilgrim's way, or the lifelong haj. At the same time, they have sometimes experienced that very order finding them, as it were 'from beyond themselves'. They have talked of the voice of the ancestors, the word of the Lord, or light from another dimension. Best estimates suggest that such language characterizes the experience of over 80 per cent of the present population of the world.[20] Even if it were strange to any particular educationist or politician, it would be an act of extraordinary arrogance to dismiss it all as worthless.

Yet it does remain true that the different beliefs and values, enshrined in separate religious traditions, can trip each other up. Closer scrutiny reveals that this may more often be true when the religious reference becomes identified with spatial, ethnic or other localized boundaries. Either way, they can only effectively be challenged, accepted or transformed, if they are first understood. And that is why what schools do with Religious Education is so important globally.

Over the years there have been initiatives that seek to identify values that are shared across religions and cultures, and with which education itself can resonate. Some naivety may be involved in these pursuits, for the historical and anthropological evidence of cultural diversity is hard to deny. For instance, how shall we reconcile animal, let alone human, sacrifice with the Jain ahimsa which hesitates even to quench a living flame? Is the prevalence of patriarchy entirely a coincidence in Semitic religious traditions? What possible compatibility might there be between an All-Powerful Cosmic Force and a crucified Palestinian? Beliefs as well as values are all too relative.

However, religious and cultural relativism is not the whole story. There is a philosophical tradition of very long standing that is not confined to Graeco-Roman roots, but which finds echoes in ancient China, India and Israel.[21] It is known as natural law, and its contemporary exposition by social scientists looks for trans-cultural continuities and a common rationality. One of its examples of pan-human valuing is the taboo against incest; those instances involving the acceptance of incest do indeed appear to be quite exceptional. Another is the acknowledgement of truth-telling as a precondition of life in community (Bok 1978). Yet another might be sympathy for suffering as a taboo against torture (see Little 1993).

It was the claim that there is a universal pattern of individual moral development, to be observed throughout the world in any and every culture, which gave Kohlberg his pre-eminent significance over twenty years. Empirical evidence does not entirely bear this out, at least not in Kohlberg's fully elaborated stage sequences; nevertheless, his concern to identify a universality of moral sense is one that continues to exercise all those who speak of Moral Education.[22]

A different initiative seeking similar effect was promulgated by the Centenary Parliament of the World's Religions in Chicago in 1993 in the form of a 'Declaration Toward a Global Ethic'. This is designed expressly to address what is diagnosed as a fundamental crisis of economics, politics and ecology, and, for its further development, acceptance and application, Hans Küng and others continue to work. They bring together the perspectives of religious diversity in a common focus on the global challenges to human survival (Küng and Kuschel 1993, cf. Küng 1991, Braybrooke 1992).[23]

The educational relevance of such initiatives deserve more direct attention from public educational agencies than they have so far been given. In the UK they deserve to be added to the formulations which have come from the Schools Curriculum Assessment Authority's Forum on Moral Values;[24] indeed, they were more than hinted at in the Inter Faith Network for the UK's Consultation on Shared Values (see Pearce 1997). What is critical in all the discussion is that the reference to religious sources and resources is freely admitted.

## The Commonwealth of human diversity

In British constitutional terms this process could be given a significant boost by celebrating the multi-faith character of the Commonwealth. It is from our historical past in Empire that the present ethnic and religious diversity of Britain largely derives.[25] Instead of playing down that diversity, near and far, its affirmation by politicians and church leaders, as also by representatives from other faiths, could be very positive and powerful.

The point is still valid even if links with the European Union and with the United States are coming to be of greater significance. In the USA the reluctance faced by religions over their admitttance to the realm of public schooling has concealed much of the now extensive religious diversity of the nation from everyday understanding on the part of the population at large (Carter 1993). More immediately, from within Europe there is much learning yet to be pursued about religious diversity, such as in France and Germany with Algerian and Turkish Muslims respectively, or in Russia and other former Soviet territories where for instance Buddhism, Islam and Shamanism have a powerful presence. Europe, America and indeed the wider world may have insights to gain from a Commonwealth tradition.

In the UK, as mooted by Prince Charles, the role of the monarch as the Defender of Faiths, and not only of Christianity, need not be the 'oddball' idea it is sometimes presented as being (see Dimbleby 1994: 528–34). It could be a highly creative symbol for a confederated framework guaranteeing the integrity of each religion and recognizing the import of faith, whether natural or supernatural, in the personal identity of individual human beings. Thus, it would indicate that the diverse faith communities now thriving in this country are actually valued in their own right as part of the national establishment. It would also demonstrate a deliberate valuing of the importance in the lives of individual citizens of their personal beliefs.

The inclusivity of the notion of 'faith' and of 'personal belief' is a critical aspect of this principle.[26] It would be as simplistic in the name of science to urge that all elements of faith should be expunged from the daily lived experience of individuals throughout the world as it is in the name of religion to proclaim that rational exploration and experiment bespeak an inferior logic. Quite deliberately, secular humanism has contributed to the Chicago statement on global ethics, also to the British consultations about shared values. In its own terms it sees itself as a living faith. It looks for an education for all which includes critical appreciation of secular perspectives, as well as enrichment by reference to the more explicitly religious faith of others.[27]

Wider recognition of this common grounding of humanity in faiths which are diverse and open to mutual scrutiny might actually make a direct contribution to health and peace. Accordingly, it is highly appropriate for the slogan 'Defender of Faith(s)' to be attached to a nation's chief constitutional office, whether royal or republican. It brings together the commitment to individual freedom and to companionability.

The articulation of such Commonwealth reference points could bring to negotiations on the future of the European Union a charity and vision that might enable Europe, both eastern and western, to come to terms with the anti-Semitism that has been at its heart and which is still latent, and at the same time to become less aggressively suspicious and defensive about Islam (see Runnymede Trust 1997). Of course, to be true to the founding vision of their faith, Muslims will live in tension with non-Muslims; theologically speaking, Dar al Islam is always at war with Dar al Harb (summarized in Schacht and Bosworth 1979: 174–7, cf. Lewis 1994: 50–3). But, by definition, tension is generated wherever there is difference, and deeply held convictions inevitably call into question those from different starting points. In both political and educational terms, however, the Commonwealth tradition of the UK holds open a moral status for Islam, as for any other faith which accepts humanity as shared and commonly gifted from beyond any one individual or group. It is in the interests of both the European and worldwide communities that tabloid distortions and invective against Islam based on highly particular episodes should not be permitted to provide the normative framework of perception with which that living tradition is condemned.

# Religion and the school's agenda

Any prediction about the imminent ending of religion in the UK and beyond is both naive and pointless, the more so when the present season of the millennium will far more probably generate an excess of its own characteristic genre of religious speculation and reflection. Of far greater significance is the end of religion, in the purposive sense, involving teleological direction. Intrinsic to religious tradition is a directional drive that affects both the individual respondent and the wider community of faith. The drive may be more internally than externally transformative. It may lead to passivity or action, solitariness or sociability. But, in this sense, the end of religion is not a tale of termination but of ambition. It strives that life in all its heights and profundity might become more abundantly appreciated by all. This is a far more interesting and challenging goal. To be sure, in its pursuit institutional religions may have some dying to do, but only if their proper end is achieved.

This end is one to which each boy and girl deserves to be introduced as they are exposed to the fundamental importance of beliefs and values in every school. Only an unthinking scepticism can doubt that questions of overall meaning and purpose for individuals, for local and national community, and for the world at large, deserve to be directly addressed by schools. As an end in itself, critically appreciative attention to religion should be a precondition for any education, religious or secular, which claims public sponsorship in a democratic society.

(2000)

Chapter 7

# *E pluribus unum:* the test and promise of Religious Education

Much is currently being made of the shared concerns of the UK and the USA. Their leaders stand shoulder to shoulder against terrorism. As nations they share a common language and their heritage is intertwined. And yet there are differences. Historically, they are the 'Old World' and the 'New World'. Ethnically, their diversity now derives from different sources. Constitutionally, the one has an established church and the other total separation of church and state. Even the leaders' apparent agreement to defeat terrorism conceals different estimations of the respective scope of the authority of nation states in relation to that shared with, or deriving from, the international community.

In common with Europe and the rest of the world, both countries are faced with social splintering and division. This chapter explores the thesis that readiness to engage with religion in the context of publicly funded education is more than ever a necessary prerequisite for community cohesion and political health.

## Preliminary reflections

### Some characteristics of the current global context

1. Although within countries and continents there may be geographical coherence and organizational drives towards unity, Asia, Africa, the Americas and Europe are culturally, politically, religiously splintered.
2. Each continent has its own rich heritage, but it is now inheritor also of the global one, as mediated through mass communications. Packaging for instant consumption may dull its distinctiveness, yet this still remains astonishingly diverse.
3. Within each continental diversity are local loyalties. These may relate to family kith and kin, or to larger tribal and ethnic groupings, extending more widely perhaps to specific region or nation. However, deep felt loyalty may just as likely be expressed in terms of support for such as a particular football team.

4. Historically, those loyalties, which have gone beyond the family and national grouping, have entailed some imperial ideology or world religion/faith. In Europe, the dominant versions of such have been Christianity, Communism and Islam. Elsewhere, they may have been predominantly Hindu or Confucian.

5. Now some would say that such comprehensive allegiances are in terminal decline. We are living in a post-Communist, post-Christian, postmodernist age. There is a multiplicity of alternative views and no independent basis for choosing between them.

6. Across the world, in place of any traditional certainties, there is a *mélange* of beliefs, in which religious and secular enthusiasms mix in the mass ecstasy of successive pop concerts or more personalized expressions of New Age sentiments, with or without the aid of alcohol or other stimulants.

7. And yet there is evidence of common currencies: those of scientific knowledge and skills (as instanced in medicine or energy generation), of monetary systems and material exchange (whether sophisticated stocks and shares or more basic bartering of pots and pans), of professional norms and routines (from air traffic control to world athletic championships).

8. There is also evidence of religion made rampant inspiration for some special cause, so much so that it appears as legitimization for actions which might otherwise be regarded as unthinkable: in the Balkans, in the Middle East, in Sri Lanka and most recently in the USA and Indonesia.

9. Almost on the sidelines there has appeared a World Parliament of Religions. It was initially mooted by Nicholas of Cusa in 1453, and actually materialized in 1893 in Chicago. Dormant during the warring decades of the twentieth century, it was convened again in 1993 and is now committed to a succession of regular meetings.

10. From this has come the Global Ethics Project associated with Hans Küng and some apparent underwriting from the United Nations (Küng and Kuschel 1993, UN 2001).

Against this backdrop, I have a particular interest in the importance of religion in our constitutional and educational future, as national and international communities. I shall argue that neglect of the centrality of religion is perilous.

## An age-old condition, in twenty-first century magnification

In some sense there is nothing new in conflicting values. The question: 'How can the one and the many be combined?' has been asked by the classical philosophers of Greece and India and China. In Europe, the apparent unity of Medieval Christendom had within it very considerable diversity, which surfaced forcefully in the fifteenth to seventeenth centuries. Indeed, that frenzy of competing nationalisms, and of ecclesiastical establishment versus more radical Christian movements, gave rise to the vision of the new world order as established in North America, with its eventual motto: *e pluribus unum*. Very clearly, tensions alongside desire for peaceful coexistence have been continually in evidence throughout history.

The chief novelty of recent times is the scale of human diversity and the extent of our awareness of it. The sheer numbers involved are mind-boggling. At 6,000 million people in 2000, the world's population has increased fourfold in the course of a century and is projected to be nearer 9,000 million by 2050. Within this total population, scholarship highlights for us the complex interface between different boundary systems: race and ethnicity, culture, nationalism and religion. Sometimes, they subsist alongside each other in mutually complementary forms; sometimes they become a more lethal cocktail mix which kills. Awareness is magnified by the greater internationalizing of that scholarship, accelerated by electronic availability on the internet, and more popularly by the omnipresent television.

By way of illustration, imagine if you will the following episode:

- Quite recently, in one of the extended rural villages outside the town of Kottayam in Kerala, Southern India, I was walking along a mud track with two students from Lancaster in the UK, who were there on a ten-week study trip. Suddenly, an excited ten-year-old boy ran up saying 'Michael Owen, Michael Owen!', nodding his head and smiling hugely. Football's World Cup and TV pictures had been there before us.

Add to this, three different sets of pictures from a year later all shown in the media:

- Asian youths (some Hindu, some Muslim) rioting in the northern cities of Bradford and Oldham in the UK, in reaction to their experience of abuse from the wider community;
- young children terrified by the explosion of a pipe bomb, thrown by members of the local Protestant community, while their parents were taking them to their Roman Catholic school in Northern Ireland;
- the demolition of the New York Trade Center by two passenger jets turned into massive petrol bombs, as from a Hollywood disaster movie, only worse.

How often has it been said that the world will never be the same again after 9/11? The truth of the claim resides, however, not simply in the act of terror itself, but in the fact that it was recorded by the full range of media. Video and film cameras, sound recordings from control towers, black boxes, mobile phones and answerphones provided the live material of desperation, dying and death, all of which could be replayed time and again. In consequence, these events and others like them (the roll-call continues: Jerusalem, Bali, Washington, Moscow) are now part of the collective psyche of the world.

In consequence also, the world has the opportunity to learn from what happened.

The same was not true at the gas chambers and ovens of Auschwitz, nor with the people surviving in Hiroshima and Nagasaki, nor in the Gulag. Neither was it true in myriad equivalent acts of human terror and degradation throughout the previous centuries. Recording and magnification by world-wide media changes the world's understanding of itself, and will continue to do so even in remote villages.

The understanding which subsequently emerges will still be incomplete, however, unless it includes particular attention to the shape and content of the beliefs and purposes which give motive force to what people do with their lives, both individually and collectively. And that means attending not only to economic needs, and to the ethnic and cultural interests, but, less fashionably perhaps, also to religious aspects of human being.

## Religious education as a global and local pivot

My thesis is a simple one. It is that the importance of religion in shaping contemporary life and civilization is insufficiently appreciated and that any related neglect of the place of Religious Education in the school curriculum will seriously damage the health of the entire world's population. What a country does with religion in its constitution is of major moment and so too is its treatment of religion in public education. Could it be that, in this respect, the model of RE provided in England and Wales is worth imitating more universally?

### Religion is a potent dimension of individual lives and whole societies

It is easy to make the judgement that the religious hypothesis is in terminal decline throughout the world. Relative to the population at large, registers of church allegiance in Europe consistently show reducing proportions of baptisms and confirmations, church weddings and even funerals. The immediate surge in Christian engagement following the demise of Communist regimes in countries of Eastern Europe has now wilted. In India or China, the forces of world development and globalization have at last exposed caste or ancestor-dominated religion as sponsoring underdevelopment; accordingly, it will be left behind. In Africa and South America the intrusions of Christianity are now exposed as covers for an imperialist presence, now largely withdrawn. Though there may be reversion to more primal and traditional religions, they will provide but fleeting interest and consolation, which will soon give way to the secular humanity already visible in China. And finally, in North America, religion may continue, like coffee drinking, as an individual habit, but otherwise have no bite in public life.

However, this kind of reasoning and conclusion that religion is a spent force is fed by other inclinations than close attention to local and global evidence. Two very different experiences speak most powerfully against it.

One is the second edition of *The World Christian Encyclopedia* (Barrett et al. 2001). From all the data, carefully gathered on a country by country basis, the following facts emerge:

- a third of the world's population wants to call itself Christian – 2,000 million (there are more Christians presently alive than lived throughout the whole of the first 1,900 years of the history of the churches);
- one-fifth identifies with Islam – 1,200 million;
- one-eighth is non-religious, including Marxists and atheists (just less than those who can be characterized as Hindu).

The fact is that for the most part humankind remains incurably religious. It is a characteristic, of many different hues, through which a sense of personal identity and meaning is articulated in response to the challenges of living and dying.

The other telling evidence, against the claim that religion is a spent force in the world, is the virulence of movements which find legitimization in religion for the use of violence in pursuit of their cause, in such diverse locations as the Balkans, the Middle East or Sri Lanka. The grim and deadly events in New York and Washington are extreme demonstrations of such inspiration. Distorted fundamentalism it may be, but before the protagonists are dismissed as entirely aberrant in religious terms, it is important to recognize that their foundations derive from the passion for social justice that is central to Jewish, Christian, Muslim and Marxist traditions. The great calculation is made that in the perspective of eternity and the welfare of larger humanity, the sacrifice of innocents is justified. The hungry have not been fed, the naked have not been clothed, the thirsty are still thirsty, therefore hellish fate of apocalyptic proportions is a predictable consequence.

Those who campaigned more peaceably for Jubilee 2000, to release the developing nations of the world from the cumulative burdens of international debt, were not for the most part guised as terrorists. However, they asserted fundamental criticisms against an established world economic order, and many of them did so as Protestant and Catholic Christians.

Arguably, recognition and understanding of this forceful presence of religion in world affairs is a model that can usefully be extended to cover those beliefs and ideologies which have functioned as equivalents or distortions of traditional religions. Thus, fighting the Lord's battle is something which may be taken on, as did Christian holy warriors in the Middle Ages. But even if the Greater God is conceptualized rather differently, as with Hitler in campaigning against the Jewish virus, or Stalin against the kulaks, impulsion by an overarching vision is clear. The actions are driven by deeply held convictions of comparably religious proportions in their determination to serve a cause greater than themselves, with the accompanying intent of transforming the world.

The potency of religion or its equivalent for social and political transformation should be no surprise to anyone who has studied Jewish, Christian and Muslim scriptures, or indeed comparable texts of Hindus and Buddhists. Religion can be a determinative dimension of individual lives and whole societies, and continues to be so for many.

## By the neglect of an open provision of Religious Education, children's capacity for world citizenship is hindered

Neglect of open Religious Education in the context of state-funded education can take many forms. I shall identify four typical ones: RE as Atheistic, RE as Non-existent, RE as Relatively Closed, and RE as Totally Open.

*RE as Atheistic* is what predominated in the USSR. Throughout the Soviet school system, the message was clear and consistent from an early age: religion is false. Thus, RE in effect took the form of induction into an atheistic world-view. The ideology was strong and bold. It expounded as fact the claim that religion is a distraction from the real world, and it deliberately downplayed the Orthodox Christian heritage, as having nothing positive to contribute to people's lives today. It did the same for Buddhism in Mongolia and for Islam in Uzbekistan and much of Central Asia. And, of course, Jews were excoriated. All religions were presented as archaeological irrelevancies. Any questions which boys and girls had about purpose and meaning in life were readily answered in terms of what works for the collective good. There was simply no need of stories involving a more transcendent faith. Any message to the contrary, which might be mediated from home, is left as highly questionable. In effect, the purported false consciousness of religion is replaced by another consciousness, whose own justification for being regarded as true or false was less open to challenge.

*RE as Non-existent* may well be what has in the past predominated in the USA, although the position is clearly changing in particular states. For many years, the constitutional separation of church and state was generally interpreted as preventing the teaching of RE in all government-funded schools. Legally, there was and is a facility to teach *about* religions, but in practice this appears to have been given minimal priority and one picked up in Social Studies or History rather than in its own right. Outside of public education, there is a more flourishing provision of RE, but this is in denominationally particular form. As such, it may be greatly enriching for boys and girls, but its quality is variable. Three risks typically follow from this approach to RE. One is the hidden curriculum message that religion belongs in the domestic sphere of life, rather than in the marketplace or political arena. A second is the knowledge deficit in respect of understanding what it means to view the world through the eyes of other faiths and cultures. And a third is the lack of criticality that is brought to bear on a dimension of human meaning which can be vulnerable to cultic enthusiasms, some of which have highly questionable credentials and aspirations.

The parallel example of this model in Europe is that of France. Constitutional suspicion of religion fed by revolutionary anti-clericalism has no study of religion in schools except in passing in the course of philosophy and history classes. There has been no RE as such. It is those same sentiments which have until the last few years prevented the building of mosques to serve the sizeable Muslim population.

*RE as Relatively Closed* is typically the model which has predominated throughout much of the world. In this, there is a common starting point according to which one religion is presented as true. Thus, in countries in which the Church or Churches have predominated, a version of Christianity has been propounded, as in many countries in Europe and Southern Africa. Similarly, in countries with a Muslim constitution, Islam has been taught as true for all. Depending on the particular country and religion, readiness to engage with other religions, as also with alternative secular claims to truth, may sometimes show itself in both the curriculum content and in the way the RE is taught. However, where the 'ownership' of the RE remains within the control of the one religious community, as is often the case, the level and vitality of engagement with the alternative starting points may suffer, even within publicly funded education. Thus, in some German *Länder*, Lutheran or Roman Catholic denominational authority has been invoked to determine both the content of the RE taught and the licence of those qualified to teach it.

From this overview, it would appear that the preferred alternative would be a fourth: *RE as Totally Open*. In such an approach any and all religions would be taught, as equally true and equally false. This would have the attraction of acknowledging the full diversity of human religions and cultures. Alongside the range of world religions which have predominated in the history of civilizations, full attention would also be given to newer religious movements, including such as Baha'is, Jehovah's Witnesses, Moonies, Mormons, Pagans and followers of New Age spirituality. None would be given priority over any of the others. In a world context in which the feuding of competing allegiances continues to create havoc, such treasuring of plurality would seem highly desirable. Moreover, it is a simple extension of the principle of Freedom of Religion with the related cautions against discrimination, as now enshrined in UN and European Union Human Rights legislation.

Effective provision for Religious Education is a far more fundamental ingredient in the promotion of children's capacity for world citizenship than is often acknowledged. In individual experience, religion pertains to the area of deepest personal meanings, broadest and most inclusive of all loyalties, and longest-term hopes and aspirations. In political terms, religion has to do with any sense of the lasting worth of social belonging, or its denial as finally futile. Inattention to it at any level is, therefore, a recipe for human diminishment. Since education is designed as the prime vehicle for transgenerational transport, the quality of how religion is treated within that process is a real test of any nation's vitality.

In the argument so far, it has been suggested that publicly funded RE provision, which is avowedly *atheistic* is too simplistically reductive and closed-minded in its suppression of human inclination to believe differently. Similarly, if RE is largely ignored or absent in a national system of education (*RE as Non-existent*), the signals sent are ones which indicate that religion is not a significant part of public life. In neither of these patterns of provision are boys and girls encouraged to engage at all directly with religious concerns and claims to truth. Where RE is provided, but in terms clearly circumscribed by one particular faith (*Relatively Closed*), the state becomes the extension of the one parental faith community. Although that may be healthier in terms of greater access to at least partial understanding, that very partiality is likely to be relatively exclusive and not really engaging with other religious concerns and claims which feature in wider society and the world at large. Even the self-understanding of the one faith is the poorer for this lack of exposure. Accordingly, the favoured alternative has appeared to be *RE as Totally Open*. Here, at last, would be a provision, which accords to every religion, and to every pupil, equal attention.

On further reflection, however, even this fourth type has some questionable consequences. Firstly, it disconnects religions from their parental faith community; any religion can be studied without reference to context, and be by implication exchanged for any other, real or fictional. Secondly, in the interests of taking in the full panorama of available religions, claims to truth may become relativized to the point of trivialization. Human sacrifice, astrological fatalism, racial superiority have all flourished in the name of religion. Simply to leave it that any one religion is as good and true as any other suspends the process of critical reasoning, and within it the invocation of moral criteria, that is otherwise characteristic of the public educational process.

Whether in Prague or Washington, Paris or Mumbai, there is good reason to look at a further, different option.

## What is so special about the model of Religious Education promoted in England and Wales?

The British context is multicultural, multi-ethnic and multi-faith. It is Christian by predominant tradition, but diversely so: between them, self-styled Anglicans, Roman Catholics and Free Church Protestants make up nearly two-thirds of the population. At the same time, it is secularizing with no more than 10 per cent regularly in church. Its formal religious diversity, beyond the Christian tradition, is estimated (2001 census figures are awaited) at around 5 per cent (cf. Weller 2001).

Constitutionally, the Church of England is the established religion of the country and the monarch is designated head of that national Church. Since state funding of schools first began in 1870, Church and State have agreed together to provide for the nation's educational needs, with public funds going into denominational church schools and county/LEA schools also providing Religious Education. That kind of RE has to be locally (typically as defined by the county education authority) agreed between teachers, politicians and representatives of the different churches; together they produced an Agreed Syllabus of RE appropriate to local context. Arguably, the dominant pattern for over a century was that of *RE as Relatively Closed* in that syllabuses were dominated by a biblical norm which was seen as conveying the essential truth of Christianity.

Reflecting both population shifts and educational arguments, that position changed dramatically in 1988. The Education Reform Act made it illegal in England and Wales only to teach Christianity. It required that in all publicly funded education, and in each year group from 5 to 18 years of age, attention should be given also to other principal religions found settled in the country. Thus, alongside Christianity, in both primary/elementary and secondary/high schools, pupils are expected to engage with Buddhism, Hinduism, Islam, Judaism and Sikhism. The truth claims of one faith are not assumed as over against those of all the others – technically the professional stance is characterized as that of 'methodological agnosticism'.

The integrity of each religion is guaranteed in National Model Syllabuses, which were produced by SCAA in 1993 after careful consultation with senior representatives of each of the named religions. In the programmes of study, there are two complementary emphases. One is 'Learning *about* Religions' and the other 'Learning *from* Religions'. Locally, the officially constituted conference is still responsible for producing the final version of the Syllabus, but its membership, alongside teacher and political representatives, now comprises people drawn from all the different religious communities found in that region.

The end result is neither *Relatively Closed* nor *Totally Open RE*, but *RE as Relatedly Open*. Its openness is guaranteed by the professional responsibility for its teaching residing not with the parental religious communities, but with the publicly trained, qualified and appointed teachers. At the same time, the genuineness of its sensitivity to the illumination and revelation found within each of these religions is open to local scrutiny by representatives of parental faith communities.

In principle these multi-faith dimensions of RE are both rooted in local community and framed in the national constitution. Most recently, a new Education Act renames publicly funded church schools as 'faith schools', and invites the other faiths to join in the creation of such. Around a quarter of all pupils are educated in church/faith schools. Most of these are Anglican or Roman Catholic; a tiny number is Jewish, Muslim or Sikh. Even so, they are all paid for out of general taxation and teach the full range of National Curriculum subject syllabuses. Together boys and girls of different faiths are welcomed to local community schools; but, they are also to be welcomed to faith schools. This is part of a system in which the plurality of religions in partnership with the state provides for the nation's schools. Curiously, too, the heir to the throne, Prince Charles, has declared his wish to interpret the traditional honorific of *Fidei Defensor* – Defender of the Faith, first given to King Henry VIII by the then Pope, more openly as Defender of Faith or Faith*s*.

There are risks with the 'Faith school' development. Unless imaginatively pursued it could reinforce the sense of separation in community development, which has been identified as contributing to the recent race riots in Bradford. For instance, if Asian boys and girls become concentrated in particular schools, with little or no regular contact with their peers from different backgrounds, a condition of mutual ignorance prevails, within which prejudice of inherited stereotypes can fester. But provided the overall prescription that school shall attend to the principal religions of the country is extended to all schools, this need not be. Faith schools are still free to be more denominationally specific as well.

More generally, I would argue that the *Relatedly Open Model of RE* warrants global imitation. It provides a basis for transforming the potentially destructive tendencies which arise from competing world-views and for releasing energies and insights that will enrich our common humanity. Critical reflection and reasoning can contribute to religious self-understanding of both insiders and outsiders to a particular tradition. For instance, as Christians, Hindus, Jews or Muslims, there is nothing to fear from rational enquiry, since reason is understood to be God-given. When followed openly, it cannot but lead to God. Similarly for Buddhists, cool dispassion and selfless concern for others go together.

But what of the sensitive question as to which religions shall be attended to? Two points are crucial. The first is that individual pupils each deserve to have their religious beliefs respected, whether in their own experience these are well developed or embryonic and however widespread or unusual the particular beliefs may be. The school should be guardian against all forms of negative discrimination amongst its pupils and teachers. Secondly, while teachers and schools retain the discretion to respond to interest generated topically on any religion, it is very important that some guidance be given at a local, regional or national level as to what selection of religions warrants most attention. Among the criteria used may well be numerical strength of allegiance, both past and present, among a country's population. By this means attention to certain minorities will likely figure in one context, but not another, such as Parsees/Zoroastrians in one or more London borough, Romas in the Czech Republic, or Native American Religion in Oklahoma.

The goal of Religious Education provided in these terms is not that boys and girls become religious, specifically as Protestants or Roman Catholics, Jews or Muslims, Buddhists or members of some New Religious Movement. They may do. This will be the legitimate ambition of teaching and learning within a particular faith community. However, the priority pursued in public education will be that they understand the nature of religious language, as expressed in myth and story, ritual and festival, art and architecture, prayer and meditation, personal and social ethics. The horizons of this learning are not just national but global, and it informs the development of their own individual self-understanding. In becoming educated in religion or 'religiate', boys and girls should discover that any particular theistic or atheistic faith which they might personally hold is qualified and complemented by insights drawn from shared humanity.

This point can be illustrated by quoting the aspirations of three parents regarding what they want from education (from Stephens 1991: 58):

As a **Christian** I believe that schools should enable children to grow openly in their parental faith. Just as a school checks the progress of a child's understanding in other respects, I expect the same to happen in RE. I know that no teacher, or school report, can possibly read all that is in the heart of a child. That would be an invasion of privacy anyway, if it were attempted. Even so, teachers should be able to tell how well each child is coming to understand the church, past and present, and important aspects of other religions. They should also know the extent to which a pupil is able to relate their own and others' faiths to living in the contemporary world.

It's no surprise that the country is in such a state of moral confusion and general uncertainty about the meaning of life. The speed of change on all fronts is so great. Schools should be doing much more to help boys and girls develop their own basic beliefs and values, around which to organize their future lives. As a **Humanist** I think an enriched provision for moral and religious education is vital. It should be matched by clear criteria that can be used to gauge what understanding has been achieved and how well implications for ordinary life have been worked through by each individual. I recognize that traditional religious beliefs deserve to be included, because they continue to matter for so many people all over the world. In turn, charity must admit that humanist convictions, agnostic about God, also make a powerful contribution that pupils need to understand.

I'm well aware that this is a land of many faiths. Islam now has a very substantial following, but it is still a minority. Nevertheless, as a **Muslim** I believe that all children should have the opportunity to learn something of my faith. It belongs in school as much as Christianity, or certain other faiths. But it must be taught well. I would welcome some means of finding out what degree of understanding of Islam boys and girls are gaining. Even though I accept that that cannot be the same as would come from attending *madrasa*, I don't want it just to be superficial. Assessment should have three purposes. It should be a check against prejudice and misunderstanding. It should help guarantee that children get a chance to appreciate the beauty of Islam. And it should indicate how far they have developed a sense of the spirit of justice and mercy for their lives ahead.

## A constitutional postscript

The question may arise, are religious values really any different from political, social and economic ones? My answer is that they are and they will interact anyway with the other values. This is not because they are fixed and unchanging, but because they express the deepest and most far-reaching sense of meaning and purpose in life and death of which humanity is capable. In this respect, while appreciating them in their own terms, they challenge the ultimate reliability and validity of all the other values.

Typically, religions, like nations, use the medium of story to articulate their identity. Humanity needs these stories. Some are highly restrictive, as is the case with Afrikaner and Third Reich stories. Happily, they are challenged and surpassed by more inclusive ones drawn from the world's religious traditions. These religious stories may give legitimization to life in a family or individual nation, but they go beyond these, even challenging their final authority. Household gods and individual nation states have their importance, but they are relativized by larger, global frames of reference.

The actual feasibility of a range of religious communities entering into partnership with an individual nation state, so that together they provide for that nation's educational needs, is tried and tested in the UK. Indeed, it may be easier to achieve in such a context, where it is directly implicit in the framework of a constitutional monarchy. Thus, the monarch is one who by office works full-time for the democratized nation, yet whose appointment derives in some sense from another source. The old tradition of the Divine Right of Monarchs is properly checked by the power of the people to hold free elections, but its birthright continues to point to a different order of givenness for any society. Thus, in religious tradition, common rationality interacts continually with the sense of revelation from beyond. Similarly, in social polity the symbol of monarch may be viewed as a means of acknowledging that, even when every human effort has been exerted to its full, the source and destiny of human life goes beyond the immediate bounds of race, cultures and country. As an honorific title, *Defender of Faith(s)* declares that. Still Christian in inspiration, it is both appreciative of diversity and affirmative of trust as a quality on which all personal life depends. Moreover, faith takes both theistic and non-theistic forms.

In the USA, the *e pluribus unum* motto, agreed by the Great Seal committee in 1776, may have had more in mind than the then plurality of 13 states, than religious and ethnic diversity as such. It has certainly come to convey a celebration of plurality. However, it is interesting to reflect on whether or not the contentious interpolation of 'Under God' after the affirmation of 'One Nation', noticeable in recent decades, is genuinely appreciative of religious diversity.

It is not easy for any one nation state to manage plurality of loyalties within itself. Culture, race and religion each can be the occasion for generating a sense of difference, which in turn may have the potential to become a challenge to others so grouped within the nation, or indeed to the whole nation. Accordingly, the rule of law is the common means of maintaining public order in the midst of competing diversities.

From time to time, however, from within the grounds of one of the groups concerned, the authority of the national rule of law is called in question. Historically, that challenge has more often than not been made on religious or pseudo-religious grounds.

Thus, within Europe, appeal has been made to the ultramontane, transnational authority of the Roman Catholic Church, to the scripture-informed conscience of a Huss or Wycliffe, or again to the interests of the greater Aryan Cause. More recently, religious inspiration has pleaded the legitimacy of terror to right a different moral wrong, or been invoked in support of rival territorial claims on the part of Israelis and Palestinians.

National and international law cannot afford to ignore religious frames of reference, as if they are yesterday's talismans. They persist, and potently so. Accordingly, there is real urgency that politicians at both national and international levels review their constitutional regard for religion, and, within that, the provision they make for it to be both prized and scrutinized in public education.

(2004)

# Chapter 8

# Signalling transcendence: beyond the National Framework for Religious Education

It is increasingly recognized both within and outside the UK that the RE tradition of England and Wales is distinctive. This may have been taken for granted by those directly involved in RE, but even among fellow educationalists its distinctiveness may not have been noticed, let alone fully appreciated. Now, however, there are signs of new interest from hardened politicians, nationally and internationally.

The salient facts are that:

- RE exists here; it is described by national law as 'basic' to the school curriculum. This is not universally the case.
- It is publicly funded, with the message that it matters for everyone; it is not an optional extra, which dependence on private finance would indicate.
- For the most part, it is not denominationally controlled; it is seen as too important to be left in the hands of each particular faith group.
- It is not left exclusively to teachers, with no acknowledgement of the debt for their subject matter to the vitality of individual and communal faith experience.
- It involves collaboration between independent professional expertise and the faith communities.

Although the ingredients in this position date back to 1870, there is much in its refined form which is Shap-shaped. From 1969 when the Shap Working Party was formed several priorities have been consistently pursued:

- the passion for the religions of the wide world on their own terms;
- the commitment to professional integrity;
- the view that understanding is the beginning of wisdom throughout all of education.

These have united its membership, drawn from a variety of contexts, including adult educationalists, advisers and inspectors, church college lecturers, photographers, publishers, the rabbinate, school teachers, university professors.

Together they have been representative of good practice from all strands of education and of the religious complexion of this country.

What further developments might now be worth pursuing after the non-statutory national framework for RE has been put in place? The suggestion which follows is deliberately different. It combines religion and politics from the past with those in the present and for the future

## A gift from an imperial past?

Ironical though it may seem, there is much in RE that gets its cue from the British Empire. This can perhaps be most simply illustrated by reference to the biographies of the founding co-chairs of the Working Party: Professors Smart, Hilliard and Parrinder. Together their names form the acronym SHAP. This is a felicitous coincidence with the actual aetiology of the working party's name, which was the place of its first meeting at the Shap Wells Hotel in Cumbria.

At that time, Ninian Smart was professorial head of the department of Religious Studies at Lancaster University. His pursuit of the intrinsic relationship between the logic of religion and secular education led him to see the foundations for the study of religion in primary, secondary and higher education as the same. They depend upon the shared challenge that everyone should come to a better and deeper understanding of the world. The location of his field experience in Ceylon/Sri Lanka and India was substantially determined by imperial inheritance, as were many of his associations with universities in Australia, Canada, India, New Zealand, South Africa.

Frederick Hilliard was Professor of Education at the University of Birmingham. He had written introductory texts for children, *Teaching Children about World Religions* (Hilliard 1961), and for teachers and world-travelling adults, *How Men Worship* (Hilliard 1965). For ten years he was based in West Africa, first at University College of Sierra Leone and then the University of the Gold Coast. Here the challenge of Christianity's relation to other world religions, which he had engaged with theoretically in his previous doctoral studies, was put to the practical test of pluralism in the context of the wider empire.

Geoffrey Parrinder was at King's College, London as Reader (later Professor) in the Comparative Study of Religions. His academic engagement with religions had developed from its base in the Christian tradition to include African religions, Islam and Hinduism. Initially it was triggered by his teaching in the French colonial context of Dahomey and the Ivory Coast, then reinforced by nine years lecturing in Religious Studies at University College, Ibadan in Nigeria. Once again the opportunities from Empire contributed to a lifetime's apologetic for the appreciation of religion globally.

In quite specific terms Shap emerged as a visible by-product of empire. Over several hundred years, the British Empire gave a minority of UK subjects the opportunity for short- and long-term location in another country, in civil servant, commercial, military or missionary capacity. This entailed exposure to other cultures and religions on an extensive scale and in considerable diversity. Long-stayers and specialists learned the local languages and customs. Their ordnance mapping of territories as of languages may have been done and paid for largely from self-interest, but it was often also individually fuelled by a sense of common humanity.

In the twentieth century tens of thousands of citizens of the British Empire travelled from their own homelands to Europe or other locations to participate in the war efforts of British Allies or large-scale building projects. More particularly, from the 1950s onwards they travelled to the mother country, responding to promised employment opportunities, first as temporary migrants, and after 1965 as settlers. It is that settlement of minorities which has brought home to the UK the religious diversity of the world previously visible only at a distance within the dispersed empire.

There is a strong temptation now to think of the imperial years in predominantly negative terms, economically driven and exploitative of any available resources, human and natural. Although there is truth in this, it is not the whole story as the historians of Empire are careful to document and the leaders of its now independent nations point out. However much motives may have been mixed, there were ingredients in that Empire which were intentionally positive. They involved mutual regard, genuine wonder at the indigenous life and culture, and a determination to engage in collaborative service.

Similarly, there is a temptation to present Christian missionary endeavour as pursuit of a controlling dominance over the hearts and minds of everyone in the world. Again, there is truth in this; however blind to it or 'alibied' from it, Christian churches and denominations are just as vulnerable to the drives of institutional self-interest as any other group. Yet the close scrutiny of Christian motivation reveals also an altruistic streak, which relishes living and working in countries and contexts which are no less God-given and God-ridden than those premised by the churches and Christianity.

Promoting attention to world religions in education is not in contradiction of a particular faith. Indeed, that faith itself may well provide some of the inspiration. Ninian Smart's engagement with Buddhism, like Geoffrey Parrinder's with African Traditional Religions or Frederick Hilliard's with Living Religions generally, was not at the expense of their Christian faith. Smart's Anglican/ Scottish Episcopalian allegiance was no less informative of his life and work than Parrinder's Methodism or Hilliard's Anglican vows. They would each say that their Christian sense was the richer from the wider understandings at which they arrived.

Though some would see it as a pathetic fig-leaf to cover a shameful past, potentially at least the change from Empire to Commonwealth is not merely a linguistic shift. And we will return to its RE dimension. Before doing so, there is the important matter of religion in political constitutions, which deserves some pondering.

## Divine/royal touch within national constitutions?

Debate about whether or not there should be some special deference to Christianity in the constitution of the European Community is as yet unresolved. There is clear contrast being made in this with the US constitution as also with those of Muslim nations. The US insists on the separation of church and state; although that same nation commonly asserts 'In God we trust'. Muslim nations, with constitutions framed by Islamic law deliberately affirm that all aspects of national life shall be ordered in accord with God-given Sharia.

The debate comes at a time when there is widespread contention over constitutional principles. The Indian constitution has been directly tested in these regards. It uses the word 'secular' to insist that no one religion has primacy, and it has survived a period in which Hindu nationalists have sought to re-establish a more exclusive priority for their majority tradition. Israel has a secular constitution, which in principle recognizes religious plurality, but its territorial claims are buttressed by appeal to a biblical basis invoked with equal fervour by some orthodox Jews and 'fundamentalist' Christians. These claims, not least regarding Jerusalem, are countered by other Jews and Christians, as also by Muslims invoking different religious authority. Issues of constitutional principle are also involved in the Orthodox Churches being acknowledged as warranting some degree of political primacy in several of the former Communist bloc countries of Eastern Europe.

That religion comes into play whenever there is consideration of national constitutions should be no surprise to anyone with a background in RE. For across all religions is a concern with order in life rather than disorder. Cosmos and Chaos vie with each other in creation myths and everyday realities. Human beings play their part in bringing estrangement and destruction. They also have a capacity for re-creation and restoration. Opportunities in life have been given to them from beyond themselves in a source rooted in the otherness of eternity, ultimate being or God.

Constitutions which foreclose on one religion to the exclusion of any others may be expressing their conviction that they have been given access to absolute truth. They have no need of any other. Indeed, they put their own faith under unnecessary pressure and by implication risk bringing insult to it. Yet, there is a common strand in religions which warns against idolatry, mistaking some human creation for the being and end of everything. Arguably, therefore, within any constitution some explicit reference to this possibility of transcendence, maybe even to cosmic and divine ordering, is a healthy guard against institutional arrogance.

According to the Hebrew Bible, the rulers of Israel were appointed by God and found wanting. Rulers of surrounding empires, irrespective of the religious tradition which locally prevailed there, were also appointed by God and used as an instrument of divine judgement against the moral failings of Israel itself. In Christian tradition from the New Testament onwards, some deference to the divine right of those in authority has been expected, whether monarchs or elected leaders, though not total or uncritical allegiance.

In the UK the arrogance of royal power is limited by the parliamentary democracy; monarchy is itself constitutionally circumscribed. At the same time, however, although government depends upon consent expressed through the ballot box, it also involves symbolic reference to a source of authority, which comes from beyond even the people. In evolutionary terms, this has been Catholic Christian, highlighted by the papal endowment to Henry VIII of the honorific *Fidei Defensor*. The involvement of the monarch in the religious leadership of the country has been maintained ever since in the nationalized Church of England and the retention of the title on the coins of the realm, but exclusiveness towards Christian denominations and other faiths has gradually been stripped away.

Comments from Prince Charles over the last fifteen years have consistently indicated his own determination to interpret *Fid Def* as involving 'Defence of Faith or Faiths', and not 'The Faith'. The logic of this position may be a move to disestablishment of Church and State; this is a matter requiring both theological and political judgement. Either way, the principle remains that monarchy is picture language for the fact that both political and religious authority come 'from beyond' as well as 'from within' vested human interests. There is no protection here for Christian imperialism; that King is dead. What is protected instead is the commonwealth of humanity

## Extending to the Commonwealth the principles of the national framework for RE?

Extension of the model of RE from England and Wales to the whole of the rest of Europe has a measure of backing in the Council of Ministers' support for Inter-cultural and Inter-religious Education and Dialogue. But the strength of feeling from within Eastern Orthodox and Roman Catholic leadership in several countries suggests progress in this direction may be slow. Similarly, although the report of Regis Debray suggested there were signs of a new readiness to attend to RE in public education in France (Debray 2002), the prising of secular separation of religion from public life is difficult to move.

Extension to the US is comparably difficult. Banished to the private sidelines by the separation of church and state, religion continues to lurk there quite potently, but precluded from public scrutiny in schools and therefore the more capable of inviting insider and outsider misunderstandings. Its capacity to inspire false judgements, not least in relation to the Middle East, also often goes unchallenged. The need for an equivalent national framework for RE might be quite strong there, but its prospects presently seem weak.

Extension to the Muslim world may seem even less likely, especially where the constitution is Sharia based. But openness is not alien to Islam. It was evident in medieval Spain and is again visible within Turkey. Its feasibility alongside

Muslim constitutions should not be ruled out, as hinted at by the involvement of the Muslim Council of Britain with the nationally agreed framework for RE (QCA and DfES 2004).

The global organization of states in which this model might find a readier prospect of extension and application is that of the Commonwealth, formerly designated as British. It is massively diverse in race and ethnicity, countries and cultures, health and wealth, and religion. Yet it shares in a variety of ways some degree of common heritage.

The heritage includes a range of religious allegiances, which in different ways has been divisive, as was the case in the Indian subcontinent following Independence, or more variously in African contexts wherein tribal religious loyalties have figured. It also includes the valuing of participatory democracy, and with it the appreciation of difference. The symbol of monarch is only minimally concerned with actual political power. It is much more about an acknowledgement that the breadth and vitality of human community depends on more than the manipulation of one group by another. It preserves the principle of common-sense reasoning, while also being open to that which draws its inspiration from some yet deeper or more exalted source.

## From transcendence in the national framework to transcendence in a Commonwealth framework

The new national framework for RE does not involve a nationalization of religion such that any of its distinctive claims to truth would be diluted or denied. Neither does it encourage the encapsulation of children, sealed as it were hermetically from any human experience and ideas which have not first been filtered in every respect by a specified religious authority. Rather it confirms a partnership between faith communities and the state in together providing for the nation's educational needs.

In community schools, as also in faith schools, children and young people are on the learning journey in which they will be encouraged to seek understanding of a faith (religious or secular) to live by and to do that in ways that are open to the beliefs of others. The Standing Advisory Councils on Religious Education (SACREs) in every LEA bring together the interests of parental faith communities with those of teachers. The parental bodies associated with the SACREs, as also with specific faith schools, accept that their resourcing from public taxation warrants acknowledgement that other faiths take no delight in religious ignorance.

More generally, the framework affirms that a public education which did not enable children and young people to grapple with the 'grand narratives' of religious claims to truth must be defective. It notices that there are invitations in abundance to play a postmodernist game in which all beliefs are deconstructed into the creations of individual members of innumerable parallel interest groups. But it is not seduced. For it recognizes that if that were all that is left of the cumulative experience which calls itself Christian or Muslim or Jewish or Buddhist or Hindu or Sikh, or some other world faith, much would have been missed. The richness of human identity would have been translated into a flatland which has levelled off the highest mountain reaches and the greatest oceanic depths. And the very substance of transcendence would not even have been glimpsed.

The timeliness of pursuing the question of how imitable the framework might be for the Commonwealth is clear. The world is no less divided now than ever. The scale of division has never been greater in respect of well-being and poverty, or the availability of destructive weaponry. Given the peculiar potency of the religious ingredient in the human mix, for so globally diverse and representative a grouping of nations as the Commonwealth to set it clearly within its educational agenda would be a distinctive contribution to justice and peace worldwide. To persuade every Commonwealth country that this is so is a challenge that would be worthy of all the energies which Shap has at its disposal. But in whose interest would it not be for such an endeavour to be successful?

(2004)

# PART TWO

# Children's religious and moral development

Discussion and decision about the nature of RE, its scope and the appropriateness of its inclusion in the basic curriculum of all publicly maintained schools involves a range of academic disciplines – philosophies and theologies of education. It also involves legal considerations and the interests of society at large, faith communities, politicians and teachers. Alongside all of them must come central attention to the interests of children and young people and their capacities to engage intelligently with this subject.

The chapters which follow in this second section focus directly on that process of understanding. They include attention to different approaches to religion, both affective and cognitive. They draw on insights from psychology and pedagogy. Above all, they are rooted in the direct experience of children themselves as exposed in personal writing and conversation with the author. The subject matter includes expressly religious themes, such as notions of God, prayer, death and any beyond to it and institutional belonging. However, they are not treated as disconnected from wider life experience. The territory explored includes scientific cosmology, social and political horizons and belonging, as well as any interfaces with religion. Learning from leisure activity, home background and peers is there, as well as school.

That much of the fieldwork was done in decades past might appear to challenge its contemporary relevance. Certainly, that is a question to be borne in mind throughout. For that reason the author is presently engaged in replicating the earlier fieldwork in the same schools, but with different pupils. First impressions indicate strong continuities in the processes of apprehension and comprehension, along with some significant variations in content. He is also following it through by re-interviewing the original participants now aged in their thirties and forties. Again, remarkable continuities are showing themselves. Rather than discarding the earlier grounding, it remains a springboard for understanding religion across the lifespan, starting with the child and looking forward from there.

The first two and the last chapters of this section provide overarching perpectives on the developmental process. Chapter 9 does so by introducing as a background context the different emphases found in the approaches to religious development which have been influential in the curriculum in England. It works with a spectrum which ranges from the more cognitive to the more affective. Chapter 10 focuses more directly the notion of God in different psychological theories. Following the intermediate chapters, Chapter 15 indicates more directly the creative and challenging contribution which RE can make to personal and social development.

In between these two chapters are four others which focus on particular religious themes which are central to any religious development. For the most part they are rooted in the author's own research. Thus, Chapter 10 sets out the range of an empirical study of the process through which children and young people make sense of religion as part of their developing understanding of the world in which they live. Drawing on the responses from those interviewed from the age group 6 to 16, and from different religious backgrounds within that, it illustrates the complex interweaving of religion within the beliefs and values which shape their respective views of the world. The collection of material consists of over 1,000 hour-long written responses, plus some 340 hours of tape recorded individual interviews. It is these that provide the resource base for what follows on Death in Chapter 12 and God in Chapter 13, as also the extrapolation to the media for teaching and learning in Chapter 14.

What is never in doubt throughout this section is the capacity of even the youngest children to engage with the concepts and feelings associated with religion or the substantial interest in this subject matter amongst even the older students. The searching out and testing of beliefs and values is an ongoing fact of life.

# Chapter 9

# 'Readiness' for religion

'Don't call me a teacher; call me a fellow-learner.' In our contemporary concern with a child-centred curriculum or with personal autonomy as the goal of education, there is a horror at the thought of *imposing* any ideas or beliefs on another. 'S/he must make up his/her own mind', 'work it out for themselves'. In the light of such thinking, formal provision of Religious Education in the the home or in the school might qualify as the major offender. 'Give me a child until the age of seven, and you can do what you like with him later' (or 'and I will form his character' – there are several versions of this saying, usually attributed to the Jesuits).

Once this kind of negative association is made, who can be surprised if a young primary teacher, charged as he or she likely will be with the responsibility for RE, were to recoil at the prospect. But imagine the relief if they subsequently heard that on psychological grounds children cannot understand religious concepts before adolescence. Here would be final proof that it is none of any teacher's business. They would be pedagogical paupers to think otherwise!

Evidently psychological considerations are relevant to both the theory and practice of RE. What understanding of religion are children and young people capable of? Is understanding religion the same as religious understanding? If not, how are they related? How does understanding develop? Though it is clear that there are divergent views on such questions, this chapter will seek to assess the conclusions drawn from recent research and comment on their potential application for the classroom.

## Religious development: spectrum of research

Two major emphases stand out in recent research on religious development. While they are sometimes presented in opposition to each other, it is helpful to see them as at different ends of the same spectrum, which runs between purely cognitive and purely affective approaches. This is done by focusing on six writers who between them range across the spectrum (see Figure 9.1).

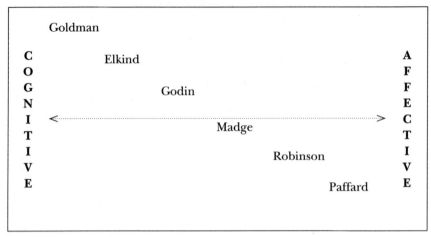

**Figure 9.1**   Spectrum of approaches to religious development

## Cognitive stage theory

Reference to a developmental sequence in the formation of concepts of number, space, time and of powers of logical reasoning has become a commonplace in educational psychology (see Beard 1969 and Furth 1970). Piaget's studies spread over half a century are better known today than ever. Latterly, attempts have been made to apply his approach to children's understanding of religion. The result is 'God-concept readiness' (Williams 1971). To demonstrate what is meant by this sort of talk we will take examples from three of its most influential exponents.

### Goldman: God and Jesus

If any one person is responsible for making teachers in England conscious of 'stages in religious thinking', it must be R. J. Goldman. His research at the beginning of the 1960s was widely reported and the evidence he presented of children's difficulties in understanding biblical concepts was a major factor in the shift from the Bible to a 'life theme' emphasis in the newer Agreed Syllabuses.

Goldman (1964) examined the understanding which boys and girls between 6 and 15 years had of three biblical stories (Exodus, Burning Bush, Temptations) and the ideas of God and Jesus contained in them. By presenting three pictures with which those interviewed might identify, he obtained further comments on their notions of biblical authorship, Church and prayer. As a result he described three main steps in religious thinking corresponding to Piaget's own schema:

INTUITIVE (pre-operational, unsystematic, egocentric, till 7/8 years)
*Why was Moses afraid to look at God?*
'He hadn't spoken politely to God.'
'Moses didn't like to see God burning in the fire.'
*Why didn't Jesus turn the stone into bread?*
'God said that if you ate bread alone you wouldn't live. You should eat something else with it – butter.'

CONCRETE (content-dominated, 8–13 years)
*Why was Moses afraid to look at God?*
'Moses thought God would chase him out of the holy ground because he hadn't taken off his shoes.'
*Why didn't Jesus turn the stone into bread?*
'Jesus didn't believe in the devil, he didn't want to do it just for him. He's bad.'

ABSTRACT (formal operations, hypothetical and deductive reasoning, 12/13+)
*Why was Moses afraid to look at God?*
'The sight of God was too much for human eyes. It's too tremendous a vision. Moses knew this and was afraid.'
*Why didn't Jesus turn the stone into bread?*
'It was a case of good against evil. It would be a victory for evil against God, if he did it.'

The order of these stages is invariant. Transition between them is apparently more related to mental age than chronological age. But at any age the limiting influence of this developmental sequence is such that all religious thinking is affected:

| | |
|---|---|
| *Ideas of God:* | omnipotence and omnipresence |
| *Miracles:* | their explanation and significance |
| *Christology:* | the distinctiveness of Jesus as a man, his perfection |
| *Good and evil:* | temptation, the devil, divine judgment |
| *Bible:* | its origin and authorship, its isolation in time or contemporary relevance |
| *Church:* | what it is and why people go |
| *Prayer:* | reasons for praying and the effectiveness of doing so |

Goldman points out that below the mental age of thirteen, thinking on any of these topics will be 'operationally' limited. This verdict applies to both the logical quality and the religious quality of thinking, since for Goldman 'theologic' depends on a prior capacity for logic. Not until late adolescence does genuine religious thinking become possible; previously it is better described as 'pre-religious' (stage 1) or 'sub-religious' (stage 2) (Goldman 1965b).

Since the topics covered by Goldman's interviews were typical of the agreed-syllabus RE that had predominated in English schools until the 1960s, the implications for teaching were seen to be dramatic. To avoid misunderstanding that might persist into adulthood, the teacher was advised to beware of direct biblical (or doctrinal) teaching and instead to concentrate on enriching and enlarging children's general experience of life. Their lives could then be illuminated by the direct use of religious language at a later stage.

### Elkind: religious identity, denomination and prayer

At the same time that Goldman was interviewing children in the West Midlands and South of England, David Elkind was extending his application of Piagetian methods to deal with children's understanding of religious identity in Massachusetts, USA (Elkind and Flavell 1969). But where Goldman had restricted his investigation to Anglicans, Nonconformists and 'Non-attenders', Elkind dealt successively with Jewish, Catholic and Protestant children (Elkind 1961, 1962, 1963). He concentrated on several components of religious identity (Elkind 1964a, 1964b):

- What characteristics are shared by all members of the group?
- How is membership attained?
- What is the distinction between membership of a religious group and any other groupings
- ethnic/national?

Again Elkind found that understanding of these various components of religious identity developed according to the familiar sequence of stages:

INTUITIVE (pre-operational, undifferentiated, egocentric, until 7/8 years)
*What is a Jew?*
'A person.'
*How is a Jewish person different from a Catholic person?*
'Because some people have black hair and some people have blond.'
*What's a Protestant?*
'I don't know.' *Really?*
'Well maybe it's something that makes you feel happy.'

CONCRETE (8–11) years)
*How can you tell a person is a Catholic?*
'If you see them go into a Catholic church.'
*What is a Jew?*
'A person who goes to Temple and to Hebrew school.'

ABSTRACT (formal operations, differentiated, 11+)
*How can you tell a person is a Protestant?*

'Because they are free to repent and pray to God in their own way.'
*What is a Catholic?*
'A person who believes in the truth of the RC Church.'

This was confirmed by his subsequent study of children's understanding of prayer (Elkind et al. 1967). Children spontaneously give meaning to religious terms that are beyond their level of comprehension, but few under the age of twelve years attain a 'proper' understanding of any religious concepts.

Especially interesting is Elkind's emphasis on denominational belonging and identity. The respective starting points of Goldman and Elkind may well reflect the different constitutional arrangements for religion in their two countries. In England, until recently, the plurality of religious communities has been 'contained' within the framework of a national Christian tradition: Protestant biblical teaching has been a common denominator for RE in schools. But in the United States provision for RE has been entirely separate from the schools and therefore carried on within the separate religious communities. Since English religious life is now increasingly recognized as plural, it is helpful to be shown what developmental considerations are operative within religious communities.

In the face of the likelihood of erroneous religious ideas being conceived during primary years, Elkind is more sanguine than Goldman about the prospect of children growing out of them. Just as Piaget showed that 'animistic' and 'artificialist' notions are gradually replaced even without systematic teaching (Piaget 1926, 1929, 1952), so Elkind anticipates that greater socialization and objectivity in thinking will extend to religious matters too.

Nevertheless, he is sceptical about RE as a deliberately intellectual enterprise during childhood. He prefers instead to concentrate on 'training the emotions', especially through exposure to the activities of the parent religious community.

## Godin: magic and sacrament

André Godin is a Belgian professor of psychology who, as editor of *Studies in Religious Psychology* (Godin 1957–68) and the Catholic RE Journal *Lumen Vitae*, has been engaged in research on children's religious development for over twenty years. He too accepts a psychogenetic stage sequence for religious understanding on the strength of various research projects carried out under his direction. Following Piaget he attributes magical notions to the primitive years of childhood and of the human race: a child prays or performs ritual acts with expectation that some aspect of the world will automatically be changed. Thus magical mentality infects a child's appreciation of the Eucharist. This is illustrated by responses to the following story put to ninety Catholic pupils aged 8, 11 and 14 years:

*What do you think of this story: it is probably not true, but if it were true, what would you think of it?*

A woman is busy cleaning in the sacristy. She finds a ciborium on the table with some consecrated hosts: the priest has forgotten to put it back in the tabernacle in the church. But the woman does not know that the hosts are consecrated; she thinks they are prepared for the morning, to be consecrated at the next day's Mass. So she eats two or three, just like that, to see what they taste like.

*Have you understood? What do you think of it? If the story were true would the consecrated hosts have produced some effect in the soul of this person?*

The responses reveal a sharp decline in magical thinking from ages 8 to 14. In constrast to older boys and girls, most of the younger children either convict the woman of sacrilege, or affirm that grace would be communicated anyway; or if they deny this, it is for 'magical reasons': 'She touched the host' (ten years), 'She ate three' (nine years).

On the basis of these and other findings, Godin suggests there is a gradual evolution from 'magical' to 'sacramental mentality'. Not every teacher shares Godin's Catholic antipathy to magic, but RE does properly encourage pupils to understand what differences there may be between magic and other religious beliefs. It is, however, very noticeable that Godin is more emphatic than either Goldman or Elkind that Christian formation must have its own theological norms transforming any *naturally given* psychological structures (Godin 1960).

Godin is also critical about the extent to which Goldman failed to appreciate the expressive power of symbols in the experiences of young children. Piaget pointed to the dawn of symbolic sense in infant thumb-sucking and doll play; similarly Godin suggests that stories and ritual acts may be passively assimilated from first contact with religious teaching. Their significance to individual children would not 'meekly follow the curve of biophysical maturation in childhood and adolescence'. But, in some hidden interior way, a child may find meaning there, deeply felt, in spite of conceptual limitations.

## The primacy of feeling

Alongside those who stress the importance of rationality in religion and the gradual construction of a conceptual framework of understanding between infancy and adolescence, there are others who focus primarily on feeling. This matches the currency of talk about fantasy and feeling in education, non-verbal methods of communication and the importance of the emotions in children's learning. Intellectual understanding is not necessarily excluded in this alternative focus; more often it is claimed that intellect without feeling is hollow. Again we will look at three examples of such an emphasis from recent research as Piaget's was to the first. But there is a common ethos derived from the mystical tradition of mankind. This ethos may be in religious form (Rudolf Otto's sense of the numinous) or poetic (Wordsworthian 'nature mysticism').

## Madge: childhood wonder

As if illustrating the contrast of ethos between the 'cognitive' and the 'affective' approaches, V. Madge relied much more on spontaneous talk and recollection than on Goldman's clinical interview technique. From extensive teaching experience in primary school, reports of student teachers and autobiographical references, she drew a picture of childhood and religion's part in it: 'children in search of meaning' (Madge 1965). Most obviously their search is represented by the varied range of questions they ask about any aspect of life:

Who made the telephone?
How does a cut in your skin heal?
How do hedgehogs grow baby hedgehogs inside?
Who is God's mummy?

In such questioning she sees the beginnings of both religious and scientific enquiry. But she also speaks of them as 'inner stirrings' of an 'elemental sense of the mysterious'. It might be prompted by iron filings wriggling under a magnet, by falling rain, or a bird, as in the child's poem 'Lark and Dove'

One morning in
lark song I heard a lovely
tone; the dark was
going, the sun was coming.
One night very early, still light,
Two loving doves came flying
To give spirit to everyone.
As they flew we saw them
From our window. (Linda, aged 7)

A sudden consciousness of beauty can compel wonder in a child – awaken a sense of 'the numinous'. But so it can for an adult. One of Madge's 'humanist-agnostic' students writes as follows after an evening stroll by the sea:

The sea pounding the beach under a starry sky is a beautiful sight any evening, but this night was different in some way. 1 stood there entranced, watching the endless cycle of the waves rolling forward, breaking on the beach, sucking back to re-form and advance once more. Something of the wonder of those minutes caused me to understand the term 'eternal' rather better than ever I had before ... Although a 'humanist-agnostic' I definitely felt something I can only think was 'spiritual-wonder', an awareness of an inexplicable 'something'. It caused me to sit down and question myself more deeply than ever before; question myself on the nature of life, whether everything can be explained scientifically in logical terms, or whether I am mistaken in this belief. I am not yet satisfied (quoted in Madge 1971).

RE, on this reckoning, from nursery onwards is rightly dedicated to arouse the sense of trust and security, of love and joy, of wonder and awe. Madge does not reject Goldman's 'stages' of development but emphasizes that sensitivity to the way young children actually think and feel is the key to religious development at this stage.

### Robinson: the taproot of experience

As Deputy Director of Sir Alister Hardy's Religious Experience Research Unit at Oxford, Edward Robinson followed up all the references to important childhood experiences mentioned in the first 1,000 adult responses to the Unit's national appeal:

> Those who feel that they have been conscious of, and perhaps influenced by some Power, whether they call it the Power of God or not, which may either appear to be beyond their individual selves or in part outside and in part within their being, are asked to write as simple and brief an account as possible of these feelings and their effects.

From Robinson's follow-up of these first returns he obtained vivid accounts of childhood recollections. These speak of powerful feelings erupting in immediate experience, but many go on to stress the long-term effect of growing on with the realization that such experiences had been had.

Many, but by no means all, of the experiences which Robinson has quoted in articles have been, triggered by nature:

> The first approach to a spiritual experience which I can remember must have taken place when I was five or six years old at the house where I was born and brought up. It was a calm, limpid summer morning and the early mist still lay in wispy wreaths among the valleys. The dew on the grass seemed to sparkle like iridescent jewels in the sunlight, and the shadows of the houses and trees seemed friendly and protective. In the heart of the child that I was, there suddenly seemed to well up a deep and overwhelming sense of gratitude, a sense of unending peace and security which seemed to be part of the beauty of the morning, the love and protection of my home and the sheer joy of being alive. I did not associate this with God, but I knew that in all this beauty was a friendliness, a protective and living presence which included all that I had ever loved and yet was something much more (quoted in Robinson 1972a).

The potency of such experiences for the people concerned convinces him that children are capable of far greater religious understanding than Goldman has seemed to allow: the fact that children may not be able to articulate their deepest feelings is no proof of their not having them or of their unimportance to children.

> I do not think it will ever be possible to do full justice to the religious experience of children unless it is unreservedly recognized that the higher (and rarer) flights of vision to which the word 'mystical' is generally applied are not generically distinct from the simpler intuitive insights which are probably a great deal more common in childhood than we are now willing to admit. (Robinson 1972a)

Any attempt to deny this is insensitive to the 'living nerve' that makes child and adult the same person. The major priority in RE is for the teacher to be able to recognize the inarticulate sense of inner spiritual awareness which may be found at any age, and to help it find expression.


## Paffard: *Inglorious Wordsworths*

Robinson takes Goldman to task for rejecting the whole idea of religious experience as a mode of awareness different from any other. Evidence can be presented, however, which suggests that the religious distinctiveness of a sense of mystery or wonder is itself doubtful. This is the thesis of M. K. Paffard's 1964 Bristol MA dissertation, now published as Paffard (1973).

Moved by recollection of the significance of solitude in his own childhood, of spiritual longings both diffuse and intense during his years at boarding school, Paffard has searched for similar experiences recorded in autobiography and fiction, or as revealed by a questionnaire he gave to 400 sixth-formers and university undergraduates. He finds transcendental experiences in abundance: feelings that ordinary consciousness is transcended, maybe involving visions or a sense of physical presence, maybe feelings of oneness, ecstasy, joy, melancholy, or fearsom awe. A C. S. Lewis may describe this sense in religious terms, but an A. L. Rowse will insist that it is thoroughly aesthetic. The difference to Paffard is one of *overbelief*. Thus he quotes, 'No Buddhist ever had a vision of the Blessed Virgin Mary, and St Benedict saw a vision of the Blessed Goddess, Kwan-Yin' (Paffard 1964). It is the experiences themselves which matter.

Few of the experiences reported in the questionnaire do actually come from the primary years; most are from adolescence. More English specialists and young people who have written poetry acknowledge having such experiences than any others. Outside, in evening solitude, is the most frequently mentioned occasion for them. All are transcendental, claims Paffard, whether the language is of Communion with God, conversion experience, or sheer aesthetic delight.

Paffard's empirical work is with younger people than that of the Religious Experience Research Unit, but his sample is from beyond the compulsory years of schooling and 'academically selective'. In principle, however, there is no reason to suppose that the capacity for such experiences is not as widespread in junior school children as he (and Marghanita Laski) (Laski 1961) claim it is in the general population. But as was also the case in the example quoted by Madge, on Paffard's reckoning, many, if not all, RE concerns will be shared by those teaching English or encouraging 'creative writing'.

## Interpreting the spectrum

It is not my present intention to declare that any one of these research wavelengths is more finely tuned than the others. On the contrary, only by trying to see these and other wavelengths in relation to each other will the total spectrum be complete – the spectrum, that is, of research and of religion itself. What then emerges?

### The spectrum of religion

To a degree this spectrum of research views reflects the fact that there are many different ways of being religious and different emphases within any one religious tradition. Yet we have examined only two expressions of these differences. To one, sophisticated theological reasoning may be the all-important characteristic of mature religious belief and understanding. To another, what matters most will be a personal encounter with God to which no words could ever do justice. It is easy enough for the philosopher to caricature all talk of mystery and mystic vision as muddle. 'The return to the catastrophic humbug masquerading as wisdom and insight that characterized medieval thought' was how one letter to *The Times Educational Supplement* dismissed an article by E. Robinson. But similarly, a mystic or an evangelical of any tradition may ask to feel the pulse that beats within reason and reject the insulting implication that until the age of thirteen or fourteen a child is sub-religious or devoid of religious insight. There is a feeling side to reason, without which he could never understand another person or 'hunch' a hypothesis. And can he not begin to do both of these in infancy?

These and other ways of being religious need appreciation by the teacher if religious development is to be understood.

### The spectrum of research

Words and how they can be used in different ways undoubtedly make problems for the researcher. Goldman entitles his book *Religious Thinking from Childhood to Adolescence* (1964), yet says he does not think religious thinking is any different from any other kind of thinking. Godin is no less concerned with cognitive structures but insists that Christian cognition might be transformed by personal revelation at almost any age. Robinson reproves Goldman for the narrowness of his conception of what it means to be human or religious: but is he in turn perhaps too broad? Though he states that religious experience may be discrete and distinct, he comes close to embracing aesthetic responses with religious. In this he is near Paffard's description of any difference between religious and aesthetic experience as 'overbelief'.

For all these apparent differences of emphasis, each in his own way is seeking to fathom the childhood of man, religious or secular. In coming to terms with their different views it has therefore to be asked just how substantial their points of difference are; are they largely semantic? Infelicitous usage may account for much misunderstanding of the respective positions. For instance, despite what their critics say of them, advocates of the cognitive stage theory are flexible about the actual age when an individual child may learn to perform certain mental operations and admit the likely difference that home culture or teacher variable can make. Goldman himself, if his debt to a Froebel training is to be properly acknowledged (Goldman 1959), is well aware of unconscious, non-rational, emotional aspects of life and even of the centrality of mystery to religion – he simply 'bracketed' these for his research purposes. Robinson, for all his distaste for compartmentalizing childhood, in turn accepts that certain qualities of mystical experience are adult phenomena. Differences remain, but not necessarily exclusive ones.

Each end of the spectrum of research on children's religious development is therefore helpful to the teacher. Between them they represent the child's gradual comprehension of the relationship between separate strands of knowledge, and the partial inaccessibility of that personal synthesis at every age to anyone but the private 'I' behind it.

## Understanding religion and religious understanding

'Secular' school and religious community are likely to have different ambitions for the children who come within their boundaries. The church, synagogue or gurdwara might well aspire to transmit the faith inherited from of old to a new generation in such a way that it becomes their own. The publicly maintained school can have no such commitment, however, to one particular religious tradition; it will seek instead to introduce its pupils to the religious facts of life as to any other aspect of human experience. In briefer terms, the hope of one will be for the child to become openly religious, of the other that s/he become 'religiate' (if we may use this term in the same sense as educators use the terms 'numerate' and 'literate' to describe a pupil equipped to deal with number and literature).

The term 'religiate' is used as a way of highlighting the practical, educational value of trying to understand what people have meant, or mean today, when, as individuals or as entire civilizations, they have ordered their lives around specific beliefs in God or gods. Even in infant school, and without any word from the teacher, children can be well aware of the existence of different religious beliefs and practices: from parents and friends, from the near neighbourhood, or farflung on the TV screen. They will try to make sense of this as of everything else, but the progress towards fully fledged conceptual understanding may be slow, as we have seen. Yet no appreciation of the convictions and dreams that have motivated their forebears and contemporaries will be complete without such learning.

The teacher in this situation is not called to proclaim his/her private faith or doubts. Faith and doubt are publicly represented in beliefs and actions which appear in stories, that are enshrined in history, in a contemporary documentary or in credal formulations; they may be the subject of songs or pictures, or even be conveyed by stylized ritual or simple gesture. In any of these forms the child and the teacher may approach them together and make of them what they are able at that particular time in their lives. Together they can talk about what they have just seen, heard, or performed; they can explore experiences just shared, checking for sense and meaning. The teacher forms a triangle, as it were, of him/herself, the children and the various expressions of religion (see Rosen 1967). He relates to the class and they to him, but they also each relate to a particular item in a whole range of experience – a specific story, ritual or example of religious truths (see Chapter 3). Concepts and feelings are both involved in the interplay. The end is understanding religion, but complementarily, it will also be an aid to a religious understanding of life.

In beginning, therefore, to open up with a class of children the manifold claims of religious belief and experience, the general primary teacher or the secondary specialist has firm ground on which to stand. In seeking an effective RE s/he need not apologize for being both learner and teacher. Religious *thinking* may begin to flourish in our teens, but religious education begins much earlier (Smith 1936) and for most people, as Gabriel Moran reminds us (Moran 1971), religious education goes on for life.

(1975)

# Chapter 10

# Sensing God

Whether within the context of a church-, gurdwara-, or synagogue-going family, or alternatively a state maintained school, the process by which a boy or girl comes to any understanding of God is complex and varied. It cannot be exhaustively described because at both poles there are qualities of infinity. This is true by definition of references to God, but arguably also with reference to the richness of individual childhood experience.

At one level, few children even in a secular western democracy grow up without any understanding whatever of religious vocabulary in general and the word 'God' in particular. It is part of their sociocultural inheritance bequeathed to them by the environment of stories, jokes, oaths, festivals, adverts, etc., within which they learn. In this respect, the degree of association with a local religious community through home or school does affect the attitude and content of their religious learning, but some minimal familiarity remains fairly universal even without explicit religious belonging.

The status of children's conceptions of God is, of course, open to dispute. There are social historians who would suggest that they are no more than the terminal moraine of yesterday's beliefs, to be acknowledged in the way that myths and legends are, but, like acne, to be outgrown by a normal healthy adolescent. There are behaviourist psychologists who are inclined to believe that God concepts are no more than miscues to stimuli that have been wrongly interpreted to mean more than they actually do: like pigeons, children are reinforced in their superstitious ideas in expectation of promised reward or punishment (Skinner 1948). Neither of these views allows much independent validity to religious belief, but both acknowledge its occurrence.

The psychoanalytic tradition presents different glosses on this same claim. According to one view, children's conceptions of God are genetically prompted, individual recapitulations of the stages of religious belief which humankind has gone through – polytheism – monotheism – atheism. Freud, too, rooted religion in the childhood of the human race, but stressed as well the individual infancy of any child's dependent relation on parents as a source for the 'religious illusion'. Faced with the harshness of the real world (war, starvation, inequality), what is a child to do but fall back on the security of a power even more protective and benevolent than the immediate parents, although ideally patterned on them. Empirical studies to check the correlation between emotions and concepts associated with parents and those associated with God indicate some interdependence, but less exclusively tied to the father than Freud suggests. In any case, the centrality or otherwise of parental motifs varies from one religious tradition to another, as also for the atheist.

It is an important characteristic of psychoanalysis that it calls attention to the conscious depths of human personality. The adult's emotional life is largely determined by childhood experiences (from earliest pre-natal ones to adolescence). Jung shared in this, but where Freud relates the unconscious life and religion to biological and physical drives, Jung makes spiritual needs and energies central. Childhood is still of major importance for emotional and religious development, but Jung sees this positively: the potential deriving from the childhood inheritances provides the path for personal integrity in middle age and beyond, when due attention can be given to more than the basic priorities of becoming materially independent in life. In a sense, for Freud, the sooner a child's religious concepts can be outgrown the better, while for Jung their promise is explored only many years after leaving school.

So far it has been claimed that concepts of God are derived from social context and emotional needs. According to developmental psychology, however, the concepts derive also from the cognitive reasoning processes. Questions about the beginning and end of the universe, as also about the whys and wherefores of life in it, are asked by young children and 'God-laden' responses are often found in this connection, whether derived from adults' comments or emerging from conversation with their peers. Piaget identified such references as typical of a myth-making stage in the development of children's thinking. Applying his general account of cognitive development directly to religious thinking, others (notably Goldman in England, Godin in Belgium, Elkind and Peatling in the USA) claim to have demonstrated that it follows the same sequence of development as do for instance mathematical, historical and moral reasoning. The earliest stage is labelled pre-operational and even pre-religious; reasoning here is restricted in that arbitrary connections are made following intuition and fancy. Father Christmas, fairies and God belong in the same sphere. This gives way in middle years, 7/8 to 11/12, to concrete thinking where reasoning is content-specific and dependent on hard evidence for its validity. God is believed in because Jesus was seen to be alive again after crucifixion, or not believed in because of spacemen failing to find the divine location. Only during adolescent years do boys and girls show themselves capable of fully operational thinking, taking into account the importance of intentions, hypothetical possibilities and the total context. God is believed in now as final source of meaning in life, or rejected as incompatible with human freedom or the facts of suffering in the world.

There is a strong implication from some cognitive developmentalists that children's God-concepts are 'sub-religious' until this last stage is reached. Such a verdict ignores the significance of the thought-forms found in earlier childhood whose apprehension of God is just differently expressed.

From these accounts it is apparent that children's conceptions of God can be approached from several different angles, some more mutually exclusive than others. They all deserve to be reckoned with when considering how to introduce children and young people to religious language. Do the child's emotions and attitudes make him/her more, or less, receptive to the content to be shared and how might receptivity be increased? If RE also goes on in middle age and beyond, what can most usefully be done earlier to peg out foundations that will not subsequently need to be changed? Do certain modes of thinking predominate at certain ages and, if so, what forms of communication will then be the most effective? What associations has the individual child already made for God from those who surround him? Above all, what point has he reached in his appreciation of God? These are all questions that a parent or teacher may well want to ask in preparation for any formal use of religious language with a child.

However, it would be a mistake to attend to only one side of the educational equation. Children need to be understood as a preliminary to any understanding of their concepts of God. But, in turn, concepts of God can affect both what is looked for, and found, in and for the children. To be sure, concepts of God are often institutionally labelled as such, deriving from specific and direct use of religious vocabulary: this is true, irrespective of the religious tradition in question. It needs to be recognized that overt familiarity with such words as God, Almighty, Lord, Allah, Vishnu, etc., is no guarantee of any particular degree of understanding. Each points to a reality which is believed to be far greater than any words could signify and each community of faith which uses any such word has generated a rich store of language to express itself and assist communication. It is vital therefore for the teacher or parent concerned for religious development to be familiar with the range of available language which can be used, i.e. not just prophet, priest and king, but father, friend or companion: artist, judge or clown: volcano, river or sun: fortress, bridge or hospital: all-loving, all-demanding, all-wise. Depending on the tradition, the words may be more, or less, personal, and with, or without, historical reference. Categories of height, or of depth, will be used, with perhaps more emphasis on the former in a tradition that stresses the 'otherness' of God, or the latter in one that stresses 'withinness'. Greatness may also be expressed in terms of the dimension of time – at the beginning and end of time, or a sense of timelessness even in the present now.

Picture language abounds throughout the religious experience of mankind and can be drawn on as a resource for apprehension of how others see God. The taboo against images, as found in Islam, Judaism and strands of Christianity, in this context may best be regarded as a warning against the misplaced concreteness of identifying one verbal or visual image with God. With this proviso, so as not to become frozen and fixed, imaging in words or pictures can be employed with even the youngest child (and surely will be by them).

Because the language which is used of God and the experiences which are referred to are so diverse, it is inevitably the case that the bounds of institutional religious labelling are exceeded. In the same way that verbal and visual images, such as those selected above, drew on a wide range of human experience, so too children may cross the religious threshold in their own experience without realizing it. They may have sensed wonder and awe in some big city-centre, on a forest pathway, or just looking up at the stars: they may have been moved to cry out at the sight of pointless cruelty on the roadside or on TV, and to follow it with an expression of fellow-feeling; or they may have been overjoyed, thrilled and delighted with a pleasure that has come to them personally for being who they are – in for example a birthday or festival celebration. Any of these can give glimmerings of the experiences that for the religious believer may be associated with a God concept and the child who has 'been there' already may be better able to make a connection or see new meaning in formal religious language. Similarly, Violet Madge used to speak of the sense of being lost and found as a model for the warmth and security of a God who seeks to be the lover of humankind. Again, a child may know inwardness from moments of quiet, solitariness, or gentle reflection in front of a fire: the isolation and desertion, the burning and transience, as well as the gentleness and warmth that may be known with feeling, can disturb and deepen, and so lead beyond the realm of surface meaning.

In many ways children introduce themselves to God concepts, but there is always the task in RE to explore much further into God-ward territory, and to help with the identification of false idols by leaving the shallows behind. This is the least that any self-respecting atheist could demand of RE. At the same time, it may also be that the initiative for conceiving God will come to a child from without his immediate world. Were that not the case, the concept of God would itself have become but a tamed superstition for children to recognize as such.

(1984)

# Chapter 11

# Religion in the child's own core curriculum

Amidst the current debate about priorities in education which has been intensified by economic crisis, religious education is once again called on to justify its claim on national resources. The largely successful efforts of the last decade to establish the educational grounds of the subject provide a basis for an effective response to be made to this challenge, especially at the level of rationale for subject content (Schools Council 1971). In addition, complementary support is available from the significant part which religion has in the life of boys and girls themselves.

## The present study

Research evidence illustrating this aspect of children's lives was gathered from interviewing a wide range of children in English schools. The sample was relatively balanced in respect of ages, sex, region, type of school and social background. For the purpose of the first (written) interview, 1,028 boys and girls were involved. They were selected from each of eight schools, four in the north-west of England, four in the south-east, and there were approximately 25 from each year group in the primary 6–10 year range and the secondary 11–15 range. In each school they were selected as a representative cross-section of their year in terms of ability spread. This provided a roughly even distribution of boys and girls of each age over the ten-year period of compulsory schooling, and a random distribution of religious belonging.

Selection for the second (individual oral) interview was made according to religious belonging: 82 Anglicans, 81 unattached, 38 Nonconformists. Numbers of boys and girls, and of each age 6–15 years, were equal and evenly drawn from each of the original school samples. In addition, 40 Roman Catholics, 41 Jews and 38 Sikhs were then selected from a further six schools and, together with 17 Muslims from another secondary school, were each given the written and oral interviews. Both interviews lasted approximately one hour and were conducted by the same person throughout. The 338 individual oral interviews were tape-recorded and subsequently transcribed.

The interviews were designed to reveal the allegiances, beliefs and values which boys and girls hold or express in the course of their trying to understand the world, and how their understanding changes as they grow older. The written one consisted of several separate items. First, comprehension and association questions were asked of two stories – a modern fairy tale *(Where the Wild Things Are)* and a Buddhist parable *(The Blind Men and the Elephant)*. Secondly, there were two sentence completion tests – on what they find important and what puzzling. And, finally, the request that the pupils should attempt to picture God and then justify their response. The oral interview was thematically structured to cover children's play and superstitions, death, thunder and lightning, atomic bomb-drop, space exploration, prayer, social and political roles and groupings, church/synagogue-going, alternative religious identities, initiation rites, present giving, loving, and beliefs in Father Christmas and God. By virtue of a semi-clinical approach to the interview (Elkind 1964c), the pupils were encouraged to spell out the meaning for them of religious and other concepts; they were prompted to use them by carefully selected photographs, role-ranking exercises, and anecdotes.

Responses were coded and computer-analysed for variations according to age, sex, religious belonging and school; they were also studied individually for their personal distinctiveness. The wealth of data was initially overwhelming and although now thoroughly analysed and written up (Gates 1976), there is yet scope for further work on it. This present chapter is a brief indication of the extensive presence which emerged of 'religious ingredients' in the thoughts and feelings of childhood and adolescence.

**1. Sense of contingency**. Human wondering at the strangeness of finding ourselves in the world at all is close to the heart of many religions. Thus creation stories in religious traditions the world over, while sensing the possibility of chaos, affirm that there is order in the universe. Among children, too, a similar sense seems to be present, anticipated perhaps by their earliest experience of insecurity; of daylight giving way to darkness, treasured objects being dropped, or loved ones being absent. It comes through vividly in playground games or in the fantasies associated with thunder and lightning.

Even in the case of so seemingly trivial a matter as treading on/avoiding the cracks in the pavement, the imagination of children makes play with its worst forebodings. This simple game has penalties built-in which relate to physical dangers or threats to personal identity. Thus whoever is careless risks falling 'over a cliff', 'down a crevice', 'into a bottomless pit', even 'into hell'; he may be devoured by animals – bears, wolves, crocodiles, lions – or more mysterious creatures – witches, wizards, bogeymen or demons. Alternatively, the features of the child's personality which encourage him to feel accepted by others may mutate, so he becomes a snake, a swine, a frog, or a monkey; not only does he look ugly, he becomes smelly and stupid, a fool, a dunce, a nutcase. Marital prospects also become the opposite of any present hopes: a rat, a stick, a black, an old lady. As well as enjoying the play with words and rhyming fun, it is as though the incongruity of what is said by very contrast confirms the orderliness of the real world.

This conclusion is made all the more compelling not so much by the fact that most of the boys and girls interviewed orally had played this game, but by each one having his or her own variant of it. Somehow, the lines which cut across their routine path are as reminders of the boundaries of being, within which any person grows. It is not surprising, therefore, to find peeping through the cosmic crack the more explicit theological associations of hell and the monstrous Leviathan.

These associations, together with a more general awareness of the contingencies of life, were evident also in relation to thunderstorms. Responses prompted by a picture of lightning in the sky and the question as to what little children feel when it is thundering and there is lightning revealed an abundance of fantasy, again almost as varied as the number of pupils describing it, whether wild animals, monsters, giants, ghosts, little men, Father Christmas, or God, their noisy activities ranged from baths to battles, furniture-moving to photography, making beds to archery practice. It might well have been God and Jesus at sport: 'rolling cannon balls', 'playing skittles' or 'soccer with the angels'; 'Jesus has just scored a goal', 'God has clapped his hands'. Less sportingly, it might be 'the devil stretching out his fingers and saying evil words that God doesn't like'. Certainly, the association of the occasion with God's wrath was very common: the world, or individuals within it, were being warned to mend their ways, otherwise they might discover for themselves that 'the lightning's been sent for you', 'God wants you with him', or 'the devils are coming for them'. However seriously, or otherwise, this precise content is taken, it is evident that fundamental human anxieties can cluster around thunder and lightning, no less than the pavement cracks.

The religious overtones found within some of the fantasy language are not just a hangover from a former era. They are a reminder of the continuing significance of the questions of personal meaning raised whensoever children are exposed to elemental aspects of life. Ironically, therefore, concern with contingency on the part of children makes it the more essential for schools to be aware of the intrinsic link between this and religion.

**2. Social inheritances**. Spontaneity was undoubtedly active in these many and varied responses. But there is evidence also of the existence of a common matrix of associations into which the children are inducted by their peers, even more than by their elders. Sociologists have latterly focused attention on 'common religion' as a neglected aspect of the adult's world; at a time of change in the institutional churches, the persistence of 'folk beliefs' is thrown into special relief (Opie and Opie 1959, Towler 1974). It now appears, however, that this sort of influence is also strong with children. The lore and language of school children, so well documented by the Opies, are both means of expressing some basic concerns and carriers of explicitly religious meanings.

The relationship between the understanding of religion that had been forged in this way, and any more formally taught religious education, was not easy to distinguish. Thus, there was much in the children's accounts of petitionary acts of prayer which sounded similar to their explanations of 'crossing fingers' – a ritual act which might easily be characterized as superstitious and therefore inferior to true religion. In fact, the evidence from the interviews points to the need to see much of what is often called 'superstition' as forming a continuum with what might be separately identified as 'religion'. At the same time, there was substantial evidence of boys and girls seeking to distinguish between religious and superstitious belief.

Be that as it may, society's bequest of the thought forms of common religion appears to be as important a source for children's understanding of religion as is any contact which they might have with more officially designated religious tradition. Even when dealing with distinctive denominational[1] self-understandings (including differences both within and between religious traditions), it may well be that some kind of folk learning process plays at least as important a role in shaping a child's understanding of the tradition as any formal 'catechizing' in the faith. Generally speaking, boys and girls were better able to give account, however limited, of the central liturgical acts (e.g. initiation, weekly services) of their own tradition than they were of those of other traditions. But much of the language of these descriptions and of their characterization of different denominational identities reflected less the influence of direct teaching, than that of diffuse, popular association.

In the case of pupils coming from a predominantly Christian background, self-knowledge and mutual caricature took fairly familiar lines: 'Church of England is better because you don't have to go to church so much and it's not so strict a religion as, say, Roman Catholic' (CE 15 b).[1] 'I don't believe in God, nor ever will. I was born Church of England (C. of E). I always thought that meant you didn't believe in God' (U 13 g). Of Catholicism: 'Guy Fawkes was one. Christians are good, Catholics are bad because they fight' (CE 6 b); 'they're the same as Christians, only a bit more flashy' (NC 12 g). Where non-Catholics spoke of an exaggerated status for Mary on the part of Catholics ('more important than Jesus') individual Catholic pupils had matching misapprehensions of other Christians: 'Protestants say the Queen is head of the church, not God' (C 13 b).

Such expressions of popular thinking occurred similarly when other religious identities were involved. Thus Jewish people were often known only in their historical role in relation to biblical times, and the object of abuse: 'you can't be a Catholic and a Jew at the same time, because a Catholic gives things' (U 12 g). Some Jewish pupils' defences against such thinking were well developed, for instance: 'Roses are red, violets are blue; if it wasn't for Jesus, we'd all be Jews' (J 11 b). Only exceptionally did the knowledge of pupils from a Christian background extend to any details of Muslim, Sikh or Hindu identities, but Muslim pupils were ready to say of Christians: 'They believe that God has sons and daughters, He's got a family. But God is really alone and one' (M 13 g). Likewise, several Sikh pupils were convinced of Muslim hostility towards them.

It is possible that some of these views may in certain circumstances have been prompted by the formal teachings of the parent religious community. Certainly, the degree of exclusiveness in attitudes to the truth claims of other religious traditions seemed to correlate with that of their parent faith (Gates 1975). It is just as likely however that they have been absorbed in the home and from casual conversations, for parents emerge as predictably powerful in their influence on both the content of their children's beliefs (theistic and atheistic) and their attitudes towards religion. Anyway, judgements such as these apparently abound and are taken for granted in the thinking of many pupils in our schools.

**3. Thinking across the curriculum**. Children bring with them to school a sense of contingency and a social inheritance; in both respects, religion is involved. As a result, therefore, religion is in the core curriculum of their seeking to understand the world and their own being in it. If comprehension in this sphere is assessed in relation to the developed canons of theological reasoning, then, as evidenced by previous research (cf. Chapter 9), severe limitations extend into the secondary years of schooling and beyond. However, when the handling of religious concepts is examined in the wider context of a pupil's thinking, it is clear that the same limitations occur in such other spheres as scientific, social and political comprehension. In so far as the same logical processes are involved in the comprehension of religion as in comprehending these other spheres, this is hardly surprising. Yet even though limited thinking in one sphere may have repercussions in others, the compartmentalized structure of the school curriculum, especially during secondary years, can easily conceal any shared framework of development.

Intellectual development during the 6–15 year group interviewed followed the familiar Piagetian stages. Summary portraits of boys or girls at each of the three main stages are now given to illustrate the *formal* continuity of thinking across the curriculum:

**Restricted/Pre-operational**. Seven-year-old Art's scientific explanations are conceptually limited. Thus thunder and lightning are 'clouds bumping together' and 'lots of lights being turned on'. His reaction to the dropping of an atom bomb would be to take to the bushes, or flee in a plane where he could even sleep. Space rockets, he thinks, can go further than the moon, perhaps to 'Mars-Bar planet', where there would be 'horrible creatures'. God used to live 'on heaven', but he is dead now, Art's brother has told him so.

Political concepts are of a similar order. An MP is 'a person who writes things – large letters – to people'. Art's reasoning on a role-ranking exercise is inconsequential: initially 'the teacher' is more important than 'the vicar', because 'she tells people off and smacks them', then the vicar has the pre-eminence because 'he prays to God and tells stories about God'. 'Father' is bottom of the list because 'sometimes he smacks people and sometimes he doesn't'. None of the social or political groupings Art is asked about can he recognize with the exception of the Scouts 'where you go for walks and do games'. He knows how you join a church: his friend has told him 'you have to go to Catholic school'. The word 'Catholic' he knows, but not 'Christian' or that of any other denomination or religion.

His other religious concepts are also restricted in formulation. Having been to church once (for his sister's marriage), he knows that there is a table there 'so the vicar can sit down and put his book on it'. More important, from time to time Art prays to God 'so I can stay alive', just as christenings are 'to make you stay alive' 'by putting the baby in a bowl of water'. However, God would not listen to Art's prayers, unless he had his hands together and his eyes closed.

Art's thinking then depends on specific items of information which he pieces together, sometimes with the aid of fantasy.

**Circumstantial/Concrete operational**. Thirteen-year-old Ann also says of thunder and lightning that it is 'clouds banging together – they just get in one another's way'. Space exploration would get no further than the moon, and no life would be found on any of the planets, because it would be either too hot or too cold. Though she cannot explain it, at death souls go to heaven; this is so far away that no one can get there, except for the fact that 'God has a special way of doing it'. An atom bomb would blow everything up, and there would be no escape unless you were '100 miles away'.

Faced with such a prospect, she would seek to cram all her life into a day by going to Buckingham Palace, 'just to look round'. This deference for the trappings of monarchy does not prevent her from defining the role of an MP as 'judging how the land should be run, how much things should cost', but she is unable to say much more about either him or the political parties, other than that they believe in different ways the country should be run, 'whether prices should go up or down'. Her 'homeland' is 'London' and she does not know what the United Nations is.

As a church-goer, she knows there is a table in church with a cross on it which 'stands for God, because Jesus was nailed to it', just as bread and wine relate to the Last Supper. In picturing God with a long cloak, she admits the influence of pictures of Jesus – 'they're supposed to be the same people'. Asked about different religious identities, she is unable to say more than that they believe differently, for instance 'Jews believe in Jesus', 'Muslims in idols'. You cannot change your beliefs from the way you have been brought up 'unless you're a king or something'; 'you've got the right then to rule over the church'.

Ann's thinking, irrespective of the extent of her factual ignorance, is largely circumscribed by continual reference to concrete manifestations.

**Elaborated/Formal operational**. Fourteen-year-old Stan was consistently able to elaborate his explanations. For thunder and lightning he referred to the weather breaking up the insulating effects between the positively charged ionosphere and the negatively charged earth, but admitted several different accounts by scientists and meteorologists. Lead and concrete shelters might serve as a way of surviving an atom bomb, but more important was the possibility of diplomatic initiative to avert the crisis. Progress in space exploration depends on possible advances in technology, but in any case there is a good statistical chance of there being other life systems in this and other universes.

Politically Stan reasons that the state would collapse without MPs to organize things; in the state's priorities, therefore, an MP would rank as top role, with 'policeman' second; for himself; however, he would put 'father' first. He is quite familiar with the constitution of different social and political groupings; for instance, he specifies that a socialist is similar to a communist, except that he wants to maintain the principles of a basic democracy without major revolution.

Stan has a rough idea of different religious identities and explains their existence by reference to separate geographical growth. In his judgement, 'religion is ignorance' and he disbelieves in heaven as a state of 'garden perfection' – 'if man were put there, he'd decay into a vegetable state'. Nevertheless, he appreciates that an altar may serve as 'a ceremonial centre on which the worshipper's attention may be focused', he describes participation in the Eucharist as 'dwelling with God', and insists that prayer can take place, if God were God, irrespective of physical posture. Neither Father Christmas nor God exist, but the former symbolizes your father, or the spirit of Christmas, the latter 'perfection'.

His thinking, again irrespective of factual knowledge, moves easily beyond the material limits of any given situation.

These portraits are but preliminary sketches of the way a child's thinking appears to be generally consistent in its formal pattern. They in no wise preclude the possibility of different kinds of awareness existing alongside intellectual understanding. But they provide a clear indication of conceptual continuities within the same thinking subject. As it turned out, throughout the sample there was a shift with age from the first to the last stage of thinking across the 20 items, religious and secular, which were assessed in Piagetian terms. Without wanting to be too tied by 'age norms', the middle years for almost all pupils were definitely the 'concrete' ones.

**4. Believers all**. The most important point to emerge from the interviews relates to consistency of a different order. Each of the pupils, including even the youngest, was revealed as engaged in constructing and checking his or her own individual loyalties and beliefs. Whether pertaining to 'superstitious' behaviour of the kind already mentioned, to Father Christmas, or to personal aspirations; whether to more explicitly religious allegiances – life after death, the efficacy of petitionary prayer, God – beliefs mattered to them and were being formed into a distinctly personal equation.

This was evident for every boy or girl interviewed. What follows of twelve-year-old Judith and thirteen-year-old Arnold are typical illustrations of how this is so.

*Judith*. Judith goes regularly to the synagogue with her family; she has heard of G-d since she was very small, so much so that she knows him 'by instinct'. Although she pictures G-d as 'fatherly, helping and loving', she says that he is more 'a sort of spirit' than 'a person': 'G-d is everywhere. He is sort of like a gas that develops everywhere.' Her trust in G-d is such that if she heard that the world was about to end, she would 'carry on as normal', believing that it would be because G-d had judged it should happen. She would still pray, however, as in an emergency when others were in great danger; G-d's plan for everyone, written at the start of each new year, might yet be changed, since G-d responds to care. Beyond death though, she has a real hope of a Messianic age, centred on Jerusalem, when all men are united under G-d, but she declined to prophesy when or how soon this is likely to happen.

At the outset, in the written interview, she specified that 'G-d and the super-natural' puzzled her most in life. This is confirmed by the way she is quite sceptical of 'calming' talk of heaven: it cannot really be called a place, 'it's mythological'. Indeed, if she starts trying to imagine beyond death, she senses there is risk of getting wrong ideas, even losing her faith. Superstition, like horoscopes, crossing fingers or talk of Father Christmas, she finds just 'funny'. In fact, touching wood is like saying 'please G-d, don't let this happen to me'. Such superstition she thinks will probably flourish 'among people from broken homes' – 'you wouldn't have much to hang on to' – but 'really you should have faith in G-d'.

To Judith the Jewish belief is the true and right one, and she thinks all other religions have stemmed from it. Nevertheless, she is reluctant to say it is actually better than the others: 'they are all true in the mind of the people who believe'. Thus earlier she had approved of what she took to be 'the moral' of the story of the Blind Men and the Elephant. G-d rules the world with kindness and not hatred and this means people 'get what they deserve'. Similarly, she seeks to love everybody – 'even when sometimes I think they're hateful' – 'because you're living together and you have to get on together, you should love your neighbour'.

*Arnold*. Arnold last went to church when he was in junior school. He thinks of church-going as for christenings and marriages, but also as sanctuary from capture. At Christmas he thinks that bread and wine is put out at the front; he is sure it stands for something, but does not know what. Holy water is important at christenings; it is taken from 'a lake or river' where Jesus is supposed to have had a bath, and therefore 'since Jesus has bathed in it, you can be part of him'.

Arnold appears to reject belief in God and any associated life after death. It is 'just a tale' that God is in heaven: 'I believe when Jesus came, when he died, someone just took him out of that cave where they carried him, and just had it as a tale.' He can picture God in human form as Jesus, crowned as 'every-one's father'; God was alive once, but he cannot see he could remain so today.

Interestingly, he had cited the whereabouts of heaven – 'if there is one' – as the thing which he found most puzzling in life.

Yet some reverence remains for both the church and God. The vicar 'teaching the word of God' he ranks as third above policeman, teacher and MP. He might himself, in desperation at the loss of his pet fish, pray to God, though he knows this would be futile since he has seen his grandma (with whom he regularly stayed) praying for his grandad to live, although he had 'had to go'. Thus he might pray to God for a miracle, while not believing in him, just as he used to carry a little stone in his pocket for luck, or to cross his fingers to stop it raining when he was playing soccer. He certainly still wishes to call himself a Christian.

Of all the different religions, he knows that Christianity is right, because it says about God and Jesus in the Bible, but not about the 'idols or statues' worshipped by the 'Hindus and Arabs'; and Jews are people who sell you toys that break. Yet he is not too dogmatic: 'others might be right if they believe in it, but I don't think they are. I might think something that they don't think, like I don't believe in God and other Christians might.' While thinking you should 'love everybody' 'because we're all one family', he is selective in both his class and on his street; he hits back at bullies. In the same way, while pointing to the applicability of the Blind Men and the Elephant story to the Northern Ireland situation, in the written interview he went on to list as the most important thing he would like to do during his life (as well as going to the moon and becoming a millionaire) as 'drop a bomb on Southern Ireland' – the army he told me later was being too soft with the IRA.

It is precisely to such centres of belief and value as Arnold's and Judith's that schools must relate if they are to help boys and girls to weigh and deepen their personal loyalties. The apparent universality, among the pupils, of positive or negative beliefs about God is a challenge to the teacher, not to dictate which belief is correct, but to help children understand more of what is involved in believing as they do, and to go on to appreciate more of the subtleties of the different ways of believing in and rejecting God. Hand in hand with this is the process also of ordering priorities for living.

## Conclusion: the core of the subject

Such a process of moral and theological refinement is one means of assisting boys and girls to grow as persons. It would provide, first of all, opportunity to work out a lasting personal response to any sense of contingency which they might have. Secondly, it would encourage them to think and feel their way through the references to religion which are their family inheritance. Instead of shuttering off religion from life, or vice versa, it would, thirdly, point up the relationship between one area of human understanding and another, so that, for instance, religion, science and politics repercuss. Finally, due priority would be given to coming to unblinkered terms with the multi-faith character and claims of our contemporary world. With this agenda, religious education would indeed be relating to the child's own core curriculum.

(1977)

# Chapter 12

# Children understanding death

It is difficult enough to speak of an adult's understanding of death and what may lie beyond, but it is even more difficult to speak of a child's understanding. For both, many different levels are involved.

As adults we are conscious that people die and that one day this must happen to us. For much of the time, we probably live in expectation of at least the biblical 'three score years and ten', but at the same time we know there are threats to this which prompt the purchase of life insurance policies. In some respects these threats are so certain that they can even be mapped in an atlas of mortality (Howe et al. 1963).

In addition to any consciousness of biological and social facts about death, there is also a less conscious awareness of what is happening. Deep down we know we are dying – eventually. This fact flickers in and out of our consciousness, brought to light perhaps by the death of a close friend, a motorway pile-up, or some incident in a television play. Psychologists make much of the presence of death in our unconscious lives and of its effect on our behaviour. It may well explain why we find 'sick' jokes funny, and perhaps why doctors reputedly have the bawdiest sense of humour.

As adults also we know very well that people hold different views about death and the prospect of some beyond it. It is less than a century since cremation was made lawful in England. Few of the then strident Christian theological objections to it are still heard, but there is no doubt that many remain suspicious of it, not least among Catholics and Muslims. We are aware of these beliefs, as of the elaborate funerary routines reported from America, or the occasional oddity of a casket being buried under the goalmouth at the home team's football ground. Equally, we know that some believe that rotting is the end of life, or that there is new life in heaven, hell, or as a result of being born again into this or another world. We also know what our own personal beliefs are in this regard; maybe clear, maybe muddled, but certainly our own personal equation.

Children's understandings are no less complex (Anthony 1971). They too are aware of the fact of death, more often than not from before going to school. It is very difficult for them not to have met the death of a grandparent, neighbour, television acquaintance or pet animal. Younger children may even show great interest in the mechanics of dying – staggering to a collapse, eyes popping and so on. Yet even without direct contact with funerals or cemeteries, there may be with them too an unconscious sense of dying, or at least potential loss of being.

This is the thrust of an experience described by James Britton:

> Alison, at the age of six and a half, took to watching her father go down the road in the mornings until he was right out of sight. One morning, after doing this faithfully for a couple of weeks, she left the window and went into the kitchen and explained to her mother, 'You see, I hate seeing things going away – even the bathwater.' Well, certainly the bathwater does go away, and some infants sometimes are distressed that it does. But Alison at six was dredging a long way back in her experience to bring this to light. Perhaps from infancy it had stood for 'things that go away and don't come back'. Like most young children she had not been easily comforted when lost or broken things were replaced by others even when they were so like the originals that she could not have told the difference. No doubt children have to learn from experience what are the possibilities, the limits of experience (and even, in due course, the probabilities, the odds for and against); they have to learn from experience what things go away and come back and what things go away and don't come back. There is no doubt that at the level of conscious expectations Alison knew her father would come back. But the uncertainty of her infancy, still alive, must have found expression in this situation – hence the need for a long, last look every morning. What her comment that morning attempted, then, may have been a deep-seated adjustment, the laying of a doubt about the world, rather than the interpretation of a daily occurrence. At all events, the morning ritual was no longer necessary and was soon given up and forgotten. (Britton 1972: 73–4)

Adah Maurer (1966) makes similar claims for the significance of young children's play where they deliberately delight in throwing toys down, or hiding themselves away, provided all can very soon be made to reappear. From our observations of children's play and singing rhymes we may well recognize some apprehension of the precariousness of life coming through. A developing consciousness of death is therefore likely to be part of the experience a child brings to school. This is illustrated by the following extract from a conversation with six-year-old Cheryl. Her words and ones recorded from others which follow are extracts from conversations with children during interviews conducted by the author with boys and girls from different religious backgrounds in English schools, as described in Chapter 11 .

> *Girls are not allowed to go to funerals, they are really not allowed, because otherwise they could cry and they could think how sad it is and they can spoil themselves and it is too dangerous.*
> Why is it too dangerous?
> *Well, just in case you think of it and you think it is really you are dead, yourself.*

Does everybody die?

*No, not everybody, only if you don't eat, if you don't feel well or your heart stops beating for a few minutes, you die.*

When do people die?

*When they don't eat anything for a few days, say fifty days.*

Just old people?

*Well, if you have something to eat everyday, say breakfast, say three times a day you won't die.*

Ever?

*Well, if you never have one; you don't die for one day without food.*

You will never die?

*No, until you stop for a few days.*

Do children ever die?

*Well, no, no, because their mothers always give them something to eat.*

Do they ever get knocked down by a car?

*Ah, now, if they don't look for their safety, they don't look right and left and listen, they can go with a car coming. They can die, really, because a wheel can go over them and they just fall.*

And what happens then?

*Well, an ambulance comes, that is the time for an ambulance comes, do do, do, do, to bib everything out of the way.*

And what happens when you die?

*Well you have to get buried, because when you put your head under the blankets you suffocate and you stop breathing, so they put you in a suffocating thing so they know you are dead now, they put them suffocating.*

Does everybody suffocate and die?

*Well, only if they think they are allowed to go under the blankets, right under and stay under overnight then they can suffocate.*

Do all old people die?

*Well not in fact all of them, if they still have something to eat.*

Then they are all right?

*Yes.*

So, how old can you be?

*Well, you can go up to, well, thirty or forty or fifty but not up to hundred, that's not allowed, no one can go up to hundred.*

Can they not? So they have to die before they are hundred?

*Yes, or ninety-nine. Nothing after that.* But does everybody have to die?

*Well, when they get old nearly to a hundred they have to die.*

Do they?

*Yes, because they get old and soggy and all horrible and they get throats and heart attacks and they die, but sometimes when you have operations you die, because it can be that your heart has no beat in it.*

Is that the end of them?

*Yes, they are finished then.*

And they don't come back to life again?

*No, they never, or it is never true that they can come back to life when they are really dead, it is never true. They just can't stop their heart, their heart is just as still as nothing.*

In places it is almost as though she can be seen working her way through to and perhaps articulating for the first time, the full facts of death.

Children of this age are not only factually aware, they are forging their beliefs on the question of any beyond to death. Cheryl, for whatever reasons, expressly rejects this prospect. Anne, another six year old in the same class affirms without hesitation that:

When you are buried, the air in you comes out and it goes up to heaven ... you go up by steps.

She knows this because her dad has told her, but apparently neither of them is sure why there are steps. If statements of belief are available for younger children, then so too are they for their older brothers and sisters, as we shall see.

Differences of belief abound, even between children from similar religious backgrounds. In quoting other individual conversations there is therefore no intent to suggest that any of them is totally typical or representative of the tradition from which they come, though some hallmarks of the parent faith are usually there. As well as diversity in expressions of the content of belief, there are wide variations in the strength of belief, almost irrespective of their formal religious label.

**Table 12.1** Percentage variations in strength of belief in a beyond to death among a sample of 340 children (aged 6–15 years) from different religious backgrounds in English schools

| RELIGIOUS ALLEGIANCE | PRO | | CON | |
|---|---|---|---|---|
| | **Strong** | **Reservations** | **Reservations** | **Rejecting** |
| Anglican | 68.5 | 12 | 13.5 | 6 |
| Unattached | 48.5 | 15.5 | 11.5 | 24.5 |
| Free Church | 76.5 | 13 | 8 | 2.5 |
| Roman Catholic | 85 | 15 | – | – |
| Jewish | 56 | 22 | 12 | 10 |
| Sikh | 61.5 | 10.5 | 7.5 | 20.5 |
| Muslim | 78.5 | – | 14.5 | 7 |

The parent religious community has its orthodox teachings and highly sophisticated interpretations, but children, like adults, may express their own beliefs in a slightly different way from what might be expected given their backgrounds. Children from Christian backgrounds, Protestant, Catholic and disaffected, generally think of a beyond to death in the forms of heaven and hell, but with wide variations in how these are conceptualized and with no shortage of additional or alternative references to spirits, ghosts, and reincarnation. The following extract from nine-year-old Alan is especially vivid:

> Heaven is just happiness, having to know that you haven't got anything dragging around you. There's nothing to stop you from doing anything, you haven't got any laws ... I think it's a normal family, but we have a ruler; he just doesn't stop you from doing anything. He's called Jesus; he's very just. You die, and it's like being put in prison for a while, while people are judging what you've done, to see what charges they can give you ... [Jesus] looks back. You might say his memory is like a drawer of files. You might say he looks at what you've done ... and whether you're going this road, that road, and whether you're going to stay here longer and whether you are going to go up the good road ... The idea of going to heaven is that you can see everyone, and you can talk with them, and you can talk as long as you like and there's no need to bother about telephone bills, because it's just natural. No one is working up there; it's just working by nothing. If you turn on the television, you don't have to say the fuse is gone, because the fuse will always be there.

Jewish boys and girls frequently refer to heaven and the soul, but more exceptionally also to mediums and reincarnation. Twelve-year-old Susanah speaks of the Messianic Israel:

> All the Jewish people will go to Israel and the people who are dead will come alive. We don't know if they'll come in their actual bodies or just their souls ... The world after we die is like a paradise, a Garden of Eden really. When the Messiah comes there won't be any more dying. They will all go to Israel, all the Jewish people, and the Christians and all the Roman Catholics will all go mainly to Jerusalem. And there is a legend that says that Israel will hold everyone that comes there.

Fourteen-year-old Jacob translates this as leisure:

> When you look at dying I consider it is the best thing that could happen to a man, because when you look at life, a person is born, he goes through his life with all the pressures of his life and then he comes to the end of his life as a man and I tend to associate this with relaxation, eternal relaxation. I believe the spirit goes and is in heaven and is in paradise. Sometimes I associate heaven with being in the upmost limits of space. Sometimes I associate it with being in the mind. Sometimes to me it is memory of dead

people, people that I can remember, not the fact that they lived but the fact that their memory lives, but I am not sure at all. I have been trying to find out myself.

Muslim boys and girls readily seem to stress the coming Day of Judgement as in the following extract from 11-year-old Belgin:

*On the Resurrection Day God calls all the people together and he tells you, or rather asks you how much wrong and how much right you have done, have you done more right than wrong. You have to answer and if you have done more bad than right then you go to hell and if you have done more right than bad you go to heaven, you stay in heaven.*
So everybody goes to heaven first?
*No, they go on to a very big kind of field, which is up there and on the Day of Resurrection he calls you. God gathers you over there and he tells you because, you see, you have got two angels on your shoulders and on the left is the one who writes the bad things you have done and on the right he writes the good things you have done. You can't see them, you can't feel them because they are invisible but they write all the good and bad and then on the Day of Resurrection they take, they go up there and they show God and God sees it.*

According to a slightly older boy from the same tradition, the difficulty of passing judgement is made easier by the aid of a video-recorder with playback facilities. Some fear for the fate of non-Muslims or stress the end of inequality in God's new day; even physical beauty or ugliness will cease to matter.

Children from Sikh families also speak of heaven and hell,' but more substantially, like Hindu children, of reincarnation:

*In the Punjab, some scatter their ashes. I don't know why they light the body of people but they light it and throw the ashes all over, over river, you know.*
Why do they throw the ashes over the river?
*It might be he will be born again to somebody and they might recognize him.*
Might be born again to somebody?
*Yes.*
What do you mean?
*He might have another life, as somebody else.*
Do you think that does happen to people, that they are born again?
*Yes, I have heard from my grandmother in India, once they had scattered the ashes and they had seen the same girl, she was going to be my aunt, you see, the same girl was seen by my grandmother in the temple, she was just going to say and she fell into tears, at seeing her.*
So what happens when they die? Is that the end of them or not?
*To some it is the end, to some it is not.*
Why to some end and not others?
*Some don't do anything before they die, and some do, like me. You see, I have killed*

*many things, and I have sworn on somebody, things like that. When I die, When you*
*lie from what I have heard from my grandmother, when we die we go to heaven.*
*God, if you have done anything, he pokes some metal things in your eyes, you see. Yes,*
*if you drop salt on the ground, you see, and you don't pick it up when you die. When*
*you die you go to pick it with your eyes, I have heard that from my grandmother.*
*She told me that he picks out your eyes and, you know, like eyes coming out and still*
*with your face, you see, and the eyes picking up the salt ... Instead of poking the metal*
*thing in your eyes. You pick, you hurt yourself for what you have done.*
What is this about not all people being born again?
*Oh, yes, some do sins you see. Then he doesn't get born again. He is just left, and I*
*don't know actually but, you know, God puts him in another life where there are wild*
*creatures, so that he can be, you know, eaten again. If an animal is killed there, the*
*animal when he dies, he will go up there and if he has done a thing he comes down at*
*the same place and is eaten. If I do a bad thing, if I am born again,' you see, I will*
*be born into another creature, like an ant, I have killed many ants, you see, and that*
*ant will kill me, you see, the ant that I have killed, will kill me when I'm an ant. Yes,*
*he will, he will have done the work, he will have taken revenge.*

The interspersing with elements of folk belief evident from this 14-year-old Sikh boy are equally forthcoming from every other background. As already hinted, such overt references to reincarnation are not confined to children from an Indian religious background. Memories of former lives and sense of déjà vu are frequently cited by children of Anglo-Saxon stock, and occasionally belief in reincarnation is the personal credo of a boy or girl who claims to be actively Christian as in the case of this 14-year-old Anglican church-goer:

*Soon after you are born again as some other being or animal or anything else – any*
*living thing. You don't 'go' for ever. After all, we are here; we must have come from*
*somewhere else. Why suddenly end a life, and not come again? This seems impossible;*
*when you die, you must be born again. That's what I believe ... I believe that we were*
*something else before we are now, and I think we continue to be like that for evermore*
*... It could be as differing things, different living things, anything, as a butterfly, you*
*wouldn't know. Like as I continue to be as I am now, the butterfly would continue its*
*life. It wouldn't know anything beforehand or afterhand, like I don't know anything*
*before or after.*

Lastly there are those who reject any possibility of a beyond to death, sometimes in the name of science, which (in spite of science fiction) is claimed to render such belief incredible, or in simple stoic resignation, as this 15-year-boy with no formal religious affiliation:

*We never really discuss death in our family. I've been very ill once or twice, so's my*
*mother, so it's something we don't like mentioning, and you daren't mention death*
*near any of my aunts, because they've had such a lot of tragic deaths. My great-uncle*

*died one Christmas Day as he was preparing the Christmas dinner, so they don't bother with Christmas dinners any more, and my grandmother on my mother's side died after a very long illness when my mother was about 11 years old.*

What do you think happens when people die?

*I think myself that once you've died you're finished with, people soon forget about you no matter how popular or otherwise you've been during your lifetime. Once you've died you're forgotten very very quickly except if you're the kind of person who likes to remember these things. Some people really enjoy to remember other people's deaths, though I wouldn't, I'd try to forget about a thing like that as soon as it's possible.*

From an inquest on such conversations as these, several conclusions emerge. First, as anticipated, the pupils whom we meet in school bear with them conscious and unconscious understandings of death and beyond, and beliefs about dying and living again. These may be limited or highly elaborated, they may be devout or sceptical, but they are certainly real and deserve to be reckoned with.

Secondly, attention to death and what lies beyond is an educational priority area. It is important for boys and girls to have the opportunity to come to understand what beliefs people have in regard to death. They deserve better than the flat-footed or inert treatment given to death in so many projects on Tutankhamun's tomb, which revealed the glitter of gold, but not the fathoming of human life and death that lay behind it. Even the facts of death themselves merit more direct attention in school than they often receive. In their absence, ethical issues regarding, for instance, differential infant mortality rates between countries or facilities for minority burials will scarcely be noticed.

It would be naive to ignore the risks which face the teacher who more deliberately treats the theme of death in school. Precisely because children are aware of the threat of death, and because the concern runs as deep as it does, they can be upset, especially at times of personal loss. Yet to avoid direct references to the subject throughout the compulsory years of schooling would be to opt for an unreal world. In practice many of the references to death that occur may well be incidental, or provoked by some news report from near or far. But there will also be a place for carefully planned project work on death and any future life. In whatever form it is tackled, it will certainly require proper professional sensitivity on the part of the teacher, both to the individual pupils in the class and to the communal realms of conviction and doubt which he/she will be seeking to share with them.

Teacher and child alike have much to learn from looking at life in the face of death. Perhaps, adapting an old Catholic custom, the curriculum should be composed annually with thoughts of mortality! The agenda then in prospect, for both the schools and families concerned, might be full of life.

(1978)

# Chapter 13

# Picturing God: a personal view

If I were to ask everyone reading this to try to picture God, I wonder what images, if any, would emerge? Different people picture God in different ways. This is apparent from iconography the world over, as indeed from those who would smash all images as in principle blasphemous. The mode of picturing may be verbal rather than visual, or 'abstract' rather than anthropomorphic, or indeed vividly available as Bonhoeffer's 'nearest thou to hand'. I came to appreciate the riches of personal picturing most clearly some fifteen years ago, when working in a hospital in New York, and I remembered the point when planning my research on children's religious development many years later.

In that research I used a great variety of prompts to open up how individual children understood the world and religion's part in it: stories – a fairy story and a Buddhist parable, sentence completion tests, a role-ranking exercise, pictures of one kind or another, such as the following:

- a picture of thunder and lightning, an occasion where, at least in childhood fancy, physical cosmology and theological cosmology can impinge on each other;
- a picture of an atomic mushroom cloud, representing the physical end of the world, and lending itself to astronomical and eschatological types of speculation;
- a picture of space rockets, again, in terms of space exploration, raising questions of the relation of divine location to the physical universe;
- and lastly, a picture of Father Christmas, to be contrasted with God when children were asked to tell what the difference between them is.

I used all of these and other prompts in encouraging boys and girls to share with me their ideas of God, and death, and prayer.

These pupils between the ages of 6 and 15 years were also requested to attempt the task mentioned at the outset: try to picture God. This is a device that has been widely used, classically by Ernst Harms over thirty years ago: he gathered thousands of pictures of God from children all over America, and carefully examined what they convey of religious experience. More recently the device was employed by Anthony Hindley in Sheffield in the early 1960s; by the government-sponsored RE research project in Sweden in the early 1970s; and latterly by Peter Pitts, in America, as reported in a recent issue of *Learning for Living*. The interviews for my own research were conducted in 1971, but the analysis and interpretation took rather longer. Along with 340 hours of tape-recorded individual interview, 1,200 written questionnaires were completed, along with which were just over 1,100 pictures of God.

The sampling was designed to be generally representative of children in English schools. Initially, eight schools were involved, four in the North-West and four in the South-East, two primary and two secondary in each region. Religious distribution among this first 1,000 pupils was random, but there were roughly equal numbers of boys and girls at each age between 6 and 15 years. Subsequently, for individual interviews, 82 Anglicans, 81 unattached, and 38 Free Church were selected from this same larger grouping. For Roman Catholic, Jewish, Sikh and Muslim pupils, another eight schools were involved; these pupils completed both a written questionnaire and an oral interview.

The pictures which the boys and girls produced were classified according to Harms' and other categorizations. Variations were examined according to age, sex, religious belonging and school, and predictably there were contrasts between the more anthropomorphic imaginings of Jesus the Christ, or God as Father, and the more abstract representations, some personal, some impersonal (Figure 13.1). Again, there was obvious contrast between religious groups, for instance, from Jewish children there were pictures of Mount Sinai, or from Sikh children pictures of Guru Nanak and even of God and his wife (Figure 13.2).

The preposterous nature of the request and the hurried context of the responses should itself serve as a warning against taking the results too seriously, a point well made by 'joke' pictures, such as the following. In the first, a ten-year-old boy gives his version of the biblical theme of Jesus as the Good Shepherd; three weeks earlier, Bishop David Shepherd had visited the school bearing his 'crook'. In the second, a 14 year old adapts the theme of man made in God's image. These joking pictures are quite salutary in that they do tell us not to expect to take the thing too seriously, but at the same time they may also be quite revealing of the conception and presuppositions held by individual pupils. The main point I would make about the 1,139 picture responses is that when I was able to check them with the verbal language and the theological imagery which came out spontaneously during the oral interviews, there was a remarkable consistency between what pupils pictured visually in their drawings and how they actually talked about God when prompted to do so. I will try to illustrate this by describing the images used by four of the pupils.

1. Six-year-old Rodney's picture is of God in the clouds. Rodney does not go to church or Sunday School, and he says that nobody has ever told him about God. However, he refers to God in a matter of fact way as 'in the sky' and joined by people when they die. He has little to say about praying, although sometimes he prays before going to bed. He has been into a church when on his holiday in Wales and also at the christening of baby Caroline (not his sister). 'At the christening they put water all over you so that you will not die

**Figure 13.1**

Try to draw a picture of God:

G O D

Now the picture is finished, say why you have done it the way you have:
I have drawn it like this because mount Sini is the mountain of God and I have always in my bible seen God as a big cloud

Now the picture is finished, say why you have done it the way you have:
Nobody living has seen God and never will

S 6g

Try to draw a picture of God:

Try to draw a picture of God:

This is The God and his wife

Now the picture is finished, say why you have done it the way you have
I have drawn the picture I have because for the time I have gone to temples for about twelve years I have seen and learnt that this is my or our Sikhs God and I have often seen it in any temple and heard from parents and grandparents that this is our God.

**Figure 13.2**

for a long time.' He believes that God and Jesus love him, as his father and mother also do, and in turn he loves them. Whereas Father Christmas lives on the ground in Iceland, God lives in the air on a cloud. From there he can send rain, frost and snow. Rodney knows his picture is right because he has seen one like it at playschool. Anyway, it is clear that his representation of God surrounded by clouds matches the imagery of his words (Figure 13.3).

2. The second picture presents rather a different view; it comes from 15-year-old David, an Anglican, in joking vein. God is pictured in man's image, with a 22 carat gold halo and smoking a cigarette. Yet David goes to church weekly, and can give a full account of the outward signs of the Eucharist and baptism; he also talks of heaven being a spiritual place which is beyond touch. Referring to his picture, he said that he had not actually meant to put in the cigarette, but this 'joking' is actually indicative of his current state of belief. He holds no store by prayer. He has never prayed at home, and though supposed to at school, would rather not. Vicar is rated bottom of the list of roles which he was asked to rank in order of importance (MP, Doctor, Policeman, etc.). He was confirmed the previous year – his Mum's idea; he is not bothered whether they go to church or not, but he says he has no choice. Pressed about his picture, he affirmed the idea of 'man's own image', but adds that 'nobody has seen him and come back'. What he produces therefore is quite appropriate to his present way of thinking. He is inclined to take church language, to which he has been extensively exposed, at its face value, and to find it wanting (Figure 13.4).

3. The next picture is from a 15-year-old Catholic boy – Ivan. When presented with a newspaper picture showing boys in a North London comprehensive school kneeling at prayer over the difficulties Apollo 13 had got into, and asked what they are doing, he told me this: 'In a way the people are God themselves. You know, the idea of one Being with all power. I can't really conceive the idea, really my interpretation of God is the whole universe. If something controls something, it's got to control itself. You know. You control yourself, the universe controls itself. It may or may not have intelligence, the universe as a whole, everything, but we are all part of it, so we are all a part of God.' Thus it is that the boys in praying are in a way God themselves. This kind of statement is quite consistent with what Ivan has to say about Father Christmas: 'he stands for God in a way. He is supposed to love everybody too ... Father Christmas is a man ... he's part of this universe, even if he is only in the mind. Therefore he is part of God and, if you are part of something then you are that thing. God is everything, the whole creation.' Ivan is not sure whether there would be God if there were no universe, but he cannot understand there being a universe without God. This theology relates not only to his picture here, but also to his interpretation of the Eucharist: 'Everybody is part of Christ, whichever way you look at it. Some people may think that if you take something that's meant to represent the Almighty to you, you become part of it; you're already part

Now the picture is finished, say why you have done it the way you have:

becoues I think its wite

**Figure 13.3**

**Figure 13.4**

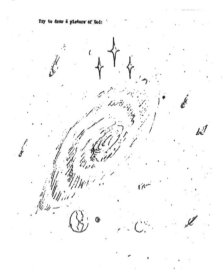

Now the picture is finished, say why you have done it the way you have

Because to define God is not really possible, but it may be possible to gain an interpretation by looking at his/her/its creations, and by this method gain some idea of the creator. In fact it may be that the whole creation, the Universe is God.

**Figure 13.5**

cos I like God.

**Figure 13.6**

of it. You might not realize it, and believe it, but it helps you to believe in something. Otherwise you might as well give up' (Figure 13.5).

This then is a third example of somebody who is matching their pictorial representation, produced when they have been asked without any warning to put something on paper, with what they subsequently tell me in a much more personal conversation about God. The individual consistency here and on the part of the others interviewed is striking.

4.  The last example is from six-year-old 'Delia', whose family are chapel-goers (Figure 13.6). In the oral interview, asked about Father Christmas and God, she says that Father Christmas is just a man dressed up; mums and dads just pretend that he is real. God is in heaven; Father Christmas is anywhere, going round the country. How does she know that God is real? 'Well, he's just sin; he is really a spirit, and he makes all the sins and the sins come, back to him when they have had enough.' Enough what? 'Enough inside somebody.' This exchange comes towards the end of the interview. Earlier in the space exploration sequence, she speaks of God in heaven with his sins. What does she mean? 'You know, inside you. When we die, our sins go to God.' How? 'They just go up or down by themselves.' What are they? 'Just nothing really, they're just thin air.' Quizzing her about her picture, she explains that this is God's bottle. It is not quite as she has drawn it, because 'God has his sins in the bottle as well.' How does she know? She just thought it: God may be something like this, perhaps 'lying straight up'. Why does God have a bottle? 'Because he thinks he's got more room in the bottle than anywhere else …' Her language is that of myth, and it rings true, even if in the perspective of others it is patently false; how is it to be interpreted?

These four examples, like all the others which might have been cited, of children picturing God, each deserves to be understood in its own terms. In this connection the term 'hermeneutics' is relevant. Theologians and philosophers, and by definition therefore individual RE teachers, are called to be expounders, translating and interpreting the faith inherited from of old in terms which make sense in the changed cultural situation of today. Otherwise, that faith would remain as frozen fruit, imprisoned in the deep freeze of yesterday's categories.

Moreover, I would like to suggest that the teacher's responsibilities be further extended, by insisting that interpretation has also to take place if children themselves are to be understood; children who are children, children who are adults, children who are students. That is to say, as teachers and as lecturers, we have to be doubly hermeneutical, in relation to the religious tradition, which we are purporting to represent to the students, and in relation to the students themselves. We have to interpret their experience, find out what is already there, understand their own categories in their own terms – in Delia's terms, in Ivan's terms.

There is one further point which I would like to make with regard to the pictorial research. It was evident that there was a very limited range of models of God available to the boys and girls in their picture making. Whether because their teaching in school was under the influence of certain forms of agreed syllabus, or because their Sunday School imaging was of a certain kind, it was very clear that of the 75 per cent who went in for anthropomorphized versions of picturing the vast majority of the pictures were 'historical-romantic' in form. Jesus was be-sandalled and cloaked; God was as father, seated and bearded. There was no sign of contemporary religious art, with one possible exception: a ten-year-old boy pictured God as he did because 'God is wherever you go', and so he has deliberately put God horizontally in the sky. Why this appears to be an example influenced by modern art is that on the wall of the corridor of the school there was a painting by Chagall imaged precisely in that way.

Now the apparent lack of examples of contemporary religious art made available to children may not be disastrous, if children are content and appropriately enlivened by the pictures to which they are otherwise exposed; but it is not clear that they are. For it emerged that children will scavenge very quickly from whatever pictures they are supplied with, however inappropriate they may subsequently seem to be. For instance, God was pictured as a masked angel seen in a film, or, rather more curiously, in the form of the Sheriff of Nottingham in a Robin Hood film. The 14-year-old girl who thinks in terms of this image does so 'not because of the way he behaves, but the way he looks'. If that seems curious, then even more so is the image of the female figure who is drawn with her extended arm holding a torch. Where has this been derived from? 'I've seen it at the front of films', that is presumably to say, thanks to Columbia Inc.

While I do not wish to be too disparaging about any of these images, I would want to suggest that insufficient use has been made of pictures and words of the imagination in RE and RS in schools and colleges in the past. It may well be that things are changing for the better.

It is crucial to Christian education, as also to RE and RS more generally, to develop 'a personal view' (others prefer 'acknowledged commitment' or 'informed prejudice'). It may well be that the forming of personal views does entail, on the teachers' part, a willingness to share our personal doubts and faith with our students. In other words, if I were to ask another person, a whole group for their own pictures of God, then it would have only have been fair for them to ask of me the same, and in school or college this would similarly apply. I should not ask for an intimacy on the part of the boys and girls with whom I conversed which I would not equally be willing to give myself – an element of personal disclosure.

However, I would not myself leave the formation of personal views simply to individual confessions of faith. Just as much, I would argue, the forming of personal views entails representing to students in college or school other pictures too, sometimes different from and even alien to the teacher's own. It means going into the Black Churches to experience Easter. It also means going to Mecca with Malcolm X of the Black Muslims, or entering a synagogue for Yom Kippur, or sensing the presence of death and suffering in the world through the enlightenment stories of Gautama. The gallery of pictures that are worthy of appreciation is even greater than that which can be personally confessed within any one classroom, and the onus is on the teacher to make available good-quality reproductions.

Reverting to our own personal views, I have little doubt that visual representation of individual faith can be very salutary, that is representations of our own faith to ourselves, as well as to the students or children we are working with. Marriage guidance counsellors tell me that couples who are being counselled are very often illuminated in their condition by having diagrammatic representations of their relationship, of how they act and react in relation to each other. Visual display of what their relationship looks like is apparently a real aid to mutual understanding. I have little doubt, similarly, that seeing my own picture of God there on paper, alongside others' pictures of God, is an aid to me in seeing my own faith, because I am thereby distanced from it and given at the same time a greater sense of perspective in relation to others.

The same point can be illustrated by reference to Milton Rokeach's *Three Christs of Ypsilanti*. This is the story of an encounter between three patients in a mental hospital, all of whom believe that they are Christ. It tells how they conduct themselves in relation to each other: confrontation with their rival images proved to be a salutary experience for them. Similarly in the field of more normal psychology, I am convinced that to see my own self-concept in relation to those of others, and in turn my picture of faith in relation to the pictures of others, can be a health-making process.

Where is all this leading? Perhaps in rounding off my personal view I may pick on two priorities, Christian priorities even, for Religious Studies. The first looks for a move towards the forging of an integral RE. It matters greatly that RE is done in a coherent way, yet still there is an attempt to carve it up into either Bible teaching or World Religions teaching, or alternatively into Life Theming or Moral Education. It seems to me that all these strands have an important part to play in the full religious education. Each of them in its own way stands for an important aspect of any particular religious tradition: the scriptures, the cumulative tradition and how they ramify in personal life and relate to other faiths. In the evolution of the subject, we are now in a position to move towards reaffirming an integral RE which no longer puts up the shutters, saying: 'I am for Farmington (Mark 1) and Moral Education'; 'I am for Shap and World Religions'; or 'I am back to the Bible with the Festival of Light'. In their different ways these and other points of view represent proper strands of RE that need to be brought into a creative relationship and tension with each other.

Secondly, as a Christian I also very much hope that in the midst of all this, the priority of working towards a Christian theology of religion, or religions, will not be missed. For the argument in favour of treating the faith of other folk seriously in English schools is not just based upon the presence of 'immigrant groups' in the country; nor is it based on some kind of nicely neutral urge to collect anything and everything in sight, with no regard for evaluation. To be sure, the presence of people of different faiths within the local community, and the plural reality of religion which is evident internationally are important incentives for developing a broader approach to RE than has been available in the past. But of no less significance is the Christian theological requirement (and its counterpart in other traditions) to make sense of the faith of other folk, because my faith says that God is aboriginally hand-shaken with the cosmos, with the whole of creation. From the beginning, humankind and God are intertwined, and thus God is not without witnesses beyond the walls of the church. Extramurally, God is there in the world to be met, to be found. This I know as a Christian, and because of it I can hardly go on to ignore the alternative claims to religious truth which come from other sources. For when a Muslim says to me 'The Qur'ān is the Word of God', or a Sikh says 'The Adi Granth is the Word of God, and I will prostrate myself before it as I move into the gurdwara', or perhaps a Hindu claims 'the *Bhagavadgītā* is God's Word', then they are all saying things that have clear implications for anything which I might wish to say about the Christian scriptures, or the Jewish Torah. Because of these facts, the theological obligation on me as Christian is clearly to take seriously the faith of others and to seek to make sense of the plural character of the facts of the religious life of the world. Indeed a Christian can rejoice and be glad in them.

Among many colleagues who have an interest in RE, there is sensitivity about confusing teaching with preaching. It may appear that I have strayed over-much into that stymatized style. Nevertheless, it is along these kinds of lines that I would like to be developing my personal view. Among other colleagues there may be a greater concern that acknowledgement of the importance of personal views will lead to relativism. That is far from the consequence which follows. For whether relating to the faith of other folk, or to more immediate pictures of God, I would willingly embrace the relativism which is made theologically necessary by its final deference only to God.

(1978)

# Chapter 14

# Children prospecting for commitment

It is not so many years since the Plowden report on primary education was published, yet many of its comments on RE seem more remotely dated. The report itself was considered by many to be progressive, but it insistently cautioned against any deviancy from Christian nurture in the infant and junior years of schooling:

> young children need a simple and positive introduction to religion. They should be taught to know and love God ... children should not be unnecessarily involved in religious controversy. They should not be confused by being taught to doubt before faith is established. (DES 1967: para 572, p. 207)

A minority disagreeing with this view argued rather differently that RE involves theology, which is 'too recondite and too controversial' for primary-age pupils, and therefore is better left until later secondary years. Neither of these views is consistent with the changes in RE that have taken place in the meantime. In connection with the first, the assumption of a practising Christian norm is increasingly perceived as inappropriate in a country which, while remaining Christian in heritage, is also secularizing and multi-faith. In regard to the second, religion is recognized as involving more than intellectual abstraction; religious behaviour, belief and belonging express themselves in many different forms.

While taking issue with any presumption about the need for Christian instruction in the content of RE in schools, we may still appreciate the Plowden emphasis on starting with the children themselves. What do we know about religion in childhood and adolescence? What are children and young people capable of understanding? Where, if at all, does commitment come into their experience? In attempting to answer these questions, this chapter offers a foundation for RE in children's experience and explorations of where their lives might lead.

## Religion in childhood and adolescence

Religion is never easily defined, and yet any judgement about the degree and depth of contact that boys and girls have with it will depend largely on what range of knowledge and experience is considered relevant. This is a problem facing social scientists and theologians generally: any working definition needs to be broad enough to reflect the variegated experience of humanity, yet sufficiently discrete to prevent blur and distortion.

One activity commonly associated with religion is that of regular attendance at a place of worship. In our own society it is clear that only a minority of boys and girls is involved in such attendance. The 1979 census of the churches conducted by a 'nationwide initiative in evangelism' registered a typical weekly attendance figure at church or Sunday school of 14 per cent of the available child population under 15 years (Nationwide Initiative in Evangelism 1980). This compares with over 30 per cent in 1950. Even allowing for some limitations in the sampling (74 per cent of English churches were drawn on, half directly, the others via their central offices), there is little reason to judge this a gross underestimate. Comparable figures for the children of Buddhist, Jewish, Muslim, Sikh and other faiths are not available, but though the parent communities might wish it were otherwise, the total number involved is unlikely to add much more than 1 per cent to the overall total.[1] Evidently, more than four-fifths of boys and girls in England are not regularly involved in attendance at a local place of worship.

It would be wrong, however, to assume that these figures represent the full extent of formal religious association. The practice of 'occasional conformity' still persists among adults, and their children, especially at Christmas and Easter. On a smaller scale a similar phenomenon may be observed on the part of the Jewish and other minority religious communities. The involvement of children with the familiar rites of passage still persists – baptisms and naming ceremonies, and weddings, if not funerals. The proportion of boys and girls who have such occasional contact with the local places of worship is significantly higher than 15 per cent, though actual figures are not available.[2]

What meaning such occasional associations with institutional religion have for the children concerned is difficult to ascertain. At worst there is little more than a superficial familiarity with the outward vestiges of an otherwise eccentric inheritance; at best, a sense of being part of a communal tradition which, along with family, region and nation provides another frame within which personal identity is forged. Self-ascription as Catholic, Church of England, Muslim, Rastafarian or whatever by a boy or girl may derive from either frequent or infrequent attendance, but in any case more often than not it will have been picked up from parents and grandparents.

An alternative or additional characteristic is that of explicit religious belief. Survey data regarding the adult population have consistently indicated a very high percentage of persons professing belief in God, a percentage which becomes higher with age (Argyle and Beit-Hallahmi 1975). Such evidence as is available pertaining to those under 18 years would suggest that among younger boys and girls belief in God is as commonplace as belief in Father Christmas, but that both are increasingly questioned during junior school years. Although the balance of belief and unbelief may in fact be shifting among young people (Francis 1981), and in any case there are regional variations (Alves 1968: ch. 3; Greer 1972), belief in God appears to persist for the majority, often accompanied by continued questioning. The content of beliefs may well be intellectually confused and reflect much ignorance, as illustrated by Loukes (1965: ch. 5) and more recently by the General Synod Board of Education's report *A Kind of Believing* (Duke and Whitton 1977).[3] However, on the basis of my own research I would claim that, generally speaking, boys and girls do all work towards a 'beliefs equation' of their own, one which is internally consistent and a key ingredient in their total attitude to life. Irrespective of the degree of belief or unbelief, it is also true that virtually all acquire some everyday connotations of the word God; that is to say, a concept of God, however simplistic, or even sophisticated, is part of their mental furniture. Intensity of religious belief varies, but exposure to it is constant.

Alongside all the explicit contact with religion in terms of belief and belonging, certain spontaneous musings on the part of the individual child may also count as relevant to his or her association with religion. Boys and girls from time to time experience certain feelings and are moved to ask particular questions, any of which may be potentially religious. A sense of wonder and awe provoked by some sound or sight of great beauty, feelings of trust and security, of gratitude or joy prompted by some act of kindness or playful merriment, or grief and sadness at some loss – these can all be the occasion for Wordsworthian sensations of mystery or presence, of greater purpose or meaning. Such experiences are now widely attested in adults[4] and it seems from children's talk, personal writing and playground lore that they abound also with them. Without presuming that the truth claims of religion are publicly proved by such stirrings, it is important to recognize that they are commonly human and religious.

The questioning referred to is typified by the young child's pressing 'Why?' It looks for relationships, causes, connections to explain anything and everything. In so pressing towards final explanations, the boy or girl is engaging in that realm of exploration and inquiry which is not satisfied with instant or interim solutions, but seeks as well for fully comprehensive cover, as ultimate as can be. Of course, such meaning may not be available, or may sometimes arise from confused thinking or mistakes in logic. Nevertheless, religion has itself been traditionally very much occupied with the question of whether there is rhyme or reason in life and death, whether there is any justice in the face of innocent suffering, and children with their questions move unwittingly into the territory of religion.

# Children's capacities for religious understanding

According to A. J. Ayer and his professional and headteacher colleagues in their minority statement on RE in the Plowden report, religion is too difficult an area for boys and girls to cope with, because it involves theology (DES 1967: Vol. 1, 489–92). This has been taken by some as the conclusion also to be drawn from Goldman's examination of the development of children's religious thinking between the ages of 6 and 15 (Goldman 1964). The responses he received to questions he had put to boys and girls regarding three episodes from the Bible and three pictures of children with reference to praying, bible reading and church-going, led him to talk of their general unreadiness for religion. Until the age of formal operational thinking in secondary schools when they become capable of hypothetical reasoning and abstract analysis, children are largely 'sub-religious'. Premature exposure to theological concepts will only encourage misconceptions and subsequent alienation. Goldman's research was extensively reported and had widespread impact on syllabus makers throughout the country; it has been widely replicated, most notably by Peatling in North America (Peatling 1977), and comparable claims have been advanced independently by others.[5] As a result, the inference may very easily be drawn that on psychological grounds RE provision should be deferred until 13-plus when a stage of more advanced intellectual sophistication will have been achieved.

It is one thing to admit that children's ability to handle religious concepts develops gradually and through a series of well-defined stages, as does their handling of for instance number, space and time. It is quite another to under-estimate how much boys and girls are able to understand about religion before they can think in an intellectually elaborated way. Much may still be refracted through to them via earlier modes of thinking – intuitive and fanciful, or concrete and circumstantial. The solution for the teacher will be to engage in more imaginative translations into terms that the children can cope with. This is preferable to waiting for a stage which may only arrive after school has been left behind. Given the extent of children's exposure to religion, whether in its institutional manifestations or their own wonderings, the raw material is already there.

Just as boys and girls, if read aright, provide their own resources for effective RE, so too there is much in religious tradition to which they can respond, in spite of their intellectual limitations. Theology, in the Plowden dissenting sense, is not ignored; it is instead expressed through a variety of media designed to convey its meaning at the appropriate level.

1. *Story* or *myth* is a basic medium for expressing religious meaning, but it also has a basic appeal to children of any age. The good story lends itself to understanding at different levels, and involves imagination and feeling as much as intellectual comprehension. It is well worth exploring as a form for work with all abilities. To this end, each teacher may wish to develop his

**Table 14.1**  Examples of stories

| Type of story | A. Implicit | B. Explicit | | |
|---|---|---|---|---|
| | | 1. Biblical | 2. Christian | 3. Other religions |
| Archetypical | Hansel & Gretel | The Flood | Grail quest | African creation stories |
| Myth/Fantasy | P. Pearce *Tom's Midnight Garden* M. Sendak *Where the Wild Things Are* | Jonah | C. S. Lewis *The Lion, the Witch and the Wardrobe* | *Ramayana* |
| Moral | Aesop's *Fables* | Naboth's Vineyard | Charles Dickens *A Christmas Carol* | Muhammad Iqbal *Guiding Crescent* |
| Exemplary | Ann Holm *I am David* | Temptations of Jesus | Saints and 'People with a Purpose' | Prophets, Gurus and Bodhisattvas |

or her list for storytelling, separated into different categories, as illustrated in Table 14.1.

2. *Ritual* or symbolic gesture is no less a basic medium for expressing religious meaning than story. It too may have a counterpart in the child's own heritage of ritual play – in the school playground, or with friends, or in connection with his or her support for a favoured team. Whether in the form of non-verbal communication ('body talk') or role-play and enacted story, ritual can reverberate with any age or ability of pupil. Again, each teacher may wish to develop an assortment of ritual acts which their pupils may be encouraged to try out, whether individually or in groups. In both cases their acts might include gestures of gratitude, affection, awe, quietness and pleading, and in groups they might also include those of trust, sadness, celebration, pledging and sharing. The power of simple action to promote a new awareness and to convey a special meaning is quickly felt. And again this is true of acts which are either implicitly or explicitly religious.

3. *Verbal and visual imagery.* Imagery in verbal or visual form is vital to religion. Taboos against making images warn us that they must be deliberately interchanged with other images or avoided altogether, to prevent any confusion between them and the reality they purport to represent. As an aid to understanding, children's picturing with words or paint is a welcome means of conveying ideas which might otherwise remain beyond anyone else's grasp.

In a culture in which the media constantly multiply the images to which a child is exposed, it is well worth the RE teacher's time to devise opportunities for sharing, exposing and inventing images that people live by – from Christmas cards to coffee adverts!

4. *Music and silence.* Music manages to be both earthy and sublime – its rhythm and beat are instantly communicable, so too is its mood; with both it can move beyond surface feeling. On occasions, it may lead to silence followed by newer appreciation. The RE teacher would do well to look to musical resources; whether as a result of listening to music or of making it, the children's responses may be surprising.

5. *Social organization and individual lifestyle.* The different shapes – ages, sizes, sexes, colours – of clubs or gangs, as of families, schools or whole nations, are quickly registered by children growing in the midst of them. The sense of belonging to one or more such grouping develops fairly early in life. There are parallel experiences here for exploring the sense of belonging that accompanies membership of a church or the *khalsa* and, perhaps, for asking about the value of membership to an individual. Social horizons can easily be restricted, but class or year/ability group labelling may itself prompt the pupil to a greater awareness of the networks of administrative and teaching arrangements that affect others. How people organize their own lives and those of their communities can be very real questions, made the more answerable by reference to the sense of social belonging and casual copying of others, already begun at home or in school.

With the aid of such vehicles as these many of the intelligibility problems that religion might be expected to present to children can be overcome.

## Autonomy – relative and committed

More and more, in practice as well as in theory, the tasks of the day school (unless it is denominational, in which case several additional considerations come into play) and of the parent religious community are acknowledged as different in respect of RE. The school has an 'appetizing' and preliminary role of endeavouring to introduce boys and girls to the wider religious experience of mankind. The end here is that they leave school religiate, though not necessarily religious. In a complementary way, outside the school, in the child's inherited or adopted community of faith, rather more, in explicitly religious terms, will be sought by and for each boy or girl.

The distinction between the educational role of the school and the community of faith is helpful in making the former's task more modest and manageable than it would otherwise be. It would be wrong, however, to polarize the two to the extent that sometimes happens when the term education is used exclusively for the school and nurture for the parent community. For what happens in both contexts may on occasion be both education and nurturing. School and parent community are at one in recognizing that a child's religious identity develops over a period of time. The parent community tends to look for a public statement of commitment, ritually expressed, during early adolescence, but the antecedents of this statement go back to birth and include family influence, formal teaching, and either through these or by other means, admit the possibility of divine initiative. The ritual may involve the laying on of hands, the wearing of a sacred vestment, the recitation of some extract from the scriptures, or some other definitive act, but even so the community responsible will scarcely identify this specific stage of the person's development with perfection, or deny that further transformation is expected. In other words, there is implicit in each religious tradition the hope that an individual's development does not finish, but continues beyond youth, even to death and possibly thereafter. Similarly, in the school context, this must be as readily admitted. CSE or GCE exams, possibly including RE, may be part of some secular rite of passage to be negotiated before adult society is entered. But any understanding of life and religion that has been achieved in school can be only at the threshold of what is to follow. Thus 'becoming religiate', like becoming numerate and literate, is a provisional condition that opens up a range of experience. Whether a girl or boy chooses to follow any of the ways further, given the help of rudimentary bearings, is beyond the school's educational brief. Nevertheless, in school the place of commitment in religion will have been clearly indicated.

On each front, the holding open of personal options is necessary on both educational and theological grounds. The school would beg too many questions if it were to favour one religious or atheistic position over all others. The parent community would be wilfully constricting (increasingly hard in a western society with its all-pervasive media) if it foreclosed on any expressions of doubt or alternative views. The autonomy to be striven for by all concerned in either context must therefore be related to the insights and affirmations of others, if it is to be other than narcissistic or blind in its dealing with commitment. There is always a danger that an individual, in working out his or her views, may become careless of every other position and closed to any claim on it from beyond.

Reference to 'commitment' being expected of the boy or girl deserves further comment, within the context of the school as well as the faith community. Since William James, it has been a commonplace among psychologists to refer to both *once-* and *twice-*born modes of personality development and religious conversion, the one gradual and long-term, the other sudden and immediately arrived at. By definition, education is more concerned with the first, though it may directly or indirectly contribute to the second. As a result of RE, some transformation in understanding of both self and the world at large should probably be expected; surface knowledge is less likely to disturb or challenge, whereas genuine appreciation and learning will give rise to deeper resonance and impact. Yet it is only when children become personally engaged – excited, frightened, charmed, provoked, challenged with a story, a festival, an intellectual ideal, a pictorial emblem of faith – that any depth of meaning can be perceived. In this sense therefore, RE calls for commitment from its participants, teacher and pupils alike, to enter into its distinctive vehicles of expression.

Commitment of this kind is not the same as making a particular confession of faith, although it ought to equip a boy or girl better to understand the implications of such. Rather, it is a willingness to try to enter into the spirit of human adventuring that has moved men and women, past and present, to respond to visions and challenges that would re-order their lives and the world around them. What moved the Pilgrim Fathers to leave the confining structures of the old world of Europe and strive to realize the new priorities of God's Kingdom in North America? Long marches, Zions – Semitic or Black, the land reform of Vinoba Bhave, the monastery that is Iona, Taizé, or Indian ashram, the believer's daily routine that is seen as shot through with divinity – these cry out to be followed and fathomed.

If this sounds too grand for a classroom, or too dangerous and difficult for children to attempt, we may need quickly to remind ourselves that comparable engagements are taking place anyway. They are found in the following and fervour given to a soccer club, the school team or the first division favourite, and when too much is expected of what after all is a simple game, it cannot bear the weight of life and death, and disorder surges out. Engagement is found in the admiration, quiet or noisy, given to the hero in some television saga, or to the latest pop star. Intellectual explanations by the boys or girls concerned of what it is they are attracted by, may be put into words only with difficulty or very briefly, but there is no doubt that they feel 'grabbed'. And, of course, the media trade and advertisers know this; they have done their market research and have developed well-tried techniques for guaranteeing take-up. They are able to devise how to trigger conscious and unconscious associations with loyalties and yearnings, hopes and fears, that are layered deep inside the adult, as well as the child. When we speak of becoming engaged in RE and developing skills for handling commitment, we too are dealing with the nerve centres of individual choice and decision which make us who and what we are.

It follows from this that there is a place in both school and parent community for putting commitments under scrutiny. If they are ignored and left to look after themselves, then any models for living or ranking of interests will be haphazard echoes and not the sources for creative selection which they might otherwise be. Only as a result of opportunity to try and test them can second-hand beliefs and rejections of belief be seen as shapeless and full of holes, or alternatively enhancing the person who decides to live with them.

## Conclusion

Any concession to child-centredness in the classroom provides an incentive to make more careful provision for RE in schools. For it is evident that religion is variously part of the 'life world' of children and young people. Any sensitivity to religious traditions provides a range of resources with which to delight and enrich our common humanity irrespective of age. Preferential teaching to establish Christian belief should indeed be avoided – not to encourage doubt, as Plowden feared, but to enable boys and girls to develop a strong sense of commitment with which they may illuminate their lives.

## Further reading

Violet Madge (1965) captures the quality of infant and junior interests and puzzlements and sets RE in this context; Harold Loukes (1961) represents the concerns of older pupils in a similar way. The limiting implications of Piagetian stages of intellectual development for a child's ability to handle theological concepts are set out in Goldman (1965a). Direct opposition to this view is expressed by Robinson (1977) in which he draws extensively on adult recollections of childhood experience. The sheer power of childhood imagination in Fynn's *Mr God, This Is Anna* (1974) is dynamite to any easy categorizations!

Most of the British literature has been written from within a framework of Christian belief, but in this respect the Duke and Whitton (1977) report sounds a caveat against assuming that an informed understanding of Christianity persists among young people; ignorance too is reported in Gates (1975). Increasingly, attention is being paid to children from other religious backgrounds. James 1974) *Sikh children in Britain* provides a close-up of one minority; Taylor (1976) in *'The Half Way' Generation* looks at new families more generally in north-east England.

The classroom implications of children's religious development in the face of diversity of belief in our society are treated positively in the Schools Council (1977b) *Primary RE: Discovering an Approach* and in Carol Mumford (1979) *Young Children and RE*. Playground encounters between boys and girls of different religious backgrounds provide the basis of a classroom text in Cleverley and Phillips (1975) *Northbourne Tales of Belief and Understanding* and Elizabeth Cook's (1969) *The Ordinary and the Fabulous* displays the treasure-trove of stories available for any teacher to dally with.

(1982)

# Chapter 15

# Development through Religious Education

Development, like music and motherhood, has got to be a good thing. Or at least that is a common assumption when the word is used. But what if development involves deterioration, regression even? What if development takes a form which so transforms the individual that they become a distortion of who they formerly were? Just as musical tastes differ, so do perceptions of what would be desirable, or less desirable, 'development'. It is even conceivable that one person's cacophony could be another's symphony. Motherhood too can be a mixed blessing. In the form of an unwanted pregnancy, it may be perceived as a curse. In the way it is experienced and managed, it can become destructive for both the mother and the child, and others can be destroyed in the process. Development may be highly desirable, but the criteria for making that judgement deserve some prior inspection if it is to be accepted with any professional confidence.

Three different sources of critical awareness regarding use of the term development warrant immediate recognition, the more so when religion is involved. These are ones from the human sciences, from humanists rejecting religion as stunting of human growth potential, and from men and women of religious faith concerned for the enrichment of common humanity. Teachers may be influenced by any or all of these sensitivities

The first source comes from the **human sciences** as applied to the context of education, as in 'child development', 'human development', 'social and psychological development'. Here, development carries evolutionary overtones which may arouse suspicion of biological determinism. That children's thought forms must go through a set sequence of stages to arrive at maturity might appear to challenge individuality. And yet, with growing boys and girls, just as there is a genetic unfolding of sequenced physical development, so there are certain continuities found throughout the world in respect of developing capacities for dependence and independence, for elaborated reasoning, for short-term and long-term aspiration, and for sense of boundaries both near and far. The forms such capacities take vary enormously, as their psychogenetic givenness is changed by human interaction and individual reflection, as also by exposure to religion. But that they do emerge as complementary expressions of our outward and inward being, as analysed socially and psychologically, remains constant. Proponents of the human sciences include a wider following than university academics. Intellectually, they all share the view that development is fundamental to human being and that it can be pursued in ways that are liberating of humanity, or quite the opposite.

The second source of critical reservation regarding the use of the word development comes from **humanists** who, on taking stock of the impact of religion in human civilization, conclude that it is divisive and stunting of human growth potential. They have seen that religious beliefs can be conflictual and contribute to war, seeming on occasion even to legitimate acts of gross barbarism. They have noted an apparent correlation between the secondary status of women and male predominance in the history of religions. They have remarked on the mixture of hypocrisy and guilt often associated with religion where sexual behaviour or personal wealth is concerned. In consequence, they fear that any promotional references to religion in relation to educational development could well be in contradiction of the development which they themselves would want. 'Humanists' in this sense may not formally use the word to describe themselves, but they are people anywhere who have read and pondered human behaviour and concluded that the role of religion is only ambiguously for the good of individuals in society. They want this wariness to be heeded

The third source of critical concern for how 'development' is best understood for education is that of **men and women of religious faith** who believe that exposure to religious tradition will contribute significantly to the enrichment of common humanity. They certainly believe this in respect of their own faith, if not also of selected others. They may be confident as individual Christians that, once experienced, the quality of life, which flows from association with God in Christ, will transform each person and relationships for the better. Likewise, as individual Muslims, they may know that the knowledge of God disclosed in the Qu'rān is creative of a sense of justice and peace for everyone. Or again as individual Buddhists, there will be clear vision that, once we are tuned in, this way enlightens the whole of life and death. Of course, these same individuals know that their respective traditions have been used on occasion to encourage human development in terms which can be characterized as exclusive, inhumane or even destructive. But by and large they would see those tendencies as going against the grain of the religious development intrinsic to the tradition at its mainstream best. Accordingly, whether as leading theologians or ordinary modest folk, they will find wanting any talk of development through education which is not open to such authentic religious insights.

Because of the process of general cultural osmosis prevalent in a society so extensively exposed to mass communications, it is very likely that RE specialist teachers in primary and secondary school, no less than specialists in other subjects, will be influenced by one or more of these kinds of critical perspective. Almost inescapably, we breathe each other's air. If not personally, then professionally, or vice versa, we will know that psychology and sociology can be used to explain religion. That may be to try to explain it away; it could equally be to acknowledge its vitality. Similarly, our general human bearings will have told us how religion can sometimes be contaminated with evil. And we will also know that religious faith has the potential to be transformative towards goodness.

Given all these different voices, what development shall we look for through RE?

## Taking the part of the other

There is a phenomenon remarked in the activity of young children, known as 'parallel play'. Two children play alongside each other, and appear to be playing together. In fact, there is little or no direct interaction between them. They are each locked into an internally coherent play world whose meaning subsists independently of anything that the other child is intending. Child A may feature in the play of child B, but entirely on the basis of meaning projected on to him and without reference to any aspect of the play in which he himself is engaged. Whether or not either child is in fact capable of more genuinely interactive play at that particular age and stage of their development matters less than that each child does come to be able to include both these forms of play in their personal repertoire (Durkin 1996: ch. 4).

There is a phenomenon known as the giving of presents. Again it is initially experienced during childhood years. It may begin with the delight of receiving such gifts, from a parent, relative, sibling or friend, but it commonly extends to pleasure also in giving gifts to others. There is often a clear pattern of reciprocation which can be interpreted as in different degrees self-serving. I enjoy receiving presents, and arguably one way of ensuring that the practice continues is to give presents to the very persons who might be expected to be givers. But there is also the experience of pleasure in giving genuinely to please the other person. This still betrays a self-satisfying element, but more in addition to that is involved.

There is a third phenomenon on which hospitals throughout the UK depend: giving blood. This gift relationship is unpaid, and though again there may be an element of self-insurance involved, it depends largely on the goodwill of a minority of men and women, who recognize the worth of being ready to share their blood with others (Titmuss 1970).

These three phenomena illustrate a developmental priority which makes good educational sense. The principle involved is that of reciprocity and it is as fundamental to human life and relationships as it is to religion. Without recip-rocal giving, the *sangha* would not survive, the sacrament of Holy Communion would make no sense, and life of dedicated professional giving would lose much of its purpose. Accordingly, it matters greatly for Religious Education that pupils are encouraged to understand the process of giving and receiving. If their under-standing is deepened in the context of learning about and from some religious story or festival, then that religious insight may prompt their appreciation of a fundamental principle for personal and social life, as well as their own enjoyment of giving. If they already know this in their own experience, they are well placed to recognize why acts of generosity are so central to religious response and tradition. Either way, they are capable of looking beyond themselves and taking the part of the other.

Such a capacity is at the root of altruistic behaviour. Though the cynic might dismiss all talk of altruism as self-serving, that is not how courageous intervention to save the drowning child or the victim of anti-Semitism feels to the rescuer or rescued. As socio-psychological research has demonstrated, an educational environment which deliberately promotes extensivity of recognition for others in their differentness will challenge any easy assumption that unquestioningly devalues what is different (Oliner and Oliner 1988: ch. 10).

Arguably, one feature which is absolutely fundamental to good RE is its promotion of empathy. Irrespective of their own individual viewpoints, it invites pupils at every Key Stage to imagine what it is like to be a Muslim, or belong to some other particular faith. This 'taking the part of the other' then feeds directly into personal and social development more generally.

It also relates to another key aspect of development.

## Extending horizons

It is remarked that primary school children, typically during Key Stage 1, may have some difficulty in conceptualizing the relationship between the village or town they live in, the country in which this is situated, and how they all relate to other towns, cities and countries. As with the phenomenon of parallel play, this was remarked by Piaget. In the aftermath of the Second World War, with encouragement from UNESCO, he was exercised about the understanding of belonging which local Swiss boys and girls were able to demonstrate in relation to their home town, nation and wider human community (Piaget and Weil 1951).

It is also remarked that youths, like or unlike their parents, can be constrained within certain cultural, ethnic, religious and other social boundaries, with potentially negative consequences for the wider community. Intensive exposure from family beliefs and attitudes, and/or from those of particular peers, can promote reductive stereotypes of other groups, thereby providing licence to think ill of them. Notorious examples of this have come in the past from Northern Ireland: vividly captured in Dominic Murray's documentation of covert pedagogy and overt stereotyping which take place in segregated schools (Murray 1985). They also come from grandparental stories of inter-religious feuding, drawn from experiences on the Indian subcontinent and told to children within the family home.

More recently they have come from Bradford. The report *Community Pride, not Prejudice* (Ouseley 2001), published in the wake of the 2001 riots, suggests that sectional community recruitment to particular schools, combined with after-school intensive teaching associated with one particular faith and culture, has had the effect of insulating whole sections of the community from other sections. In consequence, other faiths and cultures in all their wealthy diversity are never met in their own terms.

Religious Education can then be presented as creating the problem rather than contributing to its solution. But that would be a perversion of good RE and the mainstream teachings of world religions.

By definition, world religions are global in their horizons. In this respect, they contrast sharply with what might be termed 'tribal cults', in which loyalties and horizons are in effect confined to an immediate group. It is intrinsic to the Jewish tradition that there is affirmation of being both a Chosen People and simultaneously part of the whole of humanity created by God. The same is no less true for Christians and Muslims, and in all three religions there are radical demands for transformation according to the spirit of justice and generosity which flows from God. Though the Hindu tradition has until relatively recently thrived more on the sacred soil of India, its celebration of the plurality of divine forms gives licence for universal openness. Sikhs drawing parentally on that tradition, as on Islam as well, also assert a strong conviction of human oneness before God. And Buddhists diagnose dis-ease as universal to the human condition and warranting a radical re-ordering. All told, though they may do this in different ways, each of the religions which is prescribed for attention in Local Authority Agreed Syllabuses, as also in the National Models, challenges constrictions in thinking to anything less than global belonging.

Classroom RE is rich in incentives and resources from religion to promote horizons which go beyond those of any one group. Transcendent reference points in God, in Divine Reality, or in the transience of all being, give no encouragement to misplaced tribalisms. Sociologists have remarked about the historical role of religion in the challenging the 'tyranny of kin'; the same applies now to 'family firstism' and to little Englanders, as it does to the racism of the BNF or anyone else. Any local church, gurdwara, mosque, synagogue, temple or vihara points beyond itself to a wider humanity and communion of saints; schools can encourage their pupils to look through them as windows to that larger world.

'Faith Schools' are just as much committed to extending horizons as 'Community Schools'. Though their programmes for RE are different from those in Agreed Syllabuses, the 'world faith' with which they are specifically associated has global dimensions intrinsic to it. Moreover, they still operate within the framework of the 1988 Education Reform Act with its requirements that the National Curriculum be followed and that the curriculum 'promotes the spiritual, moral, cultural, mental and physical development of pupils at the school and of society' (ERA 1988: ch. I, para 1:(2)(a)).

For RE not to extend the horizons of pupils would be a contradiction in terms.

## Literal and symbolic sense

It may be said of someone, at any time, that their understanding does not go beyond surface meaning. Again, it may be said of the same person, or another, that they seem only to be interested in the literal meaning of words or pictures. In either instance, that person's human understanding would become more developed were they to learn to read and interpret how meaning is often layered and expressed on several levels.

This is an area of development that is central for RE in two respects. Firstly, religious meanings will be only partly understood without an appreciation of both letter and spirit. Secondly, the stuff of religion is richly fertile for growing such insights.

According to cognitive developmental psychology, a tendency towards concrete thinking predominates between infancy and adolescence. Whereas the younger child might delight in fantasy and fairy tale, and enjoy games of pretend that may bear little relation to matter of fact reality, it is observed that, for a boy or girl moving into Key Stages 2 and 3, matters of fact come to be of more predominant concern. Thinking becomes more readily concrete and circumstantial; symbols become brittle. And yet, from those earlier years, recollections do persist of the representative pliability of words and things. The newly dominant mode of thinking does not need to freeze out further appeal to symbolic sense, or to delay it into later adolescent years when intellectually more elaborated reasoning tends to flourish. Teachers of children across these different ages would simply recognize that their readiness to operate in terms of picture language and symbols will require appropriate classroom conjuring.

According to the theologian Paul Tillich, the great art of the religious educator is to overcome the problem of literalism (Tillich 1959). Misplaced concreteness can otherwise prevent the substance of religious teaching from having any vitality of its own and reduce its credibility to nil. That risk is perhaps especially evident in respect of scriptural text, but it extends also to all other forms of religious expression.

Take the example of biblical literalism. To be sure it is important to acknowledge that, for some Jews and Christians, biblical text should be taken literally, with its meaning still carefully pondered. But it would be wrong to give the impression that literal interpretation of the Bible has been the norm until the last hundred years, only retreated from in the wake of scientific discoveries. Picture language, powerful metaphor and colourful hyperbole abound in the Hebrew Bible, as they do also in the New Testament parables of Jesus, and in Pauline and Johannine apocalyptic. Their suggestiveness in this regard has been exploited by Christian theologians and artists across the centuries.

The Old Testament story of Jonah is demeaned if it is presented as a historical account of a man eaten by a whale. It is much more engaging as a story of a man who does not want to pass on a message to foreigners, rather than to family and friends, one who gets his 'comeuppance', and sulks. It takes on fuller force if it is then interpreted allegorically to represent the relation between Israel and the nations of the world, or as a parable about the same relationship affirming that the whole world is in God's hands. Similarly, the main point of the gospel story of Jesus walking on water is lost if it is left at the level of magical performance as found in similar stories from ancient Greece or India. Decoded as might be done for an advert, the message is that this Jesus and the power of God in him is recognized as totally dependable and present in even the most stressful of circumstances.

In approaching scriptural text, it is fundamental to RE that regard is given to the position in which it is held within its faith community. But openness to the meaning of what it says is different from deference to literalism, and scriptures are not possessions belonging exclusively to one group. They are given to humankind. Attention to the spirit and letter of text leaves space also for any student to work at it with the best intelligence they can bring to bear (Nielsen 1993).

This can also be seen in the other forms of religious language, a further example of which is that of artistic expression (Holm and Bowker 1994). There is considerable sensitivity in religions regarding visual representations of the Divine and, in a western context, an easy disdain at the very notion that God might be conveyed in, say, the form of an elephant. But this is where literal-mindedness fails a basic tuning test. Behind the friendly and strong sense of security associated with Ganesh, or Gumpati, is a living cultural experience of elephants as immensely strong and capable of removing major obstacles, as capable of great remembering and trumpeting playfulness. During the festival in his name, a carved statue of him may be fêted and reverenced, and as a way of sensing Godness and responding appropriately. But what is appropriate may well extend to processing the carved figure to the river and there allowing the elephant form to be swallowed up and carried away in the great flow of water, shortly to become one with the greater ocean which surrounds our being in the world.

Unfortunately, literalized understanding can on occasion become a very dangerous force. Caricatured versions of what is intended in a statue of the Buddha, or a Catholic image of the Virgin, have fuelled the violent antipathy of the Taliban's recent destruction by dynamite of ancient Buddhist rock carvings, or centuries ago the Protestant destruction of Christian visual expression in the churches of the British Isles. Good RE has the potential to make a real political difference!

The classroom then can be the arena for developing both literal and symbolic sense, if pupils are encouraged to bring to religious texts the quality of personal experience with which they interpret much of what goes on around them outside school, and if in turn teachers know the material well enough to prompt the links and connections that will ring true.

## Critical thinking and wondering why

Just as constraints of cognitive development can be used as a disincentive against the promotion of symbolic understanding before a certain age and stage, the same can also be invoked to discourage any priority being given to critical thinking.

It may be that, as boys and girls move into Key Stage 2, questions such as 'Did it really happen?', 'Is it true?' 'How do you know?' are more frequently asked. Similarly, comments such as 'It's just made up', 'It's not true really', and 'You can't prove it' may be more abundant. For some, perhaps later in Key Stage 3 and into Key Stage 4, this predominant emphasis may give way to different kinds of comments and questions, which may ask what is meant or intended in the first place by the statement made or belief being asserted.

However, such an age-related and linear developmental progression again strikes some as too simplistic. Children do ask these kinds of questions and may well with sensitive prompting be capable of pursuing them at a younger age than is often supposed, even in Key Stage 1 (Cam 1993/4). At the same time, questions of historical verification, scientific scrutiny and empirical check-out are more systematically asked and pursued as children get older, by both them and their teachers. Indeed, this interrogation will be encouraged as a curriculum priority. What may be overlooked in the course of this happening is that it is no less important that rigorous questioning should take place in RE than, for instance, in Science and History and Geography. Arguably, it may be even more important because RE has a special concern for 'why' questions in general, and ultimate 'whys' in particular: why is there a universe when there might be nothing? why is there cosmos and not only chaos? why does it matter that right thoughts and actions should prevail over wrong ones? (Isaacs 1930: Appendix A)

Theological and philosophical discourse has a strong place in each of the religious traditions which feature in the syllabuses. They include tracts of credal material which is didactically assertive in its form and content, but they are even richer in material which seeks to interpret, explain and justify what is being believed and taught as central to each faith. Thus, there are discussions about such questions as the following and many more besides: the injustice of innocent suffering, where life comes from, whether there is anything beyond death and what form it might take, if evil can be defeated, how to tell the difference between true and false prophecy, what God looks like, whether the individual self has any continuing identity. These all go beyond surface meanings. They connect with questions that any person might want to ask at any time in their life. Exposure to such material in RE can promote thinking skills at any age and at the same time give companionship to boys and girls in facing any tussles, in which they find themselves, regarding overall purpose and meaning in life and death.

As part of this process of scrutiny, it is important for the integrity of religion that its engagement with critical scholarship is presented so that this is recognized as an indicator of health and vitality in the tradition and not simply defensiveness. For instance, the insights from secondary disciplines – such as archaeology, ethnography, geography, history, psychology, and textual analysis – are important and variously informing of the teacher's confidence. And insights from primary sources, as generated from within each religious tradition and interrogated by scholars in its own particular terms, are even more fundamental for the teacher's repertoire. Their forms will be greatly diverse – literary and liturgical, in music, dance and drama, socially ordering and spiritually deepening, visually stimulating and morally demanding. Throughout, the questions provoked and affirmations claimed present a high order of philosophical challenge.

Religious Education does indeed have an interest in promoting cognitive development. It has vehicles and resources that lend themselves to stretching of thought and imagination. It is not at all shy of wanting to engage pupils in wondering why this, and that, and the other. A curriculum that invites them to wonder cannot help but be all about development.

## Being, knowing and sensing finitude

The contributions from RE to the social and psychological development of pupils are significant: in building empathy and sense of neighbour, in stretching horizons and loyalties beyond those nearest to hand, in creating an appreciation of the depth and power of language, and in promoting critical thinking and pursuing the question 'why?'. In the midst of all this lies another contribution which focuses in the person at the centre of all these thoughts and feelings.

This focus has been left till last for three reasons, two negative and one positive. The first of these is that there is much in contemporary western culture which takes as unquestionable norm that the goal of education is human autonomy. Enabling each pupil to think for themselves becomes the overarching goal of every curriculum subject. This is a healthy challenge to rote learning and any cultural tendency to want to predetermine the thinking and behaviour of its youth. However, the cultivation of the individual can have very isolating outcomes, which are at the expense of other relatedness and relational belonging. The 'I' is supreme, but entirely solitary.

Secondly, there is a wariness in religious traditions not only with self-centredness, but with the very notion of self having any reality. Jews, Christians and Muslims press the case that neighbour be loved as much as, or even more than, self. Buddhists challenge the very notion of an individual self: it is illusory. If therefore Religious Education were to guise itself as primarily an exercise in self-exploration, it would easily invite dismissal from across religions that it was merely navel-gazing.

Yet, thirdly, religious responses to life in the world do invariably involve a sense of contingency, of transience and of human limitation, and each of these is fundamental to personhood. Death stalks the heart of religion, as of all humanity, powerfully. Much of the sentiment expressed in petitionary prayer is admitting relative helplessness and dependence. Much of the contemplative reflection found in acts of meditation seeks to go beyond the ordinary givenness of physical sensation. Religion and RE, almost by definition, raise questions in the pupil of any age as to 'who' is the 'I' who is learning, and to what lasting end. Without sooner or later coming to recognize the relative precariousness of being, human capacity for self-deception translates more readily into delusions of grandeur.

Without engaging with the prospect of individual mortality, the opportunity to reflect on short- and long-term purpose in individual and collective life may well be delayed or dulled. Similarly, motivation, and the will to act, is less quickened than it might have been.

Children in their play already demonstrate their awareness of the transitory and of death. It is in the substance of rhymes and gestures from an early age. RE is able to work with this primal sense and to connect it with the stories and rituals that abound in religious tradition as making sense of the finitude that is involved. As the Nupe story from Africa has it: 'only the stones didn't have children and so they never die' (Beier 1966: 58–9).

Such basic 'knowing in the bones' that is often communicated through story is also connected with a developing awareness of 'ought' at the centre of individual being. Though it may be too grand to tag this straightway as 'conscience', the synoptic sense of being that accompanies more immediate knowledge and general awareness is fertile ground for growing both moral and religious insights, and with them an enriched humanity.

In the context of RE, boys and girls can be encouraged to explore their finitude in ways that heighten their sense of the specialness of human being. The awareness that emerges moves on ground which many would regard as both moral and religious. Therein too lie criteria for checking that any associated development is indeed enriching of humanity.

## And so?

In conclusion, effective provision of Religious Education has much to contribute to the development of students of every age and stage. Its absence, or poor quality of provision, is by contrast likely to be genuinely debilitating. Opportunities to enhance both social and psychological maturity are significantly missed; instead the risks of individual hollowness and communal splintering are magnified. In a very real sense, personally, socially and politically, the world suffers underdevelopment from lack of genuine RE.

(2002)

# PART THREE

# Moral Education

For different reasons in different places, it has sometimes been judged both appropriate and necessary not only to separate Moral Education and Religious Education sharply from each other, but to replace the latter with the former. The pressure for this may be political, for instance coming from a constitutional concern that religion should be kept out of public institutional life. Religion may be perceived as both diverse and contentious; by contrast, ethics may be presented as more straightforwardly agreeable or agreed. Alternatively, the pressure may come from a religious sensitivity that fears the distorting threat of religion being reduced to morality, when it is actually much more.

This section of the book examines the interplay between ethics and religion, ME and RE. It does so with direct reference to several influential reference points. The first is the work of Lawrence Kohlberg, the leading twentieth-century advocate of Moral Education, whose influence extended far beyond his Chicago and Boston bases. The second is the range of relevant insights and resources for ethics and ME available from the world's religions. And the third is a commentary on what is perceived as a dominant 'blind eye' feature with regard to religion in the operational assumptions of some members of the international Association for Moral Education.

The analysis and argument pursued here parallels those applied by the author to Citizenship and Citizenship Education in the Special Issue of the *Journal of Moral Education* (Gates 2006) in the article entitled 'Religion as cuckoo or crucible: beliefs and believing as vital for citizenship and citizenship education'. Whether unwittingly or intentionally, a similar position appears to be evident in both ME and Citizenship Education. There is a reluctance to engage with religion whose potential influence appears almost to be regarded as a contaminating one. The coincidence is actually unsurprising in that the citizenship arena is one in which the social priorities of moral education are played out on what is a directly related, if slightly different, canvas.

# Chapter 16

# ME + RE = Kohlberg with a difference

From the perspective of Religious Education (RE), Lawrence Kohlberg (1971 a and b) has evident attraction as one of the exponents of an evolutionary sequence of child development who have been so influential in the previous twenty years.[1] At a time when RE was under scrutiny and considered by many to be somewhat lacking in educational justification in public state provision, it was helpful to be able to show that there is a rationality and coherent logical structure in children's religious development. Piagetian interpretation of a child's understanding of the world was seen to include not only concepts of space, time and place, but also those of morality and religion. This was the effect of the work of Goldman (1964a) in the UK, Elkind (1964) and Peatling (1973) in the USA and, in some degree, of Godin (1971) in Belgium and France (see Chapter 9 and Elkind 1971). The shift from sub-religious intuitional thinking, through the concrete 'flat-land' thought of middle childhood to more elaborated (and therefore genuine?) religious understanding was welcomed as a basis on which the teacher might order his/her otherwise confused approach to the matter of religious belief and behaviour. Very similarly, Kohlberg seemed to provide a parallel account of stages of moral development that any teacher might refer to in understanding individual children in class.

In addition, viewed from a background of Christian moral theology, Kohlberg could be seen as validating a new and contemporary version of an ancient tradition: a 'socio-psychological' equivalent of natural law (d'Entrèves 1951). For in his view there is a natural human givenness which betrays a recognizable pattern of moral development that is invariant in sequence and universal in provenance.[2] Again, this has been welcomed when much else in social science is shifting sands.[3]

The enormous interest in Kohlberg's work ensured that his account of six stages was widely disseminated even while refinements of the developmental continuum were still being made in the light of further longitudinal and cross-cultural study.[4] Although Kohlberg himself may now be even more careful than ten or fifteen years ago to qualify the claims he makes about moral development, the basic shape of his assumptions about religion and morality, both separately and as they interconnect, has been consistent since 1958.[5] Without calling into question the total worth of Kohlberg's position, at several points it is less well grounded in common sense than it might be and accordingly more insensitive about the nature of RE than it need be.

In the pages that follow, four major areas of incompleteness will be identified: the empirical base; 'Where there's no will there's no way'; alternative religious outcomes; and religion within and without the bounds of morality. Finally, some reflections on religious and moral education are included which draw on particular experience in England and Wales.

## Exposing what is missing

### The empirical base

The care taken by Kohlberg to follow up his subjects over an extended period of time confirms that he recognizes how important it is that his theory is well earthed in ordinary human experience. This is all the more vital given the claim that natural humanity in its entirety has a moral direction which progresses with the interaction of psychogenetic inheritance and social context. It is perhaps the more surprising therefore to discover that in several respects the base is open to question. The evidence of 'regression' by subjects during the period of higher education is open to various interpretations;[6] this, and Kohlberg's recasting in recent years of the upper stages to the point of withdrawing Stage 6, if not also Stage 5, are unsettling in themselves.[7] Of greater threat, however, is the size of the database invoked to support the predictive correlation of stage of moral development with actions performed.[8] It is a commonplace of the religious experience of mankind, as of Adlerian psychology, that it is the deeds that count more than the words: do the actions that crop up match earlier verbal declarations, or were these sown on the wind? There is a fundamental snag here, and since RE must needs be specially sensitive in respect of a much-remarked human propensity for hypocrisy, we will return to it. For the moment, however, the point is registered that Kohlberg's own data may be too ambiguous to bear the weight of normative judgement attributed to them about the way the individual 'shapes up' towards moral and religious maturity.

Some doubt on Kohlberg's judgement is cast by empirical evidence from other sources, as illustrated in the following three examples. The first comes from England in the 1960s and takes the form of children responding to such quotations as 'what does naughty/bad/wrong mean?'; 'what does being fair mean?'; 'telling lies/bullying – what are they?'; 'is it wrong to tell lies/bully? If so, why?'. According to N. Williams (1969), who conducted the research with 790 children aged 4 to 18 years, responses fell into 17 different modes which were in turn reducible to Peck and Havighurst's well-established types: Amoral; Expedient (self-considering); Irrational-conscientious (self-obeying); Conforming (other-obeying); and Rational-altruistic (other-considering). On

Kohlberg's consecutive stage sequence there is a shift from amoral and expedient through role conformity to principled altruism.

According to Williams, however, all these different responses are found even in the youngest children and commonly a child answered him in more than one mode. Although a 'pecking order' may emerge in each child as she or he grows older, the different modes of thinking develop *in parallel*, initially prompted by situation-specific reactions of adults but later generalized to other areas. Thus, what the neighbours will think or a twinge of guilt may subsist alongside a generous altruism in the thinking of even the most mature of adults, and a 'primitive' altruistic reasoning may well occur in the young child.'[9] Kohlberg (1971b) admits as much from his own family experience in his four-year-old son's vegetarian protest and sympathy for seals. But this is categorized as Stage 1 because associated with a parallel judgement that Eskimos deserve to be eaten because they kill animals. The subtlety of the child's response is missed, if the fellow-feeling and basic sense of justice can be crudely put down as Stage 1; in this particular instance it is perhaps less obviously an outrageous comment in the 'land of the buffalo burger' than it would be among Jains.[10] But RE sensibilities are also aroused by the issue of whether or not evidence from children indicates a capacity for altruistic thinking of a sustained kind in earliest years, in respect of both humanity and God. Williams indicates that the evidence is not irrefutably on Kohlberg's side in this.

A second example from England in the 1970s presses this particular point further. As part of a larger study on the development of beliefs and values in children and young people, Gates (1976) includes an analysis of a subsample of 310 children's (aged 6 to 16 years) responses to the questions, 'Whom do you love?. .. Do you think you should love everybody (where you live ... in your class)? Why/why not? ... How do you decide who to love?'. Using the Williams' classification, the different modes are found across the entire age range, with one exception. Curiously, other-obeying responses (invoking personal figures, society or peer group, or the law) were rarely given in this context, although they were more frequently used by the same boys and girls elsewhere in the interview. The few which were 'other-obeying' took religious form: 'you're meant to love each other.' *Meant by whom?* 'meant by God' (11-year-old girl with no formal religious association). 'In Islam it says even if the people are people you don't like, you should still have respect for them. We are really kind of brothers and sisters to everyone in that kind of way.' *There is nobody you don't respect?* 'There are some I don't respect because they are bullies, but you still have to respect; that is what it says in Islam' (13-year-old Muslim boy). But not all the religious responses took this form, for instance, a seven-year-old Catholic girl: 'I love everybody in the world, even if they don't like me. They are God as well, they've got Jesus inside them – God the spirit.' Here the claim on her love comes simultaneously from within and without herself. Closer inspection of the relationship between religion and morality is yet to come, but alternative empirical data do not confirm that Kohlberg's stages are consecutive and invariant in sequence and confined in childhood years to instrumental hedonism or comfortable conformity.

The third example comes from South India early in 1980. It is in the form of an intensive study by Kalam (1981) of the religious and moral thinking of 150 individuals in the region of Chavakkad in the state of Kerala. In effect he achieves remarkable control of the religious variable in a non-Western setting, for his subjects share a common linguistic, cultural and political background, and similar economic status, yet there are three distinct religious groups involved: Mar Thoma Christians, Hindus and Muslims. The ages ranged from eight to 80 and each group was evenly stratified into five age bandings. As part of Form A of Kohlberg's moral judgement interview, subjects were all presented with Indianized versions of the Heinz (now Raju) and other dilemmas. They were also taken through a semi-clinical interview schedule, adapted for intelligibility, but based on Fowler's (1981) approach to faith development. Responses on both tests were then scored by Kalam and independently by Colby on the moral and Fowler and his associates on the religious.

On philosophical grounds, Kohlberg holds the view that religion and morality are logically independent, though variously interrelated. In addition, he makes the empirical claim that the trans-culturally universal pattern of moral development is necessary for and prior to the relativities of religious development (Power and Kohlberg 1980). Fowler shares Kohlberg's Piagetian heritage but puts forward the alternative claim that faith (ultimate horizon/personal centre of commitment) not only develops in a parallel series of stages, but *precedes* and is necessary for the moral stages. The result of Kalam's research is to cast empirical doubt on both their views. In half his sample Kalam finds complete agreement between moral and faith stages; of the other 74, 41 show a half-stage difference, 21 a full stage and 12 more than one stage. These differences are not confined to upper stages, but occur across the range of Stages 1 to 4 or 5. More disturbingly in this present context, 46 reveal a higher religious than moral stage, 28 a higher moral than religious. By implication Kalam goes on to question the validity of using the evidence of Shulik (1977) and Power (1979) – adduced by Kohlberg, or Mischey (1976) – adduced by Fowler, to support their respective views. Whereas in the case of his own research scoring was done by two different persons 'blind', in the other cases the same person(s) were responsible and privy to the entire scoring. In other words, the precedence of moral development over religious development, or vice versa, may relate more to scorer inclination than to a cognitively universal fact.

Kalam's study also repudiates the claim by Kohlberg to have changed successfully from content-dominated scoring procedures to criterion-based formal structure. Even with the carefully annotated Scoring Manual, Kalam argues that reference is still made to content or, if not, that arbitrary judgements occur. One instance of the difficulty of content-free scoring is illustrated by the response of an eight-year-old Muslim boy to the Heinz dilemma: 'give your (Heinz's) wife to the druggist, who will then give her the medicine and cure her so that he can have her as one of his wives'. By criterion-reference scoring this may indicate someone at Stage 1/2: although technically the solution is found within the bounds of Islamic law, the wife becomes a 'bartered bride'. The boy went on to say, however: 'If you love your wife, you want her to live, somehow or other; you wouldn't want to keep her to yourself and let her die.' It is difficult to question that this is a cognitively satisfying response of a higher stage. Similarly, Kalam draws attention to Kohlberg's attribution of Eichman to Stage 1 rather than Stage 4 in his thinking when, according to the manual, *formally* the latter seems more appropriate (Kohlberg 1980). The switch away from content would therefore appear to be a partial one.

Overall, the work of Kalam, as a moral theologian, directs its critical gaze to devastating effect at the empirical grounding of Kohlberg's and Fowler's theories. Thus a succession of questions generated by the sensitivities of Religious Education has the cumulative effect of creating scepticism that Kohlberg has really identified the proven shape of moral evolution in human beings as he had hoped.

### 'Where there's no will there's no way'

There are some versions of Moral Education which have as their priority the induction of children into well-defined routines of behaviour. Outward conformity is at a premium; inward understanding appears to count for very little. Arguably what is involved here is more 'socialization' of a particular kind than moral education. Indeed, it is one of Kohlberg's strengths, from an RE perspective, that he abhors conditioned learning as the main vehicle for moral education and instead places great stress on individual reasoning which may be sharpened by practice Thus, dilemmas are a means not only of assessing the stage of an individual's moral development, but also of encouraging his/her further progress.

It would therefore be unfair to criticize the fact that Kohlberg uses Socratic dialogue as a technique for refining personal understanding and judgement. Indeed in more recent writings, he has also set this in the context of the participatory role experience in democratically run cluster schools (Kohlberg 1980); this is seen as context for cultivating (he actually uses the term 'indoctrination') civic sense to combat a current mood of 'privatism' in society at large. With Power he has called attention to 'the social atmosphere of the school as an educational resource'. However, the medium throughout is exclusively verbal and from an RE perspective this would seem to be a mistake.

Basic beliefs and values are often verbally articulated, but they may also be nurtured, carried and expressed in gesture, image and example, in music movement and visual art (see Chapter 14). An approach to Moral Education or RE that lacks these enactive, iconic and imitative dimensions is impoverished, and the cluster school may well miss out on life if its priority is primarily cast in the following terms: 'the teacher's role is to facilitate the discussion and resolution of the conflict by encouraging students to speak thoughtfully, sharpening the points of disagreement, raising unexamined but important issues, and presenting ideas which challenge further enquiry' (Power and Kohlberg 1980: 370). Learning to think clearly and critically is important, but there is more to Moral Education than this.

It is not surprising in this light that Kohlberg has had to acknowledge a gap between the school (or prison) expression of a just community and the larger school or rest of society; societies operate not just at the diverse levels of moral sophistication, but in far more than just verbal currency. RE, because of it appreciation of ritual, myth and image in the religious experience of mankind, has to find Kohlberg wanting in these respects. Their contribution to the realm of moral experience has been remarked in disciplines ranging from anthropology and sociobiology to psychoanalysis (cf. Langer 1957), and the artistic hearts that like of an Iris Murdoch or a Maurice Sendak explore the sovereignty of good in more imaginative forms.

A restriction in Kohlberg's own perspective is also apparent in his reluctance to recognize that knowledge of what is good might not actually be translated into actions that are good. While respecting this persistent loyalty to Plato, RE is aware that by implication less respect is shown for the Hebrew tradition of humankind as fallen, a tradition replicated elsewhere in the world's great collection of creation stories, and translated theologically into a much misunderstood doctrine of original sin. The Pauline 'good that I know I don't do, the evil that I'd rather avoid I do instead' (Romans 7: 14–20) may not be a universally human experience, but it resonates for many. In individual terms, it may be dealt with under the heading of weakness of will, or sociologically, as collective aberration and estrangement that inhibits action for good through structural pressures to the contrary.[11] Either form is a further reminder of the gulf between theory and practice mentioned above. Even if the adage, 'the shinier the halo the dirtier the feet', has got it wrong, RE has to say to Kohlberg: look again at the process by which words and intentions are transformed into actions. Not only is there an affective as well as a cognitive ingredient to which Kohlberg duly insists he does justice (Conn 1981) but there is also the matter of the connative. The actor's willingness and motivation are crucial, and Kohlberg pays less attention to them than an RE perspective would sense to be both appropriate and necessary.

## Alternative religious outcomes

In spite of the widespread occurrence of the Golden Rule in different civilizations,[12] there is evident diversity in religion and culture, past and present. By virtue of his singular commitment to the principle of justice, however, and his insistence not only that moral precedes religious development, but that it does so in a unilinear way, Kohlberg shrinks reality. In effect he imposes a monochrome view of morality on an otherwise pluralistic universe. RE has its own experience of making the same mistake. There was a time when it enjoyed a confusion of identity with Christian education, and allowed privileges to be claimed for church authority that do not belong in public educational provision in an open society (see Chapters 1 and 2). There has also been a temptation to define religion as 'theistic belief', even though this religious tradition or that may even be sceptical of all talk of God or gods.[13] RE is the more wary then when a Kohlberg (or a Rawls) posits one particular model of morality.

This is not to deny that justice as a key concept figures throughout the religious experience of mankind. But the Islamic sense of justice as determined by Qur'ān is qualified differently from Judaic or Christian justice, as also from Buddhist or Hindu. Again, other key concepts are just as important in the field of social ethics, or, for instance, that of love or 'agapeistic responsibility'. Indeed, such may be more morally constructive for solving a dilemma than the principle of distributive justice mathematically applied. Would the moral theologians from any of these traditions agree with Kohlberg that the drawing of lots for suicide is the most sensitive moral outcome from the dilemma in which a pilot, an old man and a young man are marooned on a raft with survival prospects fair if there were two of them, poor if three? (Kalam 1981: 198–201).

The starting-point within a religious tradition may actually be antithetic to Kohlberg because the notion of Revelation, on some renderings, deliberately demotes the power of human reason. For instance, on certain understandings of the Bible, the Qur'ān, or the Granth as the Word of God, any definition of true justice must derive exclusively from that one source. All other sources are human counterfeit. Religious and moral development alike must be moulded towards that scriptural norm.

On these views, Kohlberg's justice is, strictly speaking, irrelevant because its autonomous logic presumes to rule when it is seen as lacking the true authority to do so. Kohlberg may retort that this sounds very like Stage 3 reasoning, but if it is, and it is therefore judged to be rationally inferior, to change the mind of someone of this persuasion will involve their theological as well as moral transformation. Alternatively, Kohlberg will need to acknowledge that the source of true revelation and morality lies beyond reasons. Kohlberg may be unable to agree to this, but the position is held with deep conviction by religious believers of many complexions.

There is also another position within religious traditions with regard to the notion of revelation. Instead of seeing scripture and reason as incompatible, with the one overwhelming the other for either believer or sceptic, they are claimed to be complementary. Special revelation fulfils general knowledge; there is a natural religious and moral sense that is completed by the grace of God. Thus, Paul and Aquinas in the Christian tradition affirm that there is a basic sense of God and ought found generally in human experience. Similar views are found within the Jewish tradition of the Noachic Covenant (Genesis 9: 8–17, with all of human and animal kind), or in Islam with the Mu'tazilite recognition of right and wrong independently of the Qur'ān itself, though underwritten by it (Hourani 1980). In the Indian tradition, the emphasis is more on progressive enlightenment and stages of spiritual discovery than on special scriptural revelation, so that the questing path of salvation is often seen as quite compatible with rational enquiry. However, in all these cases, revelation and enlightenment, while not overturning reason, anticipate a process of personal transformation whose moral outcome will not be simply the rational autonomy of Western liberalism. For such an outcome, contrary to Kohlberg's theorizing, would actually be an unnatural law.

From such critical backgrounds as these, it is not surprising to find dissenting theological criticism of Kohlberg. For instance, some evangelical Christians are impatient with the way the individual is recognized as potentially authoritative, in wilful ignorance of the grace of God from beyond (Joy 1980). Similarly, some Catholics defer instead to the Roman magisterium as determinative source for both religious and moral education, although others are able to accommodate their Catholic faith to fit the Kohlberg framework (Duska and Whelan 1977, O'Leary 1983: chapter 3). A more radical critique is that of Dykstra (1981) who thinks that Christian ethics and education are not cognitive developmental but involve instead multidimensional moral growth. He contrasts the 'juridical' ethics of Kohlberg with what he terms 'visional' ethics – mystery-encouraging rather than problem-solving, for it is imagination, the vehicle of personal illumination, that transforms someone's character. He accepts Kohlberg's account of (the first) four stages of social reasoning, but claims that any outcome in moral virtue derives from other more imaginative sources.[14] Dykstra's view chimes well with an existentialist criticism which is suspicious of any well-ordered sequence of human development. Kohlberg's 'conveyor belt' is far too predictable for the individual child or adult who may think or act discontinuously and so remain mysterious at heart (Lealman 1983, Fynn 1974).

From a Jewish perspective, Rosenzweig (1977) seizes on Kohlberg's central concern with universal justice to advance the claim that they share the same priority for fostering progress towards it.[15] However, closer inspection indicates that similarity is more apparent than real. Comparing Kohlberg with modern and Reformed Jews, Chazan (1980) identifies fundamental incompatibilities. Irrespective of any 'natural law' connection, he says that contemporary educational provision by the non-orthodox Jew aims at reinforcing a sense of Jewish group identification and teaches a specific and substantive value system markedly different from Kohlberg's. Some of the teaching methods might alone be shared with him. As to the more orthodox tradition of Jewish education, because of its preoccupation with a very specific and definitive lifestyle, Chazan finds it very different from Kohlberg's stress on patterns of thinking. Kohlberg is interested in formal principles, whereas orthodoxy stresses the oneness of principles and Jewish tradition in an all-inclusive Jewish communal setting.

Similar points of difference can be identified from other religious traditions. Even secularized versions of the world's religions have fundamental differences in expectation that derive from their distinctive theological and ethical resources.

Thus Kohlberg's understanding of moral development is the poorer from his not having recognized the different impacts that religion can have in its outward and inward manifestations. Where religion and revelation are viewed as different as chalk from cheese, then Kohlberg's ambitions for children's moral or religious development are almost certainly in conflict with those of the religious community. Where, however, they are viewed as complementary, the religious communities might still ask of Kohlberg that he show more sensitivity to their own theologically laden aspirations for children. RE, in turn, acknowledges the need for stage development talk to be open to outcomes differentiated by theologic, whether Christian or Hindu, Marxist or atheist (Oser 1980, Elias 1982).

## Religion within and without the bounds of morality

The sheer diversity of religions and world-views creates serious difficulty for any approach to religion and ethics which wants to route them all to one particular destination – along the same path. In this Kohlberg has shared the Western insularity of much moral philosphy which has allowed itself the luxury of defining its terms of reference in substantial ignorance of other traditions of reflection and value elsewhere in the world.[16] References may have been made in passing to other world-views, but even recently it is Spinoza or Santayana who are invoked for 'mystical pantheism' rather than the Indian religious tradition.[17] Thus not only is the cross-cultural base less than adequate in empirical terms, conceptually it is doubtful whether the actual diversity of religions and world-views has been taken very seriously at all.

In this, Kohlberg's understanding of the relation between religion and morality may itself be the root fault. He insists that the moral reference point comes first: in terms of the Euthyphro dilemma, good is good because it is and not because declared to be such by God. In this he is at odds with believers in a scriptural revelation which is propositionally prescriptive of right and wrong. He also fails to recognize the logic of more inductive theological positions. Because the very polarity built into this dilemma is taken as a starting point, it is the more difficult for him to allow the position that goodness and godness may mutually coinhere, or, again, that there may rationally be claims 'both ways' – from justice or love on God, or from religious conviction on moral expression.

It is possible, however, to detect some hesitation in Kohlberg on this front. His postulation of a hypothetical Stage 7 may have been immediately occasioned by the Catholic context to which he was speaking (Kohlberg 1974), but it also reflects his awareness that there is a nagging 'Why?' question to be answered in respect of any moral action. Why do right rather than wrong? Even if I have arrived at the elusive Stage 6 why does it matter? Why should I bother? At this juncture Kohlberg admits the relevance of fundamental assumptions and beliefs about the meaning of life. Curiously, they have been left to the end.

In subsequent writings, explanation of Stage 7 has been limited. Latterly, however, he appears to admit that Stage 7 concerns may be in some sense continuous with each stage of moral development, and Fowler's work on stages of faith development is seen as providing the further explanation. Yet, as has already been remarked, there is a fundamental disagreement between them over whether religious or moral development has priority over the other. The concluding section of Kohlberg's statement on this question, written in conjunction with Power, is firm that stage of moral development places a ceiling on religious development. It is not at all permissive that stage of religious development, or mode of religious thinking, may open up a new stage, let alone whole avenues, of moral development.

In this Kohlberg's thinking may yet be open to change. For Power's appreciation of the religious dimension of knowing and being, in which he follows Tillich and others, at least entails new recognition of a continuous relation of moral and religious wavelengths. Without conceding Fowler's claim that morality depends on faith (however broadly defined) and thereby abandoning notions of natural law and human autonomy, it is still possible to insist that religion contributes significantly to the content and context, grounds and bounds, of morality (Wallwork 1980). Religion may not be the necessary or sufficient basis for ethics, but ethics without religion may not be sufficient either, and the necessity of ethics, like that of religion, is no less open to debate and doubt.

The phrase 'autonomy of ethics' may actually be misleading if it has the effect of adolescent posturing of ethics against religion, as though proving some substitute machismo virtue. 'Autonomy' as expounded by Riesman in *The Lonely Crowd* has the positive connotation of independence and critical openness, as contrasted with sheepish conformity. However, as he stresses in the third edition, it can also appear narcissistic, self-centred, and even neurotic, lacking the communal warmth and sensitivity that may actually be an aspect of conformity (Riesman 1961: xvii–xxi). Perhaps the term 'relative autonomy' would better serve their general interests if the relation between ethics and religion were each described as relatively autonomous. Thus an outcome that was relative to cosmic meaning (my own and others) might be admitted as common goal.

If indeed there is flexibility in Kohlberg's thinking on this general front, the popularized impression of a monorail to the sixth stage or seventh heaven will need to be remade. How drastically will depend on the extent to which he may care to recognize divergent and convergent highways and byways by and along which men, women and children grow in moral stature, religious belief and unbelief.

## What England has that Kohlberg lacks?

Throughout this chapter the term RE has been used in an English sense to connote a form of education which is different from Christian and other particularized forms of initiatory religious education, although complementary to them. This is a distinction that was systematically hammered out in the period 1965–80 (Gates 1982b). It acknowledges the importance of specific nurture in a faith being provided by a parent religious community, but it recognizes that such is out of place in a public educational system. Instead it sees the priority of the public school curriculum to be enabling boys and girls to become not just literate and numerate, but also 'religiate', so that they leave school having had the opportunity to understand and test religious belief and unbelief on their pulses, and knowing, at least at a preliminary level, their way around the religious experience of mankind.[18]

This development has been nourished in the face of the tensions of religious diversity. Fifty or more years ago they were between different versions of Christianity and the 'Agreed Syllabus' tradition developed to provide a common biblical framework within which the disputants could feel their common interests were being served (Hull 1975a). Now it is between different world religions, including secular humanism, and again a common framework has been sought,[19] this time more inclusive of other faiths.

The result is that unlike the USSR, England and Wales public education at least potentially provides a built-in opportunity for the exploration of basic ingredients of religious beliefs and ideologies, as well as for critical thinking about them.[20] Unlike the USA, it is not customary for reference to religious belief to be extensively bracketed out from public school. In principle, therefore, there is opportunity to examine both mainstream religious traditions and quite possibly to build immunity against more hazardous flowerings.[21]

From this RE perspective the question arises whether Kohlberg's position in compartmentalizing religion and ethics may in part be a rationalization of the great divide between church and state, between beliefs and values, in the American school system (Barr and Collie 1981). The unhappy consequence of it is that other skills and resources relevant from RE for moral education and development are neglected by him.

It may even be that in the English tradition of school assemblies, not understood as sectional acts of formal Christian worship, but open explorations and celebrations of the values, beliefs and identities that undergird the school as an educational community, there is experience for Kohlberg to draw on (Hull 1975b). Here may be a means of enriching his cluster schools within schools to achieve the larger participation model of school-in-the-world for which he yearns (Kohlberg 1980).

(1986)

Chapter 17

# Religion, morality and education – constitutionally incongruent?

## Politicized perceptions?

What provision should be made for teaching citizenship and 'civilised values' in schools?

That should be done in religious education. Indeed you cannot teach religious education without teaching morality. That is its basis. It is the worth of the individual. The two great religions – Judaism and Christianity – are the two that really are based on the worth of the individual. You will not find it in some of the Far East religions.

Margaret Thatcher, (1990)

Being a Prime Minister itself provides no automatic exemption from the pall of personal prejudice. It is therefore no surprise to find, in senior politicians the world over, evidence of ignorance and distortion concerning the beliefs and values of others. Unfortunately, the consequences that flow from this are not confined to private, family feelings. They spill over to affect political judgements at both national and international levels.

In this particular instance, the view expressed about the relative superiority of some religions, as compared with others, has popular currency. It is not difficult to find examples of the judgement that the personal worth of the individual human being is devalued outside the Judaeo-Christian tradition.

On the 'Far Eastern' front, for instance, *Shinto* is commonly presented as so completely integrating its faith with the cause of nationalism that individual significance is exterminated. It becomes the archetype of Durkheim's 'altruistic suicide', where individuals are lost in their identification with a cause far greater than themselves. *Hinduism* is represented as encasting everyone hierarchically in such a way that shudra and 'untouchables' matter far less than those of higher castes, and, similarly, females than males. Moreover, post-mortem prospects only serve to confirm that individuality is transient and insignificant. *Buddhism,* it is said, cannot think very highly of individuals, when it claims that selfhood is illusory, while also rating monks more highly than other human beings.

Elsewhere too, this same judgement is made about Islam and Marxism. In the name of *Islam* the conduct of jihad, as between Iran and Iraq, or against some blaspheming book, shows, it is said, supreme disregard for the welfare of individual citizens. Hostages for this fortune are cheap. Likewise, *Marxism*, with its credo 'freedom is the recognition of necessity', camouflages the inhumanity of a Stalinist purge or Tiananmen Square for the interests of individuals in their midst. For Muslims and Marxists alike, no rule of law can have validity without the approval respectively of Qur'ānic text or Party decree.

By contrast, in the Judaeo-Christian tradition the worth of the individual reigns supreme. Or does it? *Judaism* has a different face for Palestinians, as does its orthodoxy for Jewish homosexuals. As for *Christianity*, is it certain that crusades, anti-Semitism and apartheid are entirely in the past and in any case aberrant? In Latin America, both papal opposition to birth control and protestant missionary activity among tribal peoples can seem to show indifference to individual need.

It is easy to become caught up in mutual caricature, most especially where views are expressed from within one religion of another. Education's response to Margaret Thatcher may therefore be to say: 'Your judgement against Far Eastern religions should be extended to all. There can be no effective base here for an effective moral education which gives proper priority to the worth of individuals within the human community at large. What is needed is a rationally based morality, in which teachers throughout the world endeavour to enable all boys and girls to achieve autonomy. They should be encouraged to develop their own values, independent of parental pressure and traditional beliefs. Far from providing an intellectually and emotionally satisfying basis for morality, Religious Education is an irrelevance.'

Such a position as this may be framed as Secular Humanist, or more colourfully as 'antinomian' (Partington 1984, 1990). Either way, the position commands much academic credence. There has even been some attraction in it for those engaged in RE. For too long RE has been contaminated with the 'self-righteous' associations of moral education. These have been a distraction from more intrinsic elements of religion, such as inner experience and theistic belief, artistic expression and community action. By ridding itself of all connotations of self-righteous moralizing, RE will be able to travel more lightly and strongly.

There is a fundamental problem with all these judgements, however. They are based on mistaken perceptions of the world.


## Towards a more than partial vision of the context for moral education

Before going to work, a teacher will normally get dressed. This is so usual as to be 'taken for granted' in any description of a teacher's routine. Arguably, that is equally true with the following features of the context for moral education. What might make them significantly different, however, is that a naked teacher would quickly be identified as such. Partial vision in the matter of moral education is rather less conspicuous, as the following examples show.

### Class size

Typical class sizes vary greatly from one national system of education to another. In the European Community, the general range is from 12–30, in China 30–50, and in India 50–80. Of course these figures are crude denominators and subject greatly to local variation. But they are all quite different from the more generous teacher–pupil ratio found in Boston 'schools within schools'. Their consequences for moral education are by no means certain. For instance, the larger the class the greater the likelihood of didactic teaching; but means may also be found to achieve collaborative learning which is group-based within the larger whole. In principle, however, personal values clarification and individual autonomy of moral judgement may sit more easily as the working norms in one setting as compared with another. Big may not be so beautiful for moral education.

### Friends and relations

It may be something of an occupational hazard for the professional educator to suppose that he or she has a major influence on the lives of those being taught. Research findings on the power of parents, as of peer-group pressure, arouse scepticism about the extent to which this is true. From personal experience of hour-long conversations with 340 boys and girls from 6 to 16 years of age, I was surprised how infrequently school or teachers were cited in support of any particular idea or value. Friends and relations, by comparison were omnipresent. So, too, were companions from television (Gates 1975). Consciously, or otherwise, there are more players in the moral education game out of school than in.

### Media messages

Radio, TV and newspapers reach most parts of the planet with their infor-mation. Their power to shape people's thinking is appreciated equally by government and commercial interests. They know that advertising works, whether as tabloid promotion of a sale at a local market or as wayside billboard displaying the current political icon. Whatever the form, an appeal is made to interest, and likely also to appetite, and they become significant factors in the education of child and adult alike. Ironically, irrespective of its success in promoting the sales of its drinks, the Coca-Cola jingles about the whole world family may do more to reinforce that notion in general human consciousness than many a set lesson in school.

## Stunted lives

Much moral education takes as normative that human life is a positive experience. For millions of children, past and present, that has not been the case, whether for reasons of birth defect, homelessness, starvation, child abuse, noxious disease or war. This fact may be conveniently blocked from daily consciousness, just as are more general signs of injustice. There is evidence of self-deception on a massive scale (Lerner 1980). Life for most people is not as just as we expect it to be, yet we pretend otherwise in spite of daily experience to the contrary. By the same token, at the level of initial presuppositions, moral education must address the question of the nature of the faith which it has in its own endeavours, as in the whole human enterprise (Fernhout 1989).

These examples may serve to bring to our attention that there may be aspects of the context for moral education which are commonly overlooked. A further example brings us back to the political dimension with which we began.

# Constitutional complexities

State constitutions may not be the most obvious place to look for guidance about how a nation approaches moral education, yet in reality they are of persistent significance. Historically this is immediately apparent from a scrutiny of Ashoka's India, Constantine's Rome, or Napoleon's France. A framework of beliefs and values is in each case fundamental to the nation's identity – religion, morality and education all have a part. In the world of today, this is no less true, albeit in a variety of different forms. Three contrasting types of constitution may serve to illustrate how complex is the weave involved.

## Established singularity

According to this type of constitution, there is one particular frame of reference which is all-determining. By its own confession it has total and exclusive validity, such that alternatives are by comparison rated as inferior. The constitution of Pakistan or Saudi Arabia, as Muslim states, reveals a singleness of purpose centred on Qur'ānic teaching and Sharia law. Limited rights may be accorded to religious minority groups both within Islam and of other faiths, but the notion of secular education or civil law independent of Islam is perceived as misleading and finally wrong (Metcalf 1983). Similarly, in the USSR before the dawn of perestroika the ideology of Marxist-Leninism has been all-pervasive (Lane 1972). In either of these settings, it is consistent with the constitution, whether Marxist or Muslim, for boys and girls to be inducted into one particular set of beliefs and values. Morality and education are alike determined by a prescriptive frame of reference that expects conformity from all its citizens and measures success in terms which derive from criteria generated from within the specific faith tradition. While not all Marxist or Muslim states would conform to the same extent to this particular paradigm, the features are without exception recognizably there.

## Secular pluralism

Typically in such a constitution there is overt acknowledgement of diversity. Instead of one particular world-view being institutionalized as predominant, several are recognized, all of which are on an equal footing in the eyes of the civil law. India or the USA in their respective constitutions show this tolerance. Thus, in the USA the national slogan *e pluribus unum* is matched by the political separation of church and state. In law, no particular faith has the pre-eminence over any of the others; nor can subsidy from the public purse be expected to support this faith rather than that. Religious education where it exists at all in the public school system is required to remain self-consciously at the level of descriptive 'teaching about'. Similarly, it is common for moral education to ignore religious reference points (Allen 1977). The Indian constitution, though different in some respects, is equally sensitive to differences of religious belief and practice found in the country at large (Smith 1963). Religion is deliberately prized, but not directly taught in schools. Social Studies is actually more likely to figure in the curriculum than either religious or moral education. In both these examples, education strives to be neutral in matters of beliefs and values at least to the extent that all religion is disestablished.

## Selective consensus

This third type is distinguished by some recognition of pluralism, but on carefully specified terms based on agreement as to shared values. Such constitutions are to be found, for example, in Indonesia and Japan. In Indonesia, under Sukarno's leadership a widely influential formulation known as the Pantha Sila was introduced. These fivefold principles of morality are an adaptation of a traditional Buddhist formulation to make them the more attractive to Muslims – are there not five pillars in Islam? – as well, and even to secular political interests – do we not all have five fingers? The first principle includes belief in one supreme God (Smith 1971). In Japan, the compromise has been shaped by the terms of the post-Second World War settlement and incorporates a secular principle counter to nationalist tradition and in education positive reference to Buddhism, Confucianism and Western Philosophy (Luhmer 1990).

The relative strengths of each of these types are easy to see, but so too are their weaknesses. *Singularity of establishment* has the advantage of clarity of focus.

In an uncertain world, such firm parameters can be very attractive. Moreover, if a particular world-view is believed to be fundamentally true and superior to other world-views, it is understandable that its followers will want its political priority to be reflected in education. *Secular pluralism,* by contrast, shows more sensitivity to the fact that human beliefs and values are themselves contentious. Failing any prospect of agreement between religions, it settles for a secular common ground. *Selective consensus* also acknowledges diversity of starting points, but looks for a highest common factor to bring together at least some secular and religious interests.

## Educational implications

For moral and religious education, however, each of these constitutional types has intrinsic problems. The *singular establishment* is flawed by the facts of human diversity. Even in individual terms it is in the nature of the human condition to be able to think discontinuous thoughts and to want not always to conform. This makes for serious difficulties for any approach to education which is constitutionally closed. Collectively, there is the further awkwardness that few societies anywhere in the world are now entirely monochrome in race, culture and religion. Reluctance to recognize this diversity will not make it go away.

Thus in Pakistan, the interests of remaining Hindus and Christians, plus the presence of secular Western thinking, form part of the national, as well as the international context, of which all Pakistani pupils need to make sense (Haq 1980).

Similarly in the USSR cultural and religious diversity has been latent for more than half a century, but is now suddenly manifest. The size of the Muslim population, as well as those of Buddhists, Christians and Jews (Barrett 1982), makes a constitutional preoccupation with atheistic materialism both blinkered and unrealistic. Only ambition for hypocrisy can insist that either moral or religious education should be indifferent to the distinctive starting points of the pupils from their various home backgrounds, or as found in other nation states.

*Secular pluralism* might seem to offer a better solution, but its appreciation of the subtlety of interplay between religions and values is at once curiously naive and relativizing. In the USA, because of the constitution there is disincentive to the schools to attend critically to parental reference points as background to either moral or religious education. In consequence, religious belief as such is not put under public scrutiny, but simply accepted whatever form it takes, without comment. By implication, one belief is much the same as another, their relevance for moral education is optional, and their overall significance apparently only relative.

In India, instead of serving to enhance mutual understanding, the official silence on religion in the curriculum may serve to reinforce communalism outside the school. The prevalent thrust from Hindus that the different paths to God and goodness are many and various may easily mutate into the different view that 'anything goes'.

The *selective consensus* goes some way to acknowledging the rootedness of values, for at least some people, in religion, but in the interests of consensus it risks blurring the distinctions between the views that it includes. At the same time, it marginalizes the rest. Thus, in Indonesia, and somewhat differently Malaysia (Mukherjee 1983), successive regimes have opted to maintain a common denominator approach, which is actually distorting in its inattention to religious difference. And in Japan the tendency is to show a common value base in which explicit religious reference becomes almost an optional extra, rather than a source of new insight or transforming challenge.

Constitutionally, the nations of the world are in mixed condition and this is reflected in the variety of approaches to moral and/or religious education that accompany them. It is very doubtful whether there is any single constitution which would satisfy all; different approaches to education will continue accordingly. However, from the three constitutional types there are at least two principles of potentially universal significance:

1. Religions/world-views can be placed on a continuum from *open-inclusive* to *closed-exclusive*. There is every likelihood that examples of both extremes and others in between will be found in any one society, sometimes, as in the case of Christianity, even within the same religion. Since the consequences of these views ramify outward into society at large as well as more specifically into education, ways and means need to be found of enabling them to subsist alongside each other in harmony or, if that is not possible, then in a tension that is more creative than destructive.
2. A second continuum is also evident from an overview of the different constitutions and traditions. It extends from theistic to non-theistic. Again, the contrasting views are found alongside each other in the same countries. The precise form of the theism may even vary within the same religion.

In any given context, the particular characteristics which predominate from each of the two ranges of attitudes interact and so provide checks on one another. To illustrate this, the two continua may be presented diagrammatically, with the different emphases relating to each other, as it were, orthogonally:

|  | Exclusive | Inclusive |
| --- | --- | --- |
| Theistic |  |  |
| Non-theistic |  |  |

Thus, there are many examples of theistic religions whose bent is to be exclusive; others quite the opposite. Similarly, non-theistic views may be held with different degrees of open- or closed-mindedness. To assume however, that moral education properly takes place only under the combined allegiance of the non-theistic inclusive is, in terms of an earlier comparison, a delusion of undressed academic proportions.

## Reforming tradition in England and Wales

Into which constitutional type does the educational provision of England and Wales fit? From the outside the answer might predictably be *established singularity*. There is an established Church of England, more than a third of the nation's primary schools are church-related, and in the majority – all the county maintained primary and secondary schools – since 1944 the Church of England has had the right to influence the local Agreed Syllabus for RE. There is even a legal requirement of a daily act of worship. It might therefore be concluded that Moral Education against this background is either in collusion with Christianity or provoked to secularity by it.

Another commentator might argue that the tradition is closer to *selective consensus*. There is a limited establishment ethos that has at least extended the Christian base to include Judaism. The Agreed Syllabus tradition for religious education was until the late 1960s a kind of selective compromise around the biblical foundations of the Jewish and Christian traditions. Margaret Thatcher's remarks fit this context well and MPs have repeatedly paid deference to the Bible as the source for the country's legal system and moral values.

It is more difficult to see the position as conforming to the *secular pluralist* type, yet some secular assumptions have a fundamental part in the educational tradition of England and Wales. Since the 1870 Education Act which introduced public funding for schools, it has been legally specified that no teacher should be put at disadvantage by virtue of his/her religious beliefs, religious education must not be distinctive of any particular denomination, and teacher and pupil (via parents) alike have the benefit of a 'conscience clause', with withdrawal rights, in the event of religious intrusion. In the course of the last decade, throughout the country a curriculum provision for Personal and Social Education (PSE) has been developed, especially in secondary schools. In effect this has often involved extensive work on value questions in the lives of pupils, at school, in preparation for employment and in relation to society at large. Generally speaking, in PSE very little has been made of religious reference points; instead, it can be argued that there has been a secularized approach to moral education. This may not be very far from a fully fledged secular pluralism!

In the light of the noticeable coincidence of all three typical ingredients here in England and Wales, the implications of the 1988 Education Reform Act are all the more significant (Marratt 1989). Its preamble includes the following requirement of the curriculum in every school in any sense maintained through public funding: it must promote 'the spiritual, moral, cultural ... development of pupils at school and of society'. This will be done through named National Curriculum subjects, plus Religious Education, required for all pupils throughout their years in school, up to when they leave at 16-plus or 18-plus.

*Christian establishment* references are in evidence, in that both aspects of RE – the teaching part and the assembling for collective worship – must include reference to Christianity. Every syllabus locally agreed for use in county schools must 'reflect the fact that the religious traditions in Great Britain are in the main Christian' and school worship must be 'wholly or mainly of a broadly Christian character'.

The *pluralist* context of British society is also recognized. Henceforth it will be illegal for a syllabus to be agreed which, in addition to Christianity, does not also 'take account of the teaching and practices of the other principal religions represented in Britain'. These are commonly understood to include Buddhism, Hinduism, Islam, Judaism, and Sikhism. Moreover, the Councils (referred to as SACREs) and Agreed Syllabus Conferences in each local Education Authority (116 in all), specially constituted to monitor RE provision and draw up syllabuses, should in their membership reflect such religious diversity as is found in their areas. In other words, the parental faith interests in all their diversity are formally acknowledged as by right providing a reference point for such work on beliefs and values as schools engage in. Members of the Royal Family have yet to marry outside the Christian tradition, but the educational establishment has become more inclusive, potentially to everyone's advantage.

From a *secular* humanist's point of view, it might at first seem as though education has become far too religious. The local SACREs may choose to co-opt a humanist representative, but they are not there 'by right'. However, the official National Criteria for Religious Studies at 16-plus include work on 'non-religious responses to contemporary moral issues both personal and social' alongside the specifically religious (DES 1985). In addition to the long-established deference to humanist conscience already mentioned, some further specification is given relating to one of the most morally and theologically contentious areas of school life – that of Collective Worship.

Worship in school is distinguished from worship in church, mosque, or gurdwara; it must not be 'denominational', and it is collective *not* corporate. It must be sensitive to the age, aptitude and family background of the pupils – in keeping with the educational priorities of the rest of the curriculum. Thus no assumptions should be made as to particular beliefs on their part. The specification created still includes a Christian reference; at least half the occasions should be 'in accord with the broad traditions of Christian belief'. But as a whole they are welcome to be open to the pupils and perspectives of other faiths, including secular humanism.

In fact, there is remarkable opportunity here for a coordinated approach to both religious and moral education across all the years of schooling. As well as class teaching time, there is an obligation on every school to attend daily to the matter of beliefs and values in the lives of all the pupils in a collective way. It can happen on a class year group, or other sectional basis, or indeed with the whole school together. Precisely because these occasions are distinguished from the acts of worship associated with a believing community, they provide scope to explore that which is of worth/worthship in an educational sense. Such 'target practice' has an intrinsic place in both moral and religious education.

Constitutionally in England and Wales, the establishment has undergone something of a long revolution since the seventeenth century. It was slowly extended in the nineteenth century to enfranchise 'Nonconformist' Christians and Roman Catholics, Jews and Atheists, previously denied the vote. In the settlements from Asia, Africa and the Caribbean it has the opportunity further to enlarge and enrich its ethnic, cultural and religious wealth. Although attitudes of officialdom have all too often been begrudging, in political terms the change has been achieved without reducing citizenship to 'guest-worker' status. Similarly, in education each of the three qualities – Christian, secular and multi-faith – is now, in principle at least, appreciated in its own right. In a striking way, this constitutional context for moral education holds together competing and complementary ways of goodness and truth.

## Autonomy of ethics and of religion in individual experience

Any reference to religion in connection with morality invites a ready philosophical rejoinder as to the autonomy of ethics. This is quite understandable, given the well-documented history of abuse of morality in the name of religion or an equivalent ideology. Words and actions, devaluing one section of the human community as compared with others, or involving human sacrifice and inquisition, can all be found thriving under religious sponsorship. Against such injustice, morality cries out to identify rights and wrongs in its own terms. It is stifled if it has no independent position of its own on which to base its moral judgement. What is good and true, is so because it proves itself on rational grounds without need of special licensing authority, whether scriptural, communal or charismatic.

Similarly, direct association of moral education with religious education can arouse strong, even resentful reactions. This is not simply because of sensitivity over private religious convictions, although that can be a factor if there is an implication that active membership of some religious community is a professional precondition for a teacher to engage in moral education. It is more a recognition of two other factors. First, religion can be a 'turn-off' in the thinking of boys and girls. Secondly, there is tremendous diversity of religious belief and unbelief; this may not only create shifting sands on which to attempt to engender intrinsic moral sense, but also entail conflicting moral prescriptions

It is one thing to accept the legitimate points being made on both these fronts; it is quite another to do so without qualification. Indeed, although references to the autonomy of religion are far less frequent than those to the autonomy of ethics, that also is a principle which warrants attention in discussions about both moral and religious education.

Attacks on the notion of autonomy in either sphere are familiar from versions of both psychology and sociology which seek to reduce moral values and religious beliefs to nothing but underlying emotional and economic drives. While recognizing the various conditioning factors that feature in moral and religious experience, educationists generally would be among the first to identify such reductionist arguments as themselves contentious. More insidious, because less blatant, is the view which presents the social sciences as methodologically atheistic in assumption. This is as questionable as claiming that they are nihilist about ethics. In both areas they are better characterized as agnostic – and relatively so.

In respect of both religious beliefs and moral values, education and the social sciences will hesitate to pronounce on the final claim to truth, or ultimate validity, of a particular starting point. What they may more appropriately admit is that religions matter in human affairs and contribute distinctively to moral life. Their autonomy, relative to one another, as also in relation to secular humanism and to the social sciences, warrants clear acknowledgement.

In spite of any inherent plausibility in this argument, there is still apprehension that reference to religion as part of the process of moral education will interfere with the integrity of the individuals involved. For the impression lingers that, whatever their protestations to the contrary, one by one, religions do not respect the independent claims of reason to be in any sense definitive in the life of each individual human being. Instead, they evade the issue of personal autonomy by 'pulling theological rank'.

Several examples of how the worth of individual experience can be put under attack in the name of religion were listed at the outset. As counters to them, it can be shown that from within the same religions there is genuine appreciation of both reason and conscience and a public commitment to their promotion.

Collectively, this has been advertised by inter-religious gatherings at an international level, focusing on such global issues as the environment, world peace, and, most recently, human rights (Küng and Moltmann 1990). These are matched at national or even more local levels by the existence of groups and networks for dialogue between two or more faiths. In the very act of conversation between representatives of the different traditions there is demonstrated both a readiness to listen to an alternative perspective and an attempt to express each faith in terms which will be intelligible outside the immediate theological circle. This in itself already shows deference to the force of reason. For there can be no real conversation between those who are deaf and unable to listen, or without the acceptance of some shared meanings on the basis of which mutual understanding is possible.

Taking each religion individually, it is possible to identify the same priority, not as some peripheral concern, but at the very heart of the faith. The famous Grand Inquisitor sequence in Dostoevsky's *Brothers Karamazov* captures how authority and autonomy may vie with each other, even from the best of intentions, within the same tradition. Those inside the tradition have the problem of resolving the tension to their own satisfaction. Those on the outside should shrink from a premature judgement which implies that human sense is always the loser.

## Christianity

In the case of Christianity, the tensions between human authority and that of the church, as between reason and revelation, have run throughout the tradition, typified by Tertullian's question: 'What has Athens to do with Jerusalem?' Quite central to a Christian's answer must be the New Testament picture of the freedom of adult humanity presented as fundamental to the gospel and the oft-repeated affirmations of natural theology with its claim that signals of transcendence are there within human self-awareness as well as in the universe at large. Equally, from within contemporary Roman Catholic teaching, there are statements regarding the rightful autonomy of science and its complementarity with faith (Flannery 1981). Orthodox and Protestant theologians would agree.

## Islam

Islam's dominant image, with others, if not also within the eyes of its own followers, invites the individual to submit his/her powers of reasoning to the overriding authority of Qur'ānic revelation. This impression is reinforced by the collection of stories and teachings of Muhammad in the Hadith, as also by the formal body of law contained in the Sharia and the role of community consensus – *ijma.* However, alongside these major sources of fundamental principle, there is a fourth – *ijtihad,* individual thought. Although this strand in Muslim thought may have been less conspicuous than some other emphases during various periods in the history of Islam, it is clear that recognition of the God-given powers of human reason and insight have a part in the tradition (Hourani 1985) and one to which increasing attention is being paid in Muslim university scholarship (Ahmed 1988).

## Marxism

If Christianity and Islam, along with Judaism, can be fairly characterized as prophetic religions, then arguably Marxism has more family resemblance with them than with Asian faiths. The interpretations of Marx's own writings, and the applications by his followers, include notorious examples of totalitarian thought control, the very antithesis of human autonomy. Even so, the newly announced glasnosticism is, in Eastern Europe at least, dissolving the externally imposed rigidities of the Marxist-Leninist frame of reference. In that respect, it is the heir to Marx as humanist, heralding the dawn of a more authentic autonomy, released from the precast impositions of state regulation and party decree (Lukes 1985).

### Hinduism and Buddhism

The Asian tradition is enormously diverse. Within Hinduism and Buddhism alone, there is considerable variation. Yet there is coherence. Special writings, even scriptures, exist in both religions and are greatly treasured; but in their proliferation, there is already a hint that revelation is more plural than singular. Indeed, though the light metaphor is here as much as in 'prophetic' religions, it is more commonly talked of as enlightenment than revelation; illumination, it seems, is more commonly from within than from on high. Such a built-in acknowledgement of inwardness ensures that individual experience qualifies for special attention in both religions.

In Hinduism the notional stages of life, *varnashramadharma*, through which a Hindu might pass, are themselves a template of individuation. Many of the conformist constraints that predominate earlier in life, along with the self-referring calculations of *karma*, are eventually transcended in the journey towards personal release. The heightened consciousness involved may be perceived quite differently from Western notions of autonomy, nevertheless there is no intrinsic antipathy to reason, even when transformed by spiritual knowledge (Smart 1968a).

In Buddhism the goal of enlightenment is a lifelong ambition. There is an evident ambivalence between the desire for merit acquisition on the one hand and for nirvana on the other (Spiro 1982). The one might appear as self-promoting while the other, quite literally, involves the cooling-out of self. Yet at root, there is a common thrust of moral reason that sets its priorities within a frame of compassion (Green 1978a).

In sum, contrary to superficial impressions, both religion and ethics figure autonomously in human experience throughout the world. This is true, whether they are looked at individually, or viewed as a whole. Moreover, they provide mutual reference points, so that in the name of moral worth some particular aspect of a religion may be interrogated; or vice versa, the morality of specific deeds and intentions put under religious scrutiny. There is no fixed format for morality, which can be instantly distilled from all the different world-views, religious and secular, no more than there is a perennial mystical essence of all religions. Yet, in reason, they share a common language, whose workings may be traced through comparative study as entailing trans-cultural continuities more empirically rooted than otherwise speculative talk of natural law. Their joint relevance for the enterprise of moral education, therefore, warrants practical attention to match what may otherwise remain a matter only of abstract observation. To this end, the collaboration, at a local level as in SACREs, of teachers, parents and politicians of quite different faith persuasions, in making provision for both moral and religious education, is a sign of healthy development.

## Conclusion: prerequisites for human fulfilment

It is easy to claim too much for education. At the same time, it is hard to avoid seeing the human predicament as superabundant in its promise and yet perilously close to devastation. Central to this condition is the matter of beliefs and values. As well as in the realm of personal meaning, they are fundamental also to political life, as constituted nationally and internationally. Equally, they are basic to education. Therefore, what constitutional congruence can be achieved for religion and morality, in terms of both political life and educational provision, has significance beyond exaggeration. Even Prime Ministers and Presidents may be able to learn a thing or two from so enriched a moral education.

(1990)

Chapter 18

# RE needs moral education, ME needs religious education

**Once upon a time ...**

Adam Everyman and Eve Everywoman were naively, incurably religious

- they believed in some mysterious reality/all powerful force that had given rise to the universe and life within it, and their own particular lives
- they took it for granted that this Force was present in nature – in wind, water, fire, mountains in the fortunes of their lives – from birth to death, in sickness and health, poverty and prosperity
- the ways of the Force were mightily mysterious, but partly made plain in special messages received in dreams and trances, or through gifted middle-men and, more occasionally middlewomen
- some of the messages were written down and preserved as extra-special. These writings described in some detail the Way of the Force and how Adam and Eve should behave for their own fulfilment and in appreciation of the Force of truth and justice

Adam and Eve knew that they could move closer to the Force by following this Way, and by deliberate words and actions by which they gave themselves symbolically to the Force – the source and destination of their lives.

**The story continues ...**

That was before Adam and Eve grew up. Now they've grown out of all these primitive, childish views. Religion has been left behind in the infancy of the human race

- the universe, is the universe, is the universe – it may be vast and complex, but any mystery about it is giving way to human knowledge and science
- wind, water, fire and mountain are real enough, but there's no rhyme or reason in them as such; drought and famine are savage and reveal the capriciousness of nature that needs to be brought under human control
- health is largely a matter of personal diet, hygiene and conduct – smoking when pregnant could be the death in the long run of both mother and child; but that is of their making and certainly not 'intended' by any external

Force as punishment for wrongdoing any more than Aids is typically retribution for moral delinquency
- dream and other works of the imagination in poems, plays and paintings are entertaining and illuminating, and with them the range of special writings from the past, but they are all time-bound and likely therefore to be surpassed in each new age
- any traditional pattern of behaviour/code for living is of antiquarian interest, but the changing circumstances of life demand that the decisions are taken afresh about how to live in tune with the present. To help with this, common-sense ideas of justice for all and scientifically tested truth can be relied on

Adam and Eve may yet find themselves in a world of perfect harmony, a worldwide Garden of Eden; what's needed to make it happen is clearer thinking and more disciplined effort.'

Even if this story is not an exact match for those professionally involved in the field of moral education in the western world, the correspondence with a dominant ethos within it is real. This assertion is based on professional involvement with moral education in the UK since the mid-1960s, and on attendance at the annual conference of the Association for Moral Education (see AME website: www.amenetwork.org) for over a decade. I have been aware of a tendency either to ignore Religious Education as on different tracks from Moral Education, or even to dismiss it as based on illusory foundations. There have been exceptions, but particularly from US colleagues I have been aware of what has seemed almost to be a fear of contamination from church or other religious connections. As with responses to some manifestations of character education, it has been as though the sweet reasonableness of values clarification and ethics in the curriculum has been perceived as under the threat of corruption from the dubious predilictions of religion. Or at least that religion is simply best kept out of the public domain.

One element in this attitude may well be sensitivity to the separation of church and state in the American constitution, and the consequent avoidance of RE in the public school system of many states. But that cannot be the whole story. In some, albeit few, states there is deliberate encouragement of teaching *about* religion. Nearer to home, in England the sentiments behind the 1960's Campaign to replace RE with Moral Education were subsequently evident in connection with some involved in the promotion of Active Tutorial Work and Personal and Social Education in the 1980s, and more recently on the part of influential advocates of Citizenship Education (Crick 1998, Hargreaves 1990, 1994; see Jackson 2003: ch. 4). Moreover, in spite of substantial evidence of effective and popular RE, the prevailing cultural impression as conveyed in the media has been one which combined ignorance with indifference regarding the proper significance of RE.

So recurrent is this pattern that I am inclined to think that more powerful intellectual and emotional forces, even prejudices, may be at work. Crudely speaking, this is the picture which emerges:

> The Autonomy of Ethics became a post-Enlightenment watchword. All elements of external deference in matters of moral principle were presented as secondary. This was true with parental prohibition, with public opinion and also with religion. They were all superseded in moral debate by appeal instead to the intrinsic authority of ethics defining itself according to its own logic and rationality.

I am not for a moment denying the legitimacy of the position which takes its stand on the internal coherence and consistency of moral arguments. My complaint arises only when that affirmation is made exclusively of other considerations.

The image of religion came off the worse in this exchange. In this respect Erich Fromm is a representiative advocate: religious ethics are quintessentially authoritarian (Fromm 1942, 1967). Look at the Decalogue. Look at the Qur'ān. But also at the Laws of Manu and the weighted expectation of any other religious tradition. Obedience to the external other is problematic, just as when the religious authority is secularized but yet maintaining equivalent clout as in the rule of Hitler or Stalin. If there had been any remaining doubt about it, 'obeying orders' as a potential moral stance was totally discredited by the Third Reich.

Lawrence Kohlberg knew this well and was determined to demonstrate an alternative moral way. Hence, it was important for him to be able to demonstrate the positive correlation between those dissenting in the Milgram experiment and high-stage thinking (Kohlberg and Candee 1984: 546–8). Even so, there is evidence that his bracketing of religion was a point of vulnerability in his system – so Thomas Kalam's work in Kerala, where he could work simultaneously with Muslim, Hindu and Christian subjects and control the religious variable (Kalam 1981; see above, pp. 154–5). The late appearance of Stage 7, encouraged by an audience of Roman Catholic educators, only served to illustrate the need for reconceptualization on his part, or on the part of those who would follow him (Kohlberg 1974, Kohlberg and Power 1981).

The Vancouver AME Conference of 2001 was in the immediate wake of 9/11. That event erupted dramatically on to the ME forecourt. It did so in striking fear into the hearts of those who did and did not travel to AME then or since. It did so in drawing attention to precariousness in the midst of any apparent security in modern life. And it also did so in drawing attention to the power of religious passion to challenge the established order of society.

I said as much at the time. Such religious passion in this particular instance maybe a perversion of authentic Islam. But such has been no less visible in Christian crusades or the Papal '*fatwah*' against the Queen of England in the sixteenth century. The Gunpowder Plot to blow up the Houses of Parliament was yesterday's Christian equivalent of plotting to destroy the Twin Towers. If that is a shocking comparison, then put it differently. In local and global terms, the naked have not all been clothed, the hungry not all fed, and the fact that there are now more people in prison in the Western world than have been gaoled throughout the whole of human history doesn't mean that they are all very generously visited. According to both the Gospels and the Qur'án, these failings warrant hellish punishment. The perversion is that prophetic hyperbole affirming divine prerogative has been literalized and appropriated for human implementation.

Although it is my impression that there was more visible acknowledgement of the significance of religion in relation to the springs of moral action in presentations given at more recent AME conferences, that is not true of the all the subsequent annual centrepiece Kohlberg lectures. For instance, at the Chicago 2002 conference, Elliot Turiel chose to ignore any distinctive Christian, Jewish and Muslim ingredients present in the autobiographical events he recounted in favour of more material determinants (Turiel 2003). Yet, his vaunted examples include Martin Luther King Jr, Gandhi, Druze Muslims and Fatima Mernissi, for all of whom social and political discernment, as expressed in resistance and subversion in everyday life, are a rooted in religious faith (Mernissi 1996).

## Doing things differently

This brings me to the main thesis: locally, regionally and globally, it is not in our human interests, both personal and communal, that approaches to ME and RE should continue in isolation one from another. Why? Because it is evident that religion spills into ethical consequences, and sometimes in morally questionable ways. It is equally evident that ethics draw inspiration from deepest wells of human being wherein our hopes and fears, the beliefs and values which matter most to us, reside.

There is an integrity in the autonomy of ethics. There is an integrity also in the autonomy of religion. However, the intrinsic connections between their two realms require them to be mutually attentive and indeed challenging the one of the other. Their respective autonomies are yet relative to each other.

Instead, two patterns of curriculum provision commonly predominate: *parallel play* and *mutual substitution*. In the former – typified in the USA – Moral Education in one guise or another has a significant presence throughout publicly funded education. By contrast Religious Education does not, but features instead in denominationally based provision. While they may play enjoyably alongside each other, their interaction one with another is minimal.

In the latter – typical in much of Europe – publicly funded Religious Education is controlled by the faith community, and in the event of its not being wanted it is replaced by an alternative Ethics provision. The one in effect is understood to be substitute for the other, in accord with preferences relating to parental beliefs. This pattern is found in several of the German Länden in which the RE syllabus has been controlled respectively by the Lutheran or Roman Catholic dioceses, with Ethics available as a secular humanist alternative. It has also appeared as a norm in the Eastern European countries, where, freed from the ideological yoke of state communism, Catholicism has provided the norm for RE in, for instance, Poland and Orthodoxy in Russia.

Moreover, the strains of mutual substitution have carried over into the reluctance of the European Union, at least until very recently, to speak positively about the importance of attention to religion in education. Two forces have predominated – French secularity and Roman Catholic propriety – with the combined effect that no independent and educationally grounded approach to religion in state-funded schools was considered worthy of support by the EU Council of Ministers. Instead, if religion was to feature at all, it would better be under the heading of culture/intercultural understanding.

This is disturbing – personally, politically and theologically. The stakes are too high for education to be providing such productive opportunities for misunderstanding and caricature and to be failing both to put the organic process of belief and value formation under full critical scrutiny and to guarantee it appropriate resourcing.

## A. Ignorance breeds insensitivity and can kill

Let's remind ourselves of the risks which arise from both religious and moral ignorance.

### 1. It can create a climate within which prejudice can fester with deadly consequences.

There is abundant evidence of prejudice in the name of religion, which would be exposed as a distortion of the religion in question by effective public provision for RE for all.

- From Northern Ireland, we have seen pictures of sectarian abuse of children outside the Holy Cross Primary School in 2001, prompting the cartoon caption: 'We had RE on the way to school' (for photos see www.time.com/time/photoessays/belfast/index.html). In 2006, many years after the Good Friday Peace Accords were signed, the fence separating the two communities in Belfast is in places now higher than it was before they were signed.
- From, for example, England, France and Poland, there are still attacks on Jewish cemeteries, deploying the well-known anti-Semitic imagery from yesteryear; there is also the widespread recirculation throughout the Middle East of that notorious forgery, *The Protocols of Elders of Zion* (Ben-Itto 2005). Anti-Semitism in the past has thrived especially on both Christian

and Muslim soil, and continues to do so. To this is added the new current of Islamophobia (Ramji 2005, Allen 2005).

In Europe, alongside continuing suspicions of Jews, in part accentuated by Israeli government policies, but still rooted in ignorance of Judaism, there are also suspicions of Muslims. These are highlighted by the violence of a minority, but actually reveal an ignorance of mainstream Islam. There are failures to recognize that female circumcision has no support within the Qur'ān, Hadith and Sharia; or to distinguish between 'arranged' and 'forced' marriages. Similarly, in India, there is dangerous ignorance. Though living cheek by jowl, including many instances of the celebration of each other's festivals (Katz 2004) inherited stereotypes of the other as Hindu or Muslim or Sikh still so easily in ignorance contort their individual humanity. Neither Africa (see the religious divide in Nigeria, or the Lord's Resistance Army in Uganda) nor China (see the fate of Falun Gong, or the policy towards Tibetan Buddhism) shows signs of being free from religious ignorance.

## 2. It can insulate a religious community from any need directly to face genuine moral challenges to its own operation

- For all its own protestations of peace, any morally educated outsider will point out that religion often appears to promote war: Holy warring – crusades as mentioned already and jihads; indeed the notion of *holocaust* has Biblical endorsement, in the sense of a requirement that every living being in an enemy city shall be eliminated in its entirety in an act of consecrated sacrifice (Joshua 6: 18–24; Vaux 1961: ch. 5).
- Similarly, she/he will remark that religion has a visibly strong track record of patriarchal thinking: the second-class status of women has thrived within its institutional orbit and continues to do so. The impurities associated with menstruation and even childbirth have played their part in this, and the track record of individual world religions on this front makes salutory reading.
- She/he may also observe that religious institutions can be highly hypocritical in the self-serving ways in which they seek to protect themselves from scandal, as in such instances as the Roman Catholic church's dealing with priests involved in child sexual abuse, or Hindu communal leaders in particular states in India playing down the lack of attention shown to children born with physical disabilities, or to the increasing imbalance of male children as far fewer baby girls become live births even though abortion and infanticide are at odds with a tradition that so values non-violence.

Both effective RE and effective ME have public interest grounds for challenging these manifestations in religious tradition.

### 3. Ignorance of religious vitality can be the occasion of an impoverished understanding of ethics

Why should I be bothered to love my neighbour?

- Motives and intentions are fundamental to the springs of moral action; it is no coincidence that *individuals inspired by religious conviction* stand out historically in the promotion of social justice and human compassion. This is true of key figures in the emergence of particular religious traditions, and without claiming a monopoly past or present for those with formal religious inspiration, it would be arbitrary to claim that such a resonance had ceased to exist. Learning from example remains a powerful prompt in the caring for others.
- Equally powerful is the fact that bothering to love anyone other than self, or self and particular friends, depends upon a conviction that it is right so to do. That conviction is a form of faith. *Although the faith may not always be theistic, it is centred in the same gut area as religious sentiment.* 'At the end of the day', 'when the crunch comes', 'when the chips are down' – these are all expressions of what, as an act of considered judgement and of faith, really matters. Motives make a difference.
- Rules, procedures and legislation provide important guidelines for human behaviour, but *religious experience warns that legalism* and literal compliance may unimaginatively constrict the inclination to act compassionately.
- Doing what appears to be right may easily involve the deception of both self and others; *sensitivity to hypocrisy* is not only exposed by the gospels, it is there in the teachings of Muhammad in the Hadith and of the Buddha.
- Short-termism is the subject of criticism in some moral perspectives, but attention to the full range of impact of every single word and action as they ripple their effect on others is magnified in religious traditions, with their talk of the big picture – *sub specie aeternitatis*, judgement beyond death, as in the long-term future of lives following on lives, or simply crossing into another dimension.

Moral Education is the poorer if it fails to acknowledge that there are distinctive sources and resources in religion and RE with which ethics and ME may be properly enriched.

## B. Religion featuring in all the modes of moral thinking

There is no denying that religious ethics often manifest themselves in the heteronomous mode of moral thinking. However, that does not exempt the determining authority of that other source from moral scrutiny on other grounds. Nor does it mean that religious ethics are confined to that mode. A fuller and more genuinely representative interweaving of religious and moral frames of reference can perhaps most conveniently be illustrated by invoking the fourfold classification of moral thinking: other-obeying, other-considering, self-obeying and self-considering (so, originally, Peck and Havighurst 1960, Williams and Williams 1970). Set out orthogonally, it looks like this:

|  | OBEYING | CONSIDERING |
|---|---|---|
| OTHER | **Heteronomous** | **Altruistic** |
| SELF | **Intuitive** | **Prudential** |

Where do religiously inspired ethics fit here? As mentioned earlier, a secularist view might well be that they are decidedly heteronomous and other-obeying, and the more defective because of it. However, taking the Decalogue (Exodus 20: 1–17), what do we find? Its main ingredients are familiar beyond the Jewish and Christian communities:

1. Worship only God
2. Beware idolizing what's of lesser significance
3. Don't abuse that which is God's authority
4. Observe the principle of sabbath recreation
5. Respect those who parented you
6. Do not murder
7. Do not betray marital trust
8. Do not steal
9. Do not misrepresent others
10. Don't envy what's properly others'

Analysed orthogonally, the 'command mode' is clear – albeit with a relative balance of 'Dos' and 'Don'ts'. Yet that is not the only operational mode. That of self-considering prudence also figures, in the shape of both threat and promise. The carrot is the prospect of living longer – and in a promised land, but the stick is that punishment will work itself out over several generations. The altruistic mode is also there in the encouragement to be attentive to the needs and interests of others. And, fourthly, there is expectation that recognition of the intrinsic rightness and wrongness will be part of the total response which will include the voluntary appropriation of the whole commitment. The authoritative interpreters of both the Jewish and Christian traditions would certainly resist any reduction of the moral reasoning involved merely to authoritarian ethics.

|  | **OBEYING** | **CONSIDERING** |
|---|---|---|
| OTHER | Heteronomous<br><br>DON'T! | Altruistic<br><br>SHOW REGARD TO OTHERS' INTERESTS |
| SELF | **Intuitive**<br><br>RECOGNIZING INTRINSIC RIGHT | **Prudential**<br><br>YOU'LL LIVE LONGER! |

It is too much of an oversimplification to categorize and dismiss all this as no more than 'the Divine Command' version of ethics. That is certainly part of the picture – the sense of moral ought comes from outside the individual, for the theist comes indeed from God, but it is also known from within, in terms of what might be called conscience (or mindfulness). There is deliberate use of reasoned self-interest – other-considering behaviour is a self-rewarding activity, and at the same time it matters in its own terms. Wider scrutiny shows that religious ethics are more multi-layered and sophisticated than some philosophers have acknowledged.

This is no less evident when the same analysis is applied also beyond the Judaeo-Christian tradition:

|       | OBEYING | CONSIDERING |
|-------|---------|-------------|
| **OTHER** | **Heteronomous** | **Altruistic** |
|       | The Priest, the Guru, the Imam says so. Decreed by Umma, Sangha or obligations of caste. This is what the Gita/Qurān/Adi Granth teaches. | Love of neighbour; care for poor, the sick, the stranger and lonely. Life of Muhammad, Way of the Buddha. Self-sacrifice of Krishna. |
| SELF | **Intuitive** | **Prudential** |
|       | 'I can do no other'; 'It's just wrong I know deep down'; mindful compassion, conscience, voice of God within, eternal Tao. | Prospects beyond death: heaven/hell, higher/lower being; impact on children/ succeeding generations. |

## An academic context

In academic terms, 'relative autonomy' is a more justifiable way of characterizing the relationship between religion and ethics than either of the two more usual ones. That which favours the word 'heteronomy' whenever religious language is deployed in relation to ethics misses the point that the intentional springs of moral action are rooted in fundamental belief and world-view. Theistic or otherwise, these deepest personal convictions as held by an individual take on the force of religion. Globally, given the extent of religious self-identification in virtually every country, is very likely that for many their moral sense will be informed by explicit religious exemplification and teaching. The judgement that every individual who draws on such reference points and sources of inspiration must by definition be acting in a way that disregards rational reflection betrays a certain arrogance of judgement. That judgement may even invite the person making it to examine where they get their own values from and how and why at the end of the day they are known to be right and put into practice.

The other usual characterization of ethics as singularly autonomous makes the important clarification that there is a distinctive logic of moral discourse which has its own consistency, coherence and integrity. Easy dismissal of this mode of reasoning must accept the charge of being careless of legitimate attempts to critique personal or social, political or religious, behaviour and beliefs. Invocation of external authorities, in a way that 'trumps' the force of reason, must by definition be showing indifference to common human sense. Thus, where this happens in the case of institutional religion, it has made itself immune from any application of critical scrutiny which relies on evidence which it has not itself been responsible for generating. That smacks of an arrogance which has deceived itself into thinking that it alone has an absolute authority to know what is best.

By contrast, to speak of the relative autonomy of each of these fields of human experience is a 'self-denying ordinance' on the part of both ethics and religion which serves to guard against their self-inflation. It does not preclude the fact that convictions may take on an overtly secularist form and reject all religious claims to truth as by definition necessarily false (autonomy made ultimate). Nor does it deny that some believers do operate with the assumptions that there is no truth outside their own special sphere (heteronomy made ultimate). However, it affirms that in the interests of mutual understanding within and between nations, cultures and religions, there is available a common language for learning that people have been using in different societies throughout the centuries, and which both ME and RE can and should draw.

The classical western version of this tradition is called natural law and it was the means developed by Graeco-Roman philosophers for combining the oneness of the empire with the plurality of its many nations and cultures. Less well known in the west, but no less powerful is the comparable Indian tradition of *sanatana dharma* or the Chinese *Tao*. Anthropologists too have drawn attention to recurrent motifs across cultures. A convenient exposition of such thinking is found in C. S. Lewis' *Abolition of Man* (Lewis 1947: Appendix).

Another manifestation of attempts to identify common ground without denying difference can be found in the seventeenth-century Parliament of Religions initiative of Nicola de Cusa. It was followed through in Chicago in 1894 and again in 1994, and its explicit engagement with ethics has been given renewed momentum in the work of Hans Küng and Kuschel on Global Ethics (1993). Though not without its critics, especially in judgements made regarding the interests of other living creatures than humans, as also regarding norms for sexual behaviour, this shared vision has received strong international and inter-religious endorsement.

There may be no definitive refutation in all of this against the risks of ethical or religious relativism. However, there are practical experiences that challenge their more shallow expressions which leave everything to individual taste, so that moral values have no more efficacy than a fleeting fashion choice, with religions as accompanying flavours of the moment. For instance, such dismissive scepticism does not fit at all easily with experience of the shared rationality behind international aviation regulations. Without them and their well-tried presuppositions, people would not be able to fly within and between countries with any degree of safety. Here is a universally recognized fact of life – today's secular reality.

That secularity, based as it is on common-sense reasoning, is a healthy bulwark against any indifferent relativism. It is spelt out in regulations and law, and is no less important to religion than it is to ethics. It is neither anti-religious nor, from the viewpoint of the religious believer, is religion incidental to it. For this public use of reason transcends the particular individual, nation and race. Its capacity may be appreciated as no less God-given than special revelation in Scriptures. There is a strong case that scientific developments thrived in the eleventh-century Muslim world, or the seventeenth-century Christendom precisely because of the mutuality of faith and reason. In the same way, for public health provision, law courts, leisure facilities, working routines to operate without the need for separate religious sponsorship does not mean that they must now be anti-religious. For from the viewpoint of the religious believer, they, like scientific research and discovery, are only possible because of an original and continuing gift 'from beyond'. Secularity in this sense is good, and by definition still open to moral challenge from other revelatory sources which also use the discourse of public reasoning.

To describe the academic or educational context as secular should not mean that religion is devalued or discounted. That would be a more exclusive secularist stance which closes off all alternative claims to truth. In technical terms 'methodological atheism' would have replaced the openness of 'methodological agnosticism'. The use of the word secular in connection with the Indian constitution is precisely to affirm the impor-tance of religions and to avoid singular entrenchment in one religion or indeed secularism (Baird 1992: 141–69). This arguably is also the intent of the American constitution, to recognize the plurality of 'sects' and 'civil authority' (Huntington 2004: ch. 5). But the logic of this secularity is that it should take seriously the study of both ethics and religion at the heart of its educational system

## To what then does all this add up?

I would strongly advocate that it is in everyone's interests that there be universal provision for Religious and Moral Education throughout all publicly funded education. Moral Education which brackets the relative autonomy of religion risks becoming very thin soup. Religious Education which brackets the relative autonomy of ethics risks an arrogance which will undercut its own integrity. Together they carry a powerful capacity for personal and social transformation within which compassion, courage, fairness and truth can thrive.

To be sure, there are constitutional sensitivities involved for the USA, but so there are too throughout the European Union, as for instance in France and Austria, also for India, for China and Saudi Arabia. They are complex and not easily solved. But to think that by ignoring religious claims to truth the world will become more just and peaceful is an illusion. Take the example of Jerusalem. It can never belong solely to Israel or Palestine. Its sovereignty, for the sake of all the people of the region – Jew and Muslim, Christian and Druze, secularist and Samaritan – must be seen as residing 'beyond them' all, though also shared within.

By the same token public religious education must take on the challenge of being 'passionately impartial'. Bringing to life each other's faith, understanding it in its own terms, putting their claims under critical scrutiny, and at the same time being open to their challenge and transforming capacities. Here, I would argue, is the surest way I know to comprehensive moral enrichment.

## Another instalment

Adam Everyman and Eve Everywoman came to recognize that not everyone understands the world the way they do. They even acknowledged that they did not totally agree with each other in some respects. Reflectively, they came to see religion in a different light:

- Take the universe, why is it here at all? How does there come to be anything when there might only be nothing, no one and nowhere?
- The natural environment can indeed be blindly harsh and brutal, but overall it shows extraordinary beauty, sequencing and interdependence. Caprice there apparently may be, but pattern and purpose as well.
- There's certainly human behaviour which only the word evil can describe, and some of it is done in the name of religion, but the most passionate critiques and drives which challenge evil share common ground with religious believers, who respond with comparable, even pioneering, vigour. Though different, perhaps after all ethics and religion alike rely on some deep sense of trust?
- Disease is horrible, premature death even more so, but health and healing are also astonishing, both that which is genetically given and that which human ingenuity can co-create. An apple if it is sour can give belly ache, as can greedy scoffing, or an unseen worm. But it has the capacity to grow and we to eat, and without ambiguity life might never be, or have its richness.
- Inspirational insights in the artistic expressions of theatre, cinema and concert hall may not last for ever, but there are many which do pass the test of time; their revelatory force is a reminder that special revelation does not need to remain simply as past-historic in what it has to say.

– The core beliefs of the world's religions share a profound sense of ought; might it be that they have some relevant expertise in the education of conscience?

With hearts and minds wide open, Adam and Eve realize that they cannot stop wondering ...

(2003)

# PART FOUR

# Collective worship

There is a sense of incongruity surrounding both the historical existence and present continuation of an activity called worship in the context of publicly funded education. It is felt to be odd by many within the UK, and perhaps even more so by those in other countries. Accordingly, it is important to provide a contextual comment on how and why it comes to be there.

## How does there come to be worship in state schools?

Before 1870 most schools were church sponsored; worship was part of the rhythm of the school day. After 1870, when churches and state together took on joint responsibility for the nation's educational needs, the tradition was continued in both board and church schools. Only in 1944 was an act of daily worship (subject to a conscience clause for teachers and parents) made legally obligatory in all publicly funded schools. This italicizing of Religious Education – the teaching part RI, and the assembling part Collective Worship – arose from the conviction that the prizing of shared beliefs and values would inspire new generations to resist the threat of totalitarian philosophies such as Nazism.

## Given religious diversity, is this not naively unrealistic?

The challenge in the mid-twentieth century was to work with a context whose differences were substantially shaped by the Judaeo-Christian tradition, with its considerable denominational diversity, plus both questioning and rejection of it. As expounded in Part One, in respect of the teaching, the Agreed Syllabus tradition of RE was expressly designed to appreciate local diversity and resolve its tensions. The much greater religious diversity, which has developed since 1944, is why the 1988 ERA reiterated the importance of local consensus, and also made it illegal for a syllabus to concentrate exclusively on Christianity. The development of the non-statutory National Framework for RE took that further in 2004. In curriculum teaching, Religious Education is now deliberately inclusive of mainstream religious traditions as found within the UK.

By contrast, comparable development relating to the collective worship strand of religious education has been more limited. Chapter 19 indicates many of the academic and professional sensitivities which were being increasingly articulated from the 1970s onwards. They remain no less real now in the twenty-first century, and in many ways more acutely so.

Attempts were made in the year leading to the formulation of the 1988 Education Reform Act to introduce greater changes to the legal specifications requiring worship, such that educational priorities would be evidently paramount. Other pressures, however, proved more powerful, with the result that for the first time the word 'Christian' was added to the legal requirement for worship, whereas previously the provision had been left undefined. In the associated political tussle, a powerful lobby sought to introduce Christian liturgy as daily normative for all schools. This was only avoided by the use of convoluted wording in the ERA which speaks of 'wholly or mainly of a broadly Christian kind'. This was proposed by the educational leadership of the Church of England, which was opposed to any denominational narrowing (Alves 1991). In retrospect this point is missed and it is often dismissed as gobbledegook.

Chapter 20 goes behind this controversy by focusing on what worship might mean to the learner in school. It is followed by some further observations on best options ahead which take account of current arguments and interests. Chapter 21 takes stock of the curremt postition in 2007 and projects possible ways forwards.

Chapter 19

# School assemblies and the boundaries of moral education

The setting is the large hall of a primary school.[1] Over a hundred children, their teachers, and a handful of parents are gathered for the Friday mid-morning assembly.

The teacher who is leading the assembly invites the infants to guess what the assembly is about from the mimes of the older children during the first HYMN.

MIME: Two children enter, sit at table, eat, get up, wash at chair (sink), and clean teeth. Infants successfully interpret the actions in their own words.

The teacher then announces that the assembly is on the theme of teeth and a board is turned round to reveal some children's paintings.

Several children in succession come to the front and read various pieces of information, which they have written out, on teeth.

Other children file through the hall carrying large cardboard teeth, corresponding with the particular type mentioned by the (child) narrator: together they form the plan of a mouthful of teeth.

The narrator points to a diagram of a tooth pinned to the blackboard and another child describes it.

Lower junior children then file to the front holding pictures of food; they sit in front of the teeth while the song 'Food, glorious food' is playing.

Another child appears, sits in front of the others, and recites the poem 'I wish I'd looked after my teeth ...'.

He is then inspected by the girl dentist; she checks each of his teeth in turn.

The group of children who had previously read out information on teeth now return with further information, this time about how teeth decay, what to eat and what not to eat.

The dentist explains how to brush teeth and how often to go for a check-up.

The teacher then invites everyone to PRAY
– giving thanks for dentists and toothpaste
– asking to be reminded to clean teeth
– asking to be reminded to eat properly
– giving thanks for teeth
– thinking about the school and all who spend their days in it

A child reads his own account of his last trip to the dentist.

All join in singing a second HYMN: 'I love the sun', including a verse about God making our teeth.

The teacher explains that her class have also been doing maths on the topic of teeth.

Two children appear with charts: one is a bar graph showing which is the most popular toothpaste in the class; the other shows how many points (two a day for two weeks) each child in the class has earned for cleaning teeth.

Children with maximum points are invited to the front and applauded by the other children.

Final message from teacher: visit your dentist; watch what you eat; take your toothpaste and brush on holiday with you!

Such an assembly as this can be found in any day of the week in primary schools throughout England and Wales. Not least because of seating constraints, any secondary school variant might involve only a section of the school at any one time. Yet in one shape or another, an assembly regularly takes place, albeit with differences degrees of frequency, in the majority of schools, with a similar mixture of ingredients.[2]

Reaction from an outsider will be predictably varied. An immediately critical judgement might begin by commenting that the presentation is too orchestrated and lacking in spontaneity, the tone is moralistic and, worst of all, there is confusion between belief in God and the need for dental hygiene. More positively, it might be remarked that here there is demonstrably a 'prizing of persons'. The children are involved in an occasion which encourages them to express themselves in public; care has been taken in the preparation and this is reflected in the stimuli and modes of expression that are used; and the whole experience is earthed in the children's own experience. Moreover, the clarity and warmth which are high priorities in any interpersonal morality of communication are much in evidence.

Judgements like these abound within the teaching profession, reflecting a genuine ambivalence as to the worth of assemblies. Their persistence, however, is hardly surprising in view of the tradition behind them (see Hull 1975b, Jones 1969). They were legally underwritten by the 1944 Education Act, but ante-date the establishment of Board School Education in 1870. Records suggest that, if anything, they have become the more elaborate over the years.[3] The government for its part has loosened the legal tightness of 'all together every day', while encouraging schools to maintain this communal expression of their ethos (DES 1969). Thus, school assemblies, religious education and moral education are part of some peculiar English and Welsh mix.

Yet that very mix can be painfully embarrassing. The telling portraits in the films *If* and *Kes* are matched in a wide range of educationist opinion from the last decade or so, culminating in John Hull's *School Worship: An Obituary.*[4] Where some have been keen to campaign for abolition, others have demanded as a preliminary the clarification of intent (aims and objectives), and warned against category confusion: What is an assembly? What is worship?

With those questions in mind, it is worth rehearsing the views that are forth-coming from the different educational disciplines. Somewhat artificially, they can be represented as follows:

**Sociologist:**
1. Don't be misled by appearances. Watch out for the latent as well as the manifest functions of assemblies in school. In particular, notice how the occasion can be used to underwrite the authority and position of the headteacher. One can learn a great deal about the character and structure of a particular school from the way the assemblies are organized.
2. No community known to humankind has been without its rites and rituals, its moments of anniversary, memorial and celebration – family birthday parties, weddings and funerals; the national equivalents; May Day parades, religious festivals. These are marks of the identity of that community. Where they wither and decay, so too the community itself may be withering, or at least undergoing major change. In that a school strives to be a community it is invariably involved in ritual actions. The problem then is to distinguish between ritual which authentically declares the special identity of this particular group of teachers and pupils, and ritual which is little more than an empty shell taken over second-hand.

**Psychologist:**
1. Don't be misled by appearances. When children go through the motions of an assembly, they may well be missing as persons. Concentration span is limited, especially when a reading is long and droning, and the floor uncomfortable. The range of individual levels of understanding at an assembly is enormous; how is it possible to reach them all?

2. Don't underestimate the importance of a sense of belonging in the process of individual becoming. Some opportunity for a boy or girl to see themselves in relation to both older and younger children – whether idolizing, fearing, imitating or caring – is as fundamental as the experience of being mothered and fathered.

**Philosopher:**

1. Don't be misled by appearances. An assembly to deal with notices and matters of organization is one thing, an Act of Worship is quite another. There is no justification for this in a county maintained school, law or no law. If it is compulsory, then it is immoral and offensive to individual conscience. If voluntary, then it is divisive. Either way, it is out of place in state maintained schools.
2. But an assembly of part or of the whole school can be of great educational value. If, that is, it takes seriously the differences of belief and unbelief found within the school, and then goes on to explore the different values associated with them. Throughout the curriculum, throughout the individual lives of teachers and pupils, there are presuppositions, loyalties, commitments, customs, doubts – all worth exploring, whether in the form of individual teacher, pupil, class, or subject presentation. The assembly then becomes an occasion for focusing attention on the issues and values at the heart of the school as community – for exploring them, bemoaning or celebrating them.

**Theologian:**

1. Don't be misled by appearances. An act of genuine worship is not fairly represented by a hymn–prayer sandwich. This is as distant from the real thing as it is from the multimedia mediaeval Christian liturgy, or the rhythm of an African tribal festival. Religious communities are increasingly more aware of this in their own lives and can reflect it in their own educational provisions.
2. It is theologically blasphemous, in any setting, to suppose that one can compel a person to worship. In a mixed society, it is hard to find theological justification for regular acts of Christian worship in secular schools. At the same time, school assemblies without either hymns or prayers can still be complementary to a spirit of worship, especially if they provide encouragement for dwelling on matters of substance in the life of the school.
3. Such alternative assemblies might well on occasion involve stories, music, drama, dance drawn from particular religious traditions. From time to time, there might be demonstrations by groups of believers from within the school of their own modes of worship; even on occasion attempts at some deliberately inter-faith presentation. For without some opportunity to put themselves in the shoes of those who would worship, any child is probably missing out on forms of understanding and experience that she/he might find both personally enriching and theologically challenging.

Quite how typical are the views sketched here as from the different disciplines, is open to debate. It certainly is current orthodoxy[5] that the formal act of worship in school lacks the proper educational grounds now widely credited to both religious and moral education.[6] Although any orthodoxy deserves to be questioned, in this case it also deserves to be more widely canvassed for staff-room discussion, and with it the kinds of positive alternatives which have also been mentioned.

With that prospect in mind, what might now be said about the significance of assemblies for moral education? It may help to maintain the convention of different educational perspectives and to list their questions and comments in turn.

From both philosopher and theologian we hear: 'Is the school making a proper distinction between secular assemblies and acts of worship? There is much that can be contributed to moral education from secular assemblies, for instance in the priority that is given to sharing – of ideas, interests, activities found in the life of the school – a message is articulated that would also imply a moral argument for curriculum integration.[7] Making connections, recognizing achievements, celebrating worth, deserve priority also in relation to the world beyond the school. Assemblies can provide the occasion for extending horizons into local, regional, national and international realms, whether with a visit from the 'lollipop lady' and local vet, or with some mock election, an international festival and a North–South tribunal.

Any of these examples could be set within the context of an explicit act of Christian (or other) worship, but such setting can easily be immoral in its insensitivity to diversity of starting points. On the other hand, it can also be a quite proper expression of the faith on which the school itself was founded; but, even in a church school, it will be more appropriate in some than in others to assume confessional allegiance on the part of all the pupils.[8]

Certainly there is a need to give recognition to minorities, including religious minorities, within the school.[9] An assembly can do this, and there are rich resources for doing so in many areas of the country. Although some sharing in an act of worship need not be ruled out here, more often the multi-cultural and multi-faith assembly will be designed primarily to be informing.

By the psychologist we are asked what care is taken to check intelligibility in our assemblies. Visiting speakers are at a special disadvantage when faced with wide age and ability spread and poor acoustics. Research has indicated that on the whole readings make little impact and tend not to be remembered;[10] the Welsh Office has gone so far as to suggest that the didactic approach is generally counter-productive.[11] Clearly, there are other modes of learning that can equally be deployed for an assembly.

The fact that imitation is a powerful source for moral and immoral learning suggests that special attention be given to the modelling that goes on in an assembly. Who leads? Who is mentioned? What stories are chosen and how exclusive are the heroes and anti-heroes contained in them?[12] The impact of an assembly in terms of moral education can no doubt be increased with the benefit of a wide repertoire of well-chosen stories, images and bodily gestures!

In turn, the sociologist presses for a policy in the school about how the assemblies are organized, by whom and to what end? Has this been talked through, as might a reading scheme or exam provision, for the whole school? How often are staff meetings devoted to the matter of assemblies?

He also asks how much participation there is. If the answer is 'little', is this not opportunity missed? If 'much', how is 'vying' between individuals and classes avoided? Are the children who are called on to present an assembly theme ever allowed to become a 'front' behind which I, as teacher, can hide? Finally, are there any means of exploring or expressing the sense of identity within a school as a community that are unduly neglected? Playing games in an assembly could prove to be a high-order moral activity!

With or without the benefit of academic disciplines, it is evident that there are many different sorts of school assembly. They can be arranged for clarity's sake on a simple continuum, as follows:

| | | | | |
|---|---|---|---|---|
| | | | | |
| | Administrative occasion | Informing about, e.g. special aspect of a | Sharing/ celebrating vivid | |
| NO | for sharing | curriculum subject, | manifestations of | |
| A | information | school or local | e.g. curriculum | W |
| S | about aspects of | community event, | experience, | |
| S | school routine, | achievement of an | special occasion | O |
| E | e.g. exams, | individual or group, | (group's or | R |
| M | meals, sports | occurrence of | individual's), | S |
| B | results. | festival/special day. | election, religious | H |
| L | | | festival, so it | I |
| Y | | | comes alive, | P |
| | | | debating, exploring, expressing. | |

This arrangement corresponds to that employed by the Writing Research Unit at London Institute of Education,[13] and widely used since. Their same poles of functional and expressive/poetic as applied to varieties of children's written work in school are here redeployed to interpret assemblies. Degrees of personal involvement increase towards the right-hand pole, but this is not to deny the importance also of what is on the left. Each sort of assembly is capable of becoming formality, and in all value-assumptions are implicit – more or less routinized – and judgements have been made about what matters. On the right, the values are usually more explicit, yet even here there is risk that they can still be treated in a closed way. Just as it has been important to establish that religious and moral education in schools are continuous in their enquiring methods with the rest of the curriculum, so too with assemblies, if their grounds for survival are not to beg too many questions.

At this point, the main argument of this chapter needs to be more plainly asserted. It has been suggested that assemblies are significant in a variety of possible ways for moral education. Where they do not occur an opportunity for initiative and experiment with a large community is missed and, in turn, boys and girls may have less discriminating sense to bring to their working involvement in mass meetings or leisured excitement in football crowds. In all this the aspects of moral education which have been most frequently referred to have been mainly related to interpersonal relationships, sensitivity to the views of others, social justice, community action and aesthetic delight. Equally important for moral education are questions about the worthwhileness of any action or conviction – why at the end of the day they are worth bothering about? It is here, at the level of motivation and intention, that the deepest concerns of religious and moral education overlap. It is here too that the authentic act of worship and the short play, the singing, the personal statement of political conviction, etc. trade in the realm of comparable assumptions.

A fully fledged act of Christian worship presupposes a theological focus; in effect, a belief in God. Few schools can take this belief for granted for all their pupils and staff (could they ever?); but all have, in a sense, a hole in their foundations, into which from time to time teachers and pupils alike may stare.

This image is partly prompted by the comment of the eight-year-old that 'a floor is so you won't fall through the hole your house stands on', and also by N. F. Simpson's play *The Hole*, in which a group clusters round a hole in the road and muses over the goings-on within.

The theatre critic Martin Esslin once remarked that the Theatre of the Absurd is something of a contemporary religious quest; for it expresses a tragic sense of loss of ultimate certainties and strives:

> to make man aware of the ultimate realities of his condition, to instil in him again the lost sense of cosmic wonder and primeval anguish, to shock him out of an existence that has become trite, mechanical, complacent, and deprived of the dignity that comes of awareness. For God is dead, above all, to the masses who live from day to day and have lost all contact with the basic facts – and mysteries – of the human condition with which, in former times, they were kept in touch through the living ritual of their religion, which made them parts of a real community and not just atoms in an atomized society.[14]

In similar vein the suggestion is now advanced that assemblies operate in this field. They can provide opportunity for exploring basic beliefs, loyalties and commitments; those of teachers, pupils or parents; national, international and domestic; and of specific groups. In so far as they do this, they will reveal a preoccupation with the same boundary questions of human being that no moral education that retains its salt can afford to ignore. In other words, an act of worship, a school assembly, a moral response have all at core much to do with each other.

To conclude. There is real advantage that comes from our mixed constitutional heritage. We do not have in England and Wales an impenetrable barrier between religion and the state; that American arrangement has made it difficult for critical discussion of basic beliefs to be entertained in school. Nor do we have, for the most part at least, an exclusive induction into one particular ideological framework; that Soviet programme does not encourage openness in interpretation either. Rather we have confirmed by the 1944 Education Act a mixture of secular state with parental religious community. The intervening years have seen the breadth of Christian denominationalism which was recognized there, widened in many Local Education Authorities to include other religious traditions and secular humanism.[15] There are important ramifications here for religious education, for school assemblies, for moral education and the whole curriculum. Beware of the boundaries!

(1982)

# Chapter 20

# Worship where the child is

The 1944 Education Act defined RE as comprising teaching (Religious Instruction) and assembling (Collective Act of Worship). Forty and more years on the tendency is to dissassociate RE from any school assembly for worship because the latter is 'anti-educational'. Whereas, it is said, education requires critical thinking and openness, worship has a more exclusive focus in confessing a particular faith. It is far more appropriate therefore to take up worship in the classroom as an element for study within the teaching of RE. 'Don't pray in school. Instead, strive for boys and girls to understand what it means to worship and pray.'

But how? Meeting recently with a group of secondary headteachers, I was told by one that it was useless to introduce first-year pupils to Hindu and Muslim festivals because the primary schools have left them ignorant of even Christian festivals. Instead, she said, we must concentrate on the Christian ones so the children would have a point of reference from which to move later on to other faiths. This is a beguiling argument but actually self-defeating. For it seeks to explain the unknown in terms of the equally unknown. Prayer and worship, like festivals, may actually entail quite strange language and experience for many children. For in their own family traditions overt religious activity and belonging may scarcely occur. Where then to begin?

The answer in part at least depends on the understanding of religion and worship that we as teachers are working with. If they are perceived as entirely discrete and discontinuous from all other human activity and experience then there will be little prospect of finding related or analogous elements in the everyday lives of children. Being Christian or Muslim means going to the church or mosque; worship is hymn singing or the rituals of Friday prayer. Such definition is evidently accurate, but actually inadequate. If that is the major emphasis, it is questionable what appreciation will be acquired by boys and girls who from home are unaccustomed to such activities. For the purposes of conveying the personal significance of being religious or worshipful, rather more is needed.

A common example of this failure to connect occurs in primary school textbooks that speak baldly in less than half a page of the Aztec practice of worshipping the sun. They may even add that human sacrifice was offered to this object of devotion. And then they shift their attention to Aztec pyramids or gold; religion and worship have had their passing reference and attention now properly turns to other things. What is missed in all this is any attempt to explain or explore what might have moved Aztec Indians to focus so much attention on the sun and to be prepared to make gifts of human life itself. But then again, if religion and worship are eccentric activities no one need be surprised by bizarre extremities. They can be remarked as such; teachers and taught may express momentary fascination, but that will be an end to them in all their strange religiosity. Real living experience is of a different order; that, instead, we can take for granted.

Yet it is commonplace to hear from anthropologists and social psychologists alike that religion and worship are pervasive in human experience – expressed in myth, ritual and community buildings. Trans-culturally from tribe to differentiated technological society the human context is shot through with stories and gestures that express dependence and gratitude, regret and praise, and even silent wondering. Though these may sometimes be labelled as religious, often they are not, but sing instead the plain song of humanity, plumbing heights and depths as these unnamed are stumbled on.

It is in this territory that a teacher may choose to dwell in the interests of opening up the genuine glimmer and glow of worship. If so the strategy used may be no less systematic or structured than one that begins with the overt liturgical form of synagogue or gurdwara. For these are ingredients recognizably recurrent across the range of that which is basically human or religious.

We might begin with wishing and hoping. Although estimates of it may differ from one tradition to another, this is common across religion in the form of petitionary prayer. But it is also common to children or adults who might 'hope against hope' that things could be other than they are. Buying lottery tickets, crossing fingers, or pleading before God, have a common core of desire that circumstances might change, and usually for the better. This would be well spent exploring different ways boys and girls express their hopes, the various forms that the hopes take in terms of desired outcomes, and by what power and force, or intervention, fulfilment might be achieved. It is likely that there would be no shortage of examples from a class.

I've got a lucky Cornish pixie at home. If you put it on it gets good luck[...]and when you take it off you don't get any good luck at all. I wear it on Sundays, because I always, I never get told off on Sundays if I wear it. (7-year-old girl)

When my mum was young, about 12 to 16 and she see a piece of coal she used to hack it out and wrap it in a hanky and put in her pocket, it always came lucky to her. She still does it now sometimes, she always keeps an old hanky. *And it really works?* Yes, I think so. (12-year-old boy)

Equally some ranking of hopes according to their greater or lesser worthiness might be tried out. Groups within a class might be encouraged to engage in a classification activity (e.g. self-serving/other serving, material/illuminative) before then going on to weigh their respective significance). Against the background of such activity a direct approach to specific examples of petitionary prayer might become more intelligible than otherwise would have been the case.

A second theme for preliminary exploration might be that of being sorry. Expressions of regret for what's been done or not done occur within family, between friends, or more occasionally in public life. Examples of each might be described by members of a class in pairs, perhaps orally at first, and later elaborated in letter form. Implicit in such statements will be a sense of individual responsibility for particular actions. Having begun with the experience of regret, it would be appropriate to move on to consider typical responses by the person(s) wronged. Some of these might be more punishing, others more accepting, but again, by pooling examples, a basis in common experience can be arrived at. Building on this base rather more should now emerge from direct reference to specific prayers that express comparable sentiments, as also from reference to any verbal and dramatic expressions of forgiveness that follow. By such means as these fundamental distinctions like that between accepting a person but rejecting certain actions can be exposed, and acts of penitence, individual or collective, better understood.

Being thankful is another theme that would repay this kind of attention. To whom are children commonly thankful and for what? What is the difference between 'polite thank you' and thanks that come 'from the bottom of someone's heart'? Much thankfulness quite appropriately goes on without any reference to anyone other than the friend/relative/professional/peer concerned. Yet there is a deeper sense of thankfulness that can sometimes go beyond the persons immediately involved. This is illustrated by the following extract from a conversation with an 11-year-old boy who is basically confused about the outward forms of religion and yet perceptive of some deeper meaning within:

*What's inside a church?* A cross ... I know a church near where we live which has got a bronze statue of the Mona Lisa about five foot tall and a little Jesus hanging on the top. *Why has it got a statue of the Mona Lisa?* The mother of Joseph who was the father of God. *Have you ever been inside a church?* Yes, I've been to a wedding, and once me, my mum and my friend went in a church and we prayed. *Why did you do that?* We just prayed because we're thankful for what we've got ... I've got a little dog called Santa and it kept on messing on the carpets and my brother came out of the bathroom and put his foot straight in it. Mum was going to take him to be put down – she had to sign a form and she couldn't do it so she brought him back home and we've still got him. I'm thankful for that.

An example such as this could relevantly lead on to a consideration of specific songs/hymns/prayers that have been generated by religious believers. Again, the language of a specific hymn or prayer of thanks will often deserve close inspection; so too, the different *forms* that individual and collective acts of gratitude might take. A celebration or festival within a family, nation or separate faith community may itself be intended, in part at least, as an act of general thanksgiving. Gifts too may be motivated by a sense of thankful appreciation of another or others.

Praising and cheering, being still and wondering, are some of the other recurrent ingredients of worship. They too deserve to be explored from the everyday human end as well as by reference to explicit religion. Running throughout all the themes however will be the open question of to whom the thanks, the praise, the penitence or the pleading is addressed. Much of the time they will quite simply involve the individual in relation to self or other(s). But within any one of those relationships, there may also be a religious ingredient which sets that humanity 'in italics' as extra special and pointing beyond its own immediately given form.

This 'pointing beyond', or transcendent quality, is central to worship proper. Thus, talk of God, gods or another world, is now called directly into play. Here too the same investigatory approach which moves from the experience of boys and girls to references that are beyond them is both appropriate and necessary if the question of religious claim to truth is not to be completely dodged. It has been suggested that a variety of classification work is appropriate to arrive at an understanding of the forms of prayer and worship. Equally important would be some analysis of the qualities of transcendence in whatsoever form it is found or affirmed. Thus the God who is believed to be welcoming of human sacrifice may be very different from the God who is healing hospital for humankind; rather closer to a Nazi nationalist cause that is stubbornly indifferent to the wholesale gifts of followers' lives its policies take for granted.

Take the sun: what are its qualities? It generates warmth and light. It is reliable, even predictable. Yet, it is high up and beyond reach; it is outside human control and gives its benefits to poor and rich alike. Without the sun there would be no life, but with it there is also drought and burning.

Take an oak tree. Like the sun it is not of my own making. It is strong and bears fruit, but it is also vulnerable to disease, fire, old age and the human axe. It has been known to give shelter and shade. Its roots reach down under our feet, but its branches reach up higher than ten of the tallest humans. It began to grow decades, even centuries, before us and may well continue long after we die. As a tree it is obvious for all to see, but it also bridges into unknown worlds.

Take a nurse. What qualities here? Physical warmth and shelter; bringing light, nourishment and healing potions according to human need. Not just aloof, standing over and beyond, but patient and approaching close and expressing personal care and interest. The nurse is other than you or me but yet somehow nearer to us than tree or sun can ever be. The very nearness in time and space that makes the human closeness possible also restricts the outreach and coverage of nurses' care.

The sun, the tree of life and the healer's companion are all images that have recurred in religious experience the world over, as expressions of the immanence and/or transcendence of God. But so too are mountain, river, thunder; manufacturer, destroyer, rescuer; child, wise one and clown. Without first exploring in relation to their own experience the personal thoughts and feelings associated with each, children will have difficulty making any sense of the evocation of god-ness that is variously represented by them. Transcendence with a capital T may not be coterminous with transcendence but the one is apprehended in its correspondence with, as well as its distinction from, the other.

There is in other words a very important activity of moral, humanity-testing scrutiny to be begun with boys and girls if they are ever to fathom for themselves the different doubts and affirmations which move men and women to worship so doggedly and in such diversity. Acts of worship in this sense remain central to good RE.

(1985)

# Chapter 21

# Where now with collective worship?

**How can the notion of 'compulsory worship' have any educational credibility?**

Strong philosophical and theological arguments make it difficult to understand how the legal requirement for worship in schools can any longer be justified in a modern liberal democracy. It seems to be intrinsically self-contradictory, potentially invasive of individual pupil's conscience and entirely inappropriate in an institution funded for educational purposes and from public taxation.

Two lines of defence do however carry some weight, one pertaining to the voluntary aided provision, now designated as 'faith schools', and the other to Local Authority community schools.

In the category of faith schools, which are expressly associated with one particular faith community (Gates 2005b), the supporting arguments take the following form:

> We have existed with a particular denominational link since state education began in 1870. Most have been related to the Christian churches, principally Anglican and Roman Catholic. A few have been Jewish, and more recently Hindu, Muslim and Sikh schools have been established. We have served our own faith community, though Anglican ones have also sought to serve the wider community especially in neighbourhoods and villages where they are the only school. Indeed, this notion of wider service has now been affirmed by the other faith communities as appropriate also in the admissions policies for their schools. We now provide education for around a quarter of all those of school age and the parents and other members of the faith communities pay their taxes for education like anyone else.
>
> As part of the ethos of our schools, we consider it right and educationally sound to encourage all the pupils and teachers to participate in worship which expresses our faith. Although this requirement will always be sensitively managed and the worship will be alive to the learning interests of all concerned, it will remain a prerogative of parents to be able to invoke the conscience clause for their sons or daughters to be withdrawn from such worship.

In the category of Local Authority community schools, which also includes those church schools whose status is 'controlled' rather than 'voluntary aided', the supporting arguments take the following form:

'Collective worship' in school is different from 'corporate worship' in church, mosque or synagogue; there is recognition that there is no unanimity of religious belief within the school community. The 1988 Act specifies that in arranging collective worship there should be regard for 'age, aptitude and family background' of the pupils in each school. Accordingly, collective worship should be designed as an open educational activity which invites attentive listening and participation, while making no assumptions as to the religious allegiance of individual pupils or teachers. The law is deliberately permissive in these regards. It states that collective worship may be wholly and broadly Christian in character, but Christian breadth includes expressions of thankfulness or regret, of striving that the world might be transformed for the better, and of wonderment. Words, music and other activities, as well as silence, may be deployed which express this. Equally, while this might cover much of the provision, it allows that substantial parts of what is done (technically up to half) might be drawing more explicitly on other religions and on more secular traditions. The whole is left in the responsibility of headteachers who have the opportunity to be creative and imaginative in what is done to invoke aspects of the school's curriculum and setting within the local, national and global community in ways which will illuminate each pupil's sense of identity.

Such arguments as these meet with varied responses. For instance, what is used as justification in relation to faith schools may be generally accepted by those who accept the worth of such institutions, but for others who object on principle to the very existence of faith schools the argument simply reinforces their view that public money should not be used to instil and reinforce what they regard as singular sectarian beliefs. Or again, what is indicated in defence of even 'collective' worship in Local Authority schools may be perceived as simply special pleading.

## Would it not be far more sensible therefore to end all talk of worship and have regular school assemblies instead?

The practice of worship in school has long since been abandoned in most other liberal democracies; it therefore seems all the more likely that it should be discontinued in England and Wales. After all, though the practice continues in most primary schools, in secondary schools it is a more occasional feature of the school day, with most being found guilty of non-compliance by the government office for standards in education (Ofsted). Moreover, the challenge to maintain an open and flexible interpretation of the requirements of the 1988 ERA was actually made much more difficult by the advisory Circular 1/94 (DfE 1994) which went beyond that Act's introduction of the word Christian by specifying deference to Jesus as the Christ.

The Circular immediately provoked contention. It reinforced the antagonisms of those who were already critical of collective worship. It aroused the suspicions of some members of minority faiths that all of religious education in community schools was covertly designed as as exercise in conversion. Yet others sought to use it as a justification for arguing that corporate worship for individual minority faiths should be allowed in community schools.

A major attempt to arrive at a satisfactory resolution to all the sensitivities was made by the Inter Faith Network for the UK, the National Association of SACREs and the RE Council of England and Wales (REC 1996, Gay 1998). It achieved a near consensus, however, not a unanimous one and, in the absence of that, the government shied from initiating any changes. Subsequent mappings of the continuing condition in schools only serve to reinforce the scale of the challenge (Gill 2000a and 2000b, Cheetham 2004)

In Scotland, by contrast, a significant alternative was not only explored (Gray 1999) but formally enacted (Scottish Executive 2005)

## What is at stake?

Contrary to commonplace judgement, contemporary culture within the UK has not ceased to engage in worship. The total numbers participating annually in services and festivals associated with individual religions is in excess of 5 million. They have such names as Easter and Pentecost, Yom Kippur and Holocaust Day, Ramadan and Eid, Holi, Diwali and Wesak (Brown 1986, Shap Working Party 2007). That these events are now a significant feature of the British cultural landscape should serve as an invitation to schools to find ways and means of acknowledging, exploring, and even celebrating something of their meaning and distinctiveness by exposure to verbal prayers, visual emblems, songs and ritual actions. In their own ways they are each reminders of a larger global humanity and belonging, beyond that of the immediate school or wider nation state.

Alongside these, collective worship is still in evidence on great state occasions involving a centenary or millennium, remembrance of war dead, some favoured royal personnage, or some more local victim who has suffered untimely death. Even more, it is there in the crowds gathered for major sporting occasions, in huge music concerts and festivals; they express devotion and adulation, and sometimes sadness and despair. Behaviour in a large group is indubitably a powerful experience, and not always for the good. All the more reason therefore that while yet young, everyone should have the opportunity to learn to become critically aware in their appreciation of any sentiments and messages involved.

Within the school as well, there are special priorities that can too easily be missed or only partially acknowledged. One of these is awareness of others across the full age range of the school or college on occasions warranting recognition of achievement or response to tragic circumstance. Opportunities for regular exposure between those younger or older to each other, as to teachers grouped as an even 'older generation', is all the more welcome in a society which can disintegrate when mutuality across the full age span becomes attenuated. Another is collective consciousness of the best experiences which individual subjects are able to generate and express. Opportunities for such sharing can do much to make connections across the whole curriculum. A third is to have that curriculum continually exposed to 'big picture' dimensions of deepest meaning and purpose in life. In addition to reflection, worship by definition usually involves the direction of energies to what matters most. Without opportunity for collective 'target practice' which heightens critical awareness of what is more or less ephemeral or lasting, institutional education will have failed its participants.

Such ambitions as these are complementary to those of the classroom teaching of RE. They are even less likely to be successfully arranged unless they are worked at through appropriate training and support for the staff responsible. However, if carefully designed and delivered they have the potential to be transformative for whole year groups, school communities and making a lasting impression on generations of children and young people. And, as with the RE teaching, they have the underdeveloped potential for local regional backup in the form of SACREs, containing the range of representatives of faith communities, plus professional and political interests.

## Opportunity knocking or knocked?

From another, and probably a professionally predominant point of view, such a replenishment of the collective worship tradition is a time-wasting pipedream. With the exception of 'faith schools', there is evidence that, in many, especially secondary, schools and almost all post-16 age range provision, the practice of collective worship has withered on the branch. Singing has long gone. Invitation to be attentive to another's prayers is rare. Exposure to global exemplary lifestyles is very unusual. Pruning would be a far more sensible response.

Before that final execution occurs, there are two further considerations which are relevant. The first is the once daily declaration in the US:

I believe in the United States of America as a Government of the people, by the people, for the people; whose just powers are derived from the consent of the governed; a democracy in a republic; a sovereign Nation of many sovereign States; a perfect union, one and inseparable; established upon those principles of freedom, equality, justice, and humanity for which American patriots sacrificed their lives and fortunes. I therefore believe it is my duty to my country to love it; to support its Constitution; to obey its laws; to respect its flag; and to defend it against all enemies.

If a comparable creedal affirmation of loyalty to the nation is unthinkable within the UK, it may be that the absence of any equivalent in schools leaves a hole in national consciousness.

Therein lies the second consideration. Debate is ongoing about what it means to speak of 'British identity'. Such is not unusual in other nations. Simultaneous with a heightened awareness of transnational citizenship, there is also a drive to establish more individual nations and within them greater regional and local autonomies. Within the UK in particular, there is sensitivity over English, Welsh and Scottish, not to mention Northern Ireland and the Irish Republic (Davies 1999, Richardson 2000), and there are experiments in regional devolution. There is also sensitivity about prospective European citizenship, and whereas Commonwealth citizenship is, sadly, largely overlooked, a sense of global citizenship has achieved some greater popularity. Alongside this comes the greater ethnic and religious diversity, plus a dominant cultural input from the US, most especially through film and television. The consequential mix in terms of overall sense of human identity is too easily one of confusion.

It is precisely in relation to identity questions that public educational provision is expected to make direct response. That most commonly occurs in the construction of a national curriculum, with its various subject components. Debates about these and their respective contents take place within individual nations. As already indicated, that is variously true with regard to any provision for RE.

The proposal here being advanced is that, just as the established approach to RE+ME **teaching** in England and Wales is worth consolidating here and maybe following elsewhere in other countries, this is also the case with a replenished model of RE+ME **assembling** – an open collectivity regarding that which warrants valuing most – locally, nationally and globally.

Schools and colleges are in part creatures of the communities within which they are set and as such they will want to reflect the best from those local communities in their own communal lives. Schools and colleges are in part creatures of the national subject curricula which they have been given, and again they are challenged to realize the best they can for every young person on all these fronts.

In addition, however, schools and colleges have the opportunity to develop their own sense of communal belonging, with and for the all the individuals who spend much of their waking lives within them. That will have its ups and downs, since any school, any community may sometimes be buoyant, and sometimes broken. But it also deserves to create its own opportunities to be musically delighted, theatrically enthralled, scientifically gobsmacked, historically chastened, morally inspired, and religiously reflective. In any deliberation about how the whole curriculum experience in schools can more effectively equip students for their future lives, collective exploration of worth and identity is an aspect that deserves not to be knocked. Public agencies addressing education for the future are myopic to ignore worship as a social universal, as well as a distinctively confessional activity. As an aspect of collective life does it not need to be openly addressed?

# Notes

## Notes for chapter 1

1.  In England two opposing viewpoints are represented in B. Brophy, *RE in State Schools*, London, Fabian Society, 1967; and P. R. May and O. R. Johnston, *Religion in Our Schools*, London, Hodder, 1968. For a summary of the debate and official reports, cf. C. Alves, *The Christian in Education*, London, SCM. Press, 1972. The extent of the American controversy is documented in L. C. Little, *Religion and Public Education in the News, 1957–67*, Westminster, The author, 1968 and *Religion and Public Education: a Bibliography*, 3rd edn, Pittsburgh, University Book Center, 1968.
2.  Cf. M. Cruickshank, *Church and State in English Education, 1870 to the Present Day*, London, Macmillan, 1963.
3.  The first of these was issued by the West Riding of Yorkshire in 1923, followed in 1924 by Cambridge. Their evolution is summarized in Institute of Christian Education, *RE in Schools*, London, SPCK, 1954, ch. 2, pp. 21–54.
4.  Just as the reading of Homer was once universal in Greek schools, the Bible had a rightful place in the English school curriculum – so Matthew Arnold in *Reports on Elementary Schools, 1852–82*, London, Macmillan, 1889, pp. 139–40.
5.  Charted and documented in: Sheffield University Institute of Education, *RI in Secondary Schools: A Summary and a Syllabus*, London, T. Nelson, 1961; H. Loukes, *New Ground in Christian Education*, London, SCM Press, 1965, Ch. 4; and C. Alves, *Religion and the Secondary School*, London, SCM Press, 1968, pp. 78–81. Cf. a new 'Syllabus and Handbook' produced in 1965 for use in county and Protestant voluntary grammar schools in N. Ireland; and for this usage in Scotland, Millar Report *Moral and Religious Education*, Edinburgh, HMSO, 1972; 2.27, 29; 2.50, 53.
6.  Cf. A. Wainright, 'RE in the English Examination System' in Moray House College of Education, *Curriculum and Examinations in RE*, Edinburgh, Oliver Boyd, 1968; Schools Council, *Examination Bulletin 17. CSE Trial Exams: RK.* London, HMSO, 1967; H. Lupton, *RE in the CSE*, CEM., Teachers' Dept Paper, London, Annandale, 1970.
7.  As listed in: Christian Education Movement, *A Bibliography for the Use of Teachers*, 6th edn, London, CEM, 1966; Educational Foundation for Visual Aids, *Visual Aids: films, filmstrips and transparencies Part I, RE*, London, 1968, pp. 5–72.

8. This amendment to the 1870 Forster Education Bill provided that in schools 'hereafter established by means of local rates, no catechism or religious formulary which is distinctive to any particular denomination shall be taught.' Cf. discussion in M. Cruickshank, op. cit., pp. 29–30 and *passim.*

9. For a review of the then university position: A. Vidler, 'The Future of Divinity' in J. H. Plumb (ed.), *Crisis in the Humanities*, Harmondsworth, Penguin, 1964, pp. 82–95. On Colleges of Education, cf. F. H. Hilliard, 'Divinity Studies in Teacher Training' *Theology*, (67 532,) October 1964, pp. 438–42; N Naylor, 'An analysis of courses in Religion in Colleges of Education with critical comments' in Religious Studies Section *Bulletin No. 2*, A.T.C.D.E., June 1971, pp. 1–17.

10. The Rt. Rev. R. Stopford, Bishop of London, 'Christian Education and Christian Unity' in A. Wedderspoon (ed.), *RE 1944–84*, London, Allen Unwin, 1966, pp. 11–29.

11. G. M. Trevelyan, *English Social History*, London, Longman, 1944, p. 452.

12. On the indebtedness of this type of RE to biblical theology, cf. E. Kinniburgh, 'Theology and the Teacher of Religious Knowledge', *Scottish Journal of Theology* **23**(2), May 1970, pp. 183–90.

13. Cf. J. Webster, 'Teaching the Gospel', *Learning for Living*, **2**(1), September 1962. Certain 'Bible as literature' courses in American high schools have also sought to bracket out theology in Bible study, e.g. T. Warshaw, 'Studying the Bible in Public School', *English Journal* **53**(2), February 1964.

14. Loukes, op. cit. chs 5, 6; and R. J. Goldman, *Religious Thinking from Childhood to Adolescence*, London, Routledge Kegan Paul, 1964, Ch. 15.

15. Cf. E. A. Peel, *Nature of Adolescent Judgement*, London, Staples, 1972.

16. Most blatant in the unqualified title 'Scripture' for RE work in general.

17. A phrase derived from J. A. T. Robinson, *New Reformation*, London, SCM Press, 1965, Ch. 2. As in much contemporary Christian theology, there is an emphasis on the immanence of God in this type of RE

18. H. Loukes, *Teenage Religion*, London, SCM Press, 1961, chs 5, 6. Cf. I. H. Birnie, *Encounter*, London, McGraw-Hill, 1967; J. Hills Cotterill *Facing Life's Challenge*, London, Nelson, 1969.

19. E.g. *'Which and Why' Cards, Talk Abouts, Focus Wallcharts, Projects,* from Christian Education Movement, London, NW11 Annandale.

20. West Riding, *Suggestions for RE*, 1966; Northamponshire, *Fullness of Life: an Exploration of Christian Faith for Primary Schools* and *Life and Worship* (Senior section); Lancashire, *Religion and Life*, 1968; Inner London, *Learning for Life*, 1968; Hampshire, *Approaches to RE*, 1970; Cambridgeshire, *RE* 1970.

21. R. J. Goldman, *Readiness for Religion*, London, Routledge & Kegan Paul, 1965b. Cf. Goldman, *Symbols, Bread, Myself*, London, Hart-Davis, 1965–; K. N. Smith, *Themes*, London, Macmillan, 1969; K. E. Hyde (ed.), *Topic Books: The Senses 1 and 2; Neighbours 1 and 2*, London, Lutterworth Educational,

1970; C. Alves and M. Stanley, *Exploring God's World*, London, Macmillan, 1972; and M. Evening, *Approaches to RE*, London, Hodder, 1972, ch. 1.

22. K. Russell and J. Tooke, *Learning to Give*, Oxford, Pergamon, 1967; CEM, *Focus on Service*, London, Annandale, n.d.; M. Evening, op. cit., ch. 6.

23. A refrain familiar also in the romanticism of certain forms of 'religionless Christianity'.

24. Cf. the symposium on 'The New Agreed Syllabuses' in *Learning for Living*, **8**(5), May 1969; in particular J. Bowden, 'The Bible, Dodging the Main Question', pp. 20–3. For examples of this happening in integrated work, G. Kent, *Projects in the Primary School*, London, Batsford, 1968, pp. 89, 102.

25. Cf. S. Marshall, *Experiment in Education*, Cambridge, Cambridge University Press, 1963.

26. E.g. S. Clements et al., *Reflections*, Oxford, University Press, 1962; G. Hacker et al., *Conflict 1 and 2*, London, Nelson, 1969; A. Hancock and R. A. Robertson, *People Today*, 1. *Ourselves*, 2 *Our Society*, London, Longmans, 1965; P. Grosset, *Things that Matter*, London, Evans, 1966; R. Mabey (ed.), *Connections: A Teachers' Guide*, Harmondsworth, Penguin, 1970.

27. For attempts at clarification: J. Holm, 'Life Themes: What are They?', *Learning for Living* **9**(2), November 1969, pp. 15–18; J. M.Hull, 'The Theology of Themes', *Scottish Journal of Theology*, (**25** 1), February 1972, pp. 20–31.

28. i.e. recipes consisting of biblical references: 1lb of Jg. 5: 25, a pinch of Lev. 2: 13, etc. Follow Prov. 23: 14 for an unbeatable cake! Cf. nineteenth century arithmetic via the Bible: 7 days between Christ's birth and circumcision, and 5 to epiphany. How long was it from the nativity to the epiphany?

29. An 1869–70 Cincinnatti court case, in line with the Church and State separation in the Bill of Rights and the 14th Amendment, upheld the exclusion of RI, Bible reading, and hymn singing from local public schools. Cf. R. Michaelson, *Piety in the Public School: Trends and Issues in the Relationship between Religion and the Public School in the US*, New York, Macmillan, 1970; L. C. Little, 'The Role of Religion in Public Education' in M. P. Strommen (ed.), *Research on Religious Development*, New York, Hawthorn, 1971, ch. 8.

30. Non-compliance has been at its greatest in the south and mid-west: K. M. Dolbeare and P. E. Hammond, *School Prayer Decisions*, Chicago, University Press, 1971.

31. M. J. Taylor, *Religious and Moral Education*, New York, Centre for Applied Research in Education, 1965, pp. 23–4; but cf. n. 74.

32. It would be difficult to find a more noticeable contrast in English and American parish life than that between their respective programmes for RE. In America the responsibility is clear and the provision elaborate.

33. Cf. P. Phenix, *Religious Concerns in Contemporary Education: A Study of*

*Reciprocal Relations,* New York, Columbia UP, 1959; *Education and Worship of God,* Philadelphia, Westminster, 1966.

34. Cf. J. R. Whitney, 'Religion in Public Schools: Some Pluralist Arguments for Religious Studies in the Public School Curriculum', *Bulletin,* Council on Study of Religion **3**(2), June 1972, pp. 15–20.

35. Cf. W. A. Christian, *Meaning and Truth in Religion,* Princeton UP, 1964; N. Smart, *Reasons and Faiths,* London, Routledge & Kegan Paul, 1958; and F. Ferré, *Basic Modern Philosophy of Religion,* New York, Scribner, 1967a.

36. Cf. B. Wilson, *Religion in Secular Society,* Harmondsworth, Penguin, 1969 (Watts, 1966), ch. 6.

37. Cf. C. Alves, *Religion and the Secondary School,* London, SCM, 1968, p. 181.

38. P. Phenix, *Realms of Meaning,* New York, McGraw-Hill, 1964, pp. 250–2; cf. *Philosophy of Education,* New York, Holt, 1958, chs 5 and 25.

39. P. H. Hirst, 'Liberal Education and the Nature of Knowledge' in R. F. Dearden et al. (eds), *Education and the Development of Reason,* London, Routledge Kegan Paul, 1972, pp. 391–414; 'The Role of Religion in Public Education' in T. R. Sizer (ed.), *Religion and Public Education,* Boston, Houghton Mifflin, 1967, pp. 329–39.

40. N. Smart, *Secular Education and the Logic of Religion,* London, Faber, 1968b *Religious Experience of Mankind,* London, Fontana, 1969a *The Phenomenology of Religion,* London, Macmillan, 1973a.

41. e.g. S. Ogden commenting on J.-P. Sartre: 'The Strange Witness of Unbelief' in *The Reality of God,* London, SCM, 1967, ch. 4.

42. P. H. Hirst, 'Morals, Religion and the Maintained School' in *British Journal of Educational Studies* **14**(1), November 1965.

43. J. Wilson et al., *Introduction to Moral Education,* Harmondsworth, Penguin, 1968. For an extension of this procedural analysis to religion cf. J. Wilson, *Education in Religion and the Emotions,* London, Heinemann, 1971.

44. e.g. learning games and role play, *Introduction to Moral Education* op. cit., ch. 9 and Appendix A, cf. *Education in Religion,* op. cit., ch. 11. and especially: *Practical Methods of Moral Education,* London, Heinemann – J. Wilson's last work before leaving the Trust in 1972. The practice advocated reflects perhaps the best in the English Public School tradition of moral education; it includes separate subject work on 'Moral Thinking', language exercises for handling real-life problem situations, the making and testing of rules and contracts, and a carefully operated house-system with 'super-parents'.

45. The Secondary Project (1967–72) was attached to the Oxford University Department of Education; the Primary Project (1972–5) similarly attached to Hughes Hall, Cambridge. Publications (London, Longman, 1972) by the project team are entitled *Lifeline* and include handbooks *Moral Education in the Secondary School* (Mcphail 1972*), Our School* (on the practice of democracy by pupils) and packs of materials *In Other People's Shoes; Proving the Rule; What Would You Have Done?*

46. *Moral Education in the Secondary School,* op. cit, Pt 1; cf. M. Argyle, *Psychology of Interpersonal Behaviour* (2nd edn), Harmondsworth, Penguin, 1972.

47. P. McPhail reports wide use of the materials in so diverse a range of subjects as Domestic Science, Biology, and English. *Moral Education in Secondary Schools,* op. cit., 154–68.

48. Director of the influential Schools Council Nuffield Humanities Project 1967–72; then at the Centre for Applied Research in Education at the University of East Anglia, where one of the new tasks was to try out in Britain the Bruner, 'Man – A Course of Study' materials from Harvard, cf. J. Ruddock, *Cambridge Journal of Education* **22**, Easter, 1972.

49. London, Heinemann Educational Books, 1970–.

50. e.g. science and responsibility, crime, family, conflicts, education – materials for 15–18 year olds: General Studies Project, The King's Manor, York.

51. Schools Council Integrated Studies, e.g. Units 2: Communicating with others, and 3: Living together; Oxford, University Press, 1972.

52. P. J. Tansey and D. Unwin, *Simulation and Gaming in Education,* London, Methuen, 1969a; 'Simulation the Games Explosion', *Social Education* **33**(2), February, 1969a, pp. 175–99; Decisions Kit; Siting an Oil Terminal, Merstham, School Gov't Publishing Co.; Man and His Environment, Coca Cola Export Corp.; Blacks and Whites, Runnymede Trust/Delmar, CA. Comprehensive lists in J. L. Taylor and R. Walford, *Simulation in the Classroom,* Harmondsworth, Penguin, 1972, Pt. 3.

53. Cf. D. J. O'Connor, *Introduction to the Philosophy of Education,* London, Routledge, Ch. 6; R. F. Dearden, *Philosophy of Primary Education,* London, Routledge, 1968, pp. 53–9, 75–8, 153–61.

54. Quoted in a section on 'primary religion' by R. Hoggart, *Uses of Literacy,* Harmondsworth, Penguin, 1958, pp. 112–19.

55. P. R. May, *Moral Education in School,* London, Methuen, 1971.

56. The SMC. was set up for joint study and action on moral issues by religious believers and non-believers, with the specific object of 'promoting morality in all aspects of the life of the community'.

57. Published thrice yearly by Pemberton Publishing Co., London. Its editorial board was then virtually identical with serving members of the SMC.

58. e.g. D. Konstant, *Syllabus for Catholic Primary Schools* (1966); *Secondary Schools* (1967), London, Burns & Oates; D. Lance, *11–16. A Complete Course for RE at the Secondary School Level,* London, Darton, Longman & Todd, 1967. Cf. D. Brennan, *A Guide to Audio-Visual Aids for RE,* London, Chapman, 1969.

59. Cf. *Media I* (1969) and *II* (1970) *Guide to materials for Christian Formation,* Dayton, G. Pflaum.

60. Durham Report, *The Fourth R,* London, SPCK, 1970, pp. 61–3, 102–3; cf. the speech by the late Ian T. Ramsey, Bishop of Durham, introducing a parliamentary debate on 'Education in a Multi-Racial Britain', *Hansard:*

*House of Lords Official Report*, 326:23, 15 December 1971. 'Confessional RE' does not have to be closed.

61. Shap Working party, World Religions in Education: Islam '*Learning for Living*,' **11**(3), January 1972; cf. the fourth issue of CEM's *Primary Mailing: RE in a Multi-Faith Society*, London Annandale, May 1972.

62. R. Richardson, *Frontiers of Enquiry, 4. The Gods*, London, Granada, 1972.

63. J. Hick, 'The Re-construction of Christian Belief for Today and Tomorrow: 2. Other World Religions', *Theology* **73**(603), September, 1970, pp. 399–405; cf. W. A. Christian, *Opposition of Religious Doctrines: A Study of Dialogue among Religions*, London, Macmillan, 1972. For full bibliographical review article: E. J. Sharpe, 'Christian Attitudes to Non-Christian Religions' in *World Religions: Aids for Teachers*, London Community Relations Commission, 1972.

64. This has been the thrust of meetings of representatives of the differerent religious communities in the country sponsored by the government (DES) and the British Council of Churches; cf. the consultative document *Inter-Faith Dialogue in Education*, BCC, 1972. At a local level collaboration of this kind is producing new RE syllabuses for the Birmingham and Bradford areas.

65. So N. Smart writing in the *Guardian*, 29 August 1972; but cf. his more detailed suggestions in 'Comparative Study of Religion in Schools' in C. Macy (ed.), *Let's Teach Them Right*, London, Pemberton, 1969b, pp. 61–9; and 'The Structure of the Comparative Study of Religion' in J. R. Hinnells (ed.), *Comparative Religion in Education*, Newcastle, Oriel, 1970c, pp. 20–31.

66. Relevant work in the psychology of religion is summarized by D. Elkind, 'The Developmental Psychology of Religion' in A. H. Kidd and J. L. Rivoire (eds), *Perceptual Development of Children*, London, University of London Press, 1967, ch. 8; cf. D. Wright, 'A Review of Empirical Studies in the Psychology of Religion', *ARE Bulletin*, Extended Supplement 1, 1972 (from Highcroft House, Sutton Coldfield, Warwicks). But further work in the religious understanding of children and young people is very necessary.

67. Project on RE in the Primary School, Director C. M. Jones, at Leeds University Institute of Education 1969–71; report *RE in the Primary School*, Evans Methuen, 1972. Project on RE in the Secondary School, Director N. Smart, Deputy Director D. Horder, University of Lancaster, 1969–72; report *RE in the Secondary School*, London, Evans Methuen, 1971. (This second project was then extended into the primary field, 1973–6, and based in Lancaster.)

68. Coordinating Secretary P. Woodward, Borough Road College, Isleworth, Middlesex.

69. On such themes as: religious language, suffering, science and religion, nature of belief, introduction to Hindu tradition, etc., and subsequently published by Hart-Davies, 1973.

70. Shap Working Party, *World Religions: Aids for Teachers*, London, Community Relations Commission, 1972a.
71. Associated Examining Board, Aldershot and Joint Matriculation Board, Manchester. Similar revisions for both Ordinary and Advanced Level are in process in other Boards.
72. E.g. Ontario: cf. Ontario Department of Education, *World Religions* 1971.
73. Described by S. Rodhe in G. Parrinder (ed.), *Teaching about Religions*, London, Harrap, 1971, pp. 77–98; cf. National Swedish Board of Education Newsletter: *School Research*, Stockholm, May 1971.
74. A National Council on Religion and Public Education (founded 1971) is active 'to provide a means for cooperative action among organizations concerned with religion as a constitutionally acceptable and educationally appropriate part of a secular programme of public education'. Cf. R. U. Smith (ed.), *Religion and the Public School Curriculum*, New York, Religious Education Association, 1972 (Pt 2 of *Religious Education*, July–August 1972). Also: Symposium on Religion in American Public Schools in *Religious Education*, Englewood Cliffs **64**(2), March–April 1969 and 'Units, Courses, and Projects for Teaching about Religions' in *Social Education*, December 1969.
75. Cf. J. F. Smurl, *Religious Ethics: A Systems Approach*, Prentice-Hall, 1972.
76. Cf. the position referred to in note 9 above. For corrective: N. Smart, 'Religion as a Subject', *Church Quarterly Review* **23**, January 1970, pp. 227–33. One such course in a college of education is described in a paper by C. Alder, 'Education in Religion', Goldsmiths' College, 1971.
77. Cf. the study of education, not least in colleges of education; it too can be 'wagged' by its second-order disciplines.
78. Cf. the course advocated in H. L. Miller', PhD 'The Preparation for Teaching Religion in the Public School'. Athens, OH: Ohio State University ens 1966.

## Notes for chapter 3

1. In law, Religious Education is the only subject with parental right of opt out; in practice, the 'RI Clauses' of the 1944 Education Act have occasioned considerable resentment. The shortage of secondary specialists in the subject and the inadequacy of training provisions to prepare prospective primary teachers for their responsibility for moral and religious education are documented in the Marratt Report (1971).
2. On the 'messianic pretensions' of sociology, cf. D. MacRae (1964).
3. Other teachers do, however, recognize that the logic of both religion and education leads to an exploration of world religions generally. For this uneasy tension, cf. op. cit., pp. 13, 18–23, 39–44, 58–61.
4. The direction of the English political tradition is described in R. Williams (1961). For an imaginative affirmation of this potential as applied to our

present situation, cf. the House of Lords (1971) debate on 'Education in a Multi-racial Britain', in particular the speech of the late Ian Ramsey, then Bishop of Durham (Cols. 1137–49).

5. Chairman (1973–81) Edwin Cox, Senior Lecturer in Religious Education, University of London Institute of Education.

6. It is interesting to note the way a TV Western series (today's 'morality tales') has 'gone East': the Lone Ranger is transposed to Kung Fu, Puritan backdrop becomes Confucian.


## Notes for chapter 4

1. Agreed syllabuses have served a dual purpose. They have defined a common basis for religious education in a society which disagrees over questions of religious truth. Yesterday the disagreement was primarily between different Christian denominations, today between religions and over non-religious stances for living. They have also provided help for teachers seeking to teach the subject without any specialist knowledge. They have existed since the 1920s, but were required of all local education authorities by the 1944 Education Act. Cf. Hull (1975b).

2. For the shift from Bible to Life themes, see Chapter 1. The preface to the West Riding Syllabus singles out Dr R. J. Goldman for special thanks for his assistance.

3. Academic pressure to change this legal requirement has accumulated to such an extent that its death-knell has been sounded: J. M. Hull, *School Worship: An Obituary* (London, SCM Press, 1975b). Public outcry at the publication of the book indicates the likelihood of delay in the funeral arrangements.

4. The extent of 'secularization' in England is disputed; for contrasting analyses, cf. Wilson 1966 and Martin 1967. On the 'minority' status of the Church of England today, cf. Ling 1973.

5. Chairman Rabbi Hugo Gryn; Hon. Sec. John Prickett (both now deceased. Though SCIFDE itself lost momentum, its energy for promoting dialogue was carried forward into the Inter Faith Network for the UK).

6. D. Brennan, Religious Education Centre, Borough Road College, Isleworth, Middlesex; M. Grimmitt, Religious Education Centre, Westhill College, Birmingham. The Church's centre is at St Gabriel's College, London. It has a satellite at the College of Ripon and York, St John's, Lord Mayor's Walk, York. (Each of these centres has now been closed as a separate entity.)

7. Ninian Smart, Professor of Religious Studies at the University of Lancaster, has been Director of two of the Schools Council Projects on Religious Education, the Secondary one 1969–72, and the Primary one 1973–6 (Smart 1975). The model has become the basis for the Projects' own

approach and publications, and that of others, e.g. Grimmitt 1973, Kronenburg and Longley 1972.

## Notes for chapter 6

1. Thus the Jewish Continuity/Joint Israel Appeal, Chief Executive Jonathan Kastenbaum. Cf. Sacks (1994).
2. Absent since 1851, when fears were expressed that it would not be in the national interest to publish the strength of Christian pluralism alongside the established church.
3. See discussions in religious press.
4. What proportion of the UK Chinese community would describe itself as Buddhist? It is they who might significantly swell the numbers of those meeting regularly in Buddhist centres, viharas and monasteries. Cf. Weller (1997).
5. Not only has the number of weddings decreased by two-fifths in the last 25 years, but of those only 49 per cent are held in church (Church 1996: ch. 2, tables 14–16).
6. 'In the history of the spread of faith you will find little else but epidemiology, and causal epidemiology at that ... Happily, viruses don't win every time. Many children emerge unscathed from the worst that nuns and mullahs can throw at them' (Dawkins 1993).
7. Cf. Church (1996: table 2.11) on divorce, which has doubled since 1971; table 2.1 on births outside marriage, now four times as many as in 1971 and accounting for a third of all live births. Reliable data on child abuse are more difficult to come by. There were 90,000 emergency calls to Childline in 1995–6, which is four times as many as in 1986–7.
8. Cf. Centre for the Study of Implicit Religion and Contemporary Society, recently established at Middlesex University, see Bailey (1986 and 1997).
9. Cf. *Religion, State and Society*, quarterly journal of Keston Institute, 4 Park Town, Oxford.
10. Although not named in the text of the 1988 Education Reform Act, Buddhism, Hinduism, Islam, Judaism and Sikhism were identified as the principal religions of Great Britain, alongside Christianity. This was so in publications from the National Curriculum Council and including new agreed syllabuses from local education authorities.
11. Hence the famous Cowper-Temple amendment in the 1870 Forster Education Act which specified that in schools 'hereafter established by means of local rates, no catechism or religious formulary which is distinctive to any particular denomination shall be taught'.
12. For historical background, see Cruickshank (1963) and a more recent treatment, Waddington (1984).
13. On the evolution of syllabuses, see Hull (1975a). The claim of contribution to ecumenical cohesion was made more than thirty years ago by the then Bishop of London (Stopford 1966: pp. 11–29).

14. Hence the arrangements for public inspection. Whereas the school as a whole, and the curriculum delivered within it, is scrutinized by Ofsted on the same basis as in any other, special arrangements are made for the inspection of religious education. The legislation specifying this is contained in section 13 of the 1992 Education Act. Cf. Keiner (1996).

15. There are 96 primary schools (24 voluntary aided, the rest controlled), and four secondary (only one of which is voluntary aided) related to the Free Churches, as compared with nearly 6,500 C of E and RC primaries and 600-plus secondaries.

16. There are seventeen primary and five secondary Jewish voluntary aided schools.

17. The racial dimension of the slowness of this change was apparent in the recommendation against 'separate schools' in the Swann Report (1985) and is discussed again in Comper (1994, ch. 12).

18. The evidence from Ofsted reports on school inspections is highly revealing in these respects; cf. National Association of Head Teachers (1994). For a more general review of the debates surrounding collective worship, see Religious Education Council of England and Wales (1996).

19. On the joint initiative of the Inter Faith Network UK, the National Association of SACREs, and the RE Council of England and Wales, a year-long consultation is taking place with a view to establishing what consensus there might be that would achieve such changes as would effect greater sensitivity to educational priorities and the range of religious and secular sensibilities. See *Collective Worship Reviewed*, (Gay 1998).

20. See *Worldwide Adherents of All Religions by Six Continental Areas Mid-1995* available on: wwwzpub.com/un/pope/relig.html. This information is developed from a combination of recent UN population figures, the data in the 1982 *World Christian Encyclopedia*, edited by David Barrett, and other sources.

21. Not in any fixed and static sense, but dynamic and evolutionary, rooted in a purposive sense of humanity seeking fulfilment.

22. A recurrent theme within the *Journal of Moral Education*'s Moral for the Millennium conference held at St Martin's College, Lancaster in July 1996, and of the pages of that journal.

23. As an indication of the proponents' interest in engaging a consensus of world with the specific text of the Global Ethic, specially created web pages invite browsers to indicate their preferences for alternative wordings on the more contentious statements in the original; see www.silcom.com/-origin/poll.html.

24. Cf. SCAA's Revised Consultation Document arising from the National Forum for Values in Education and the Community, January 1997.

25. Principally from India, Pakistan and Bangladesh (in part, via the Commonwealth East Africa of Kenya and Uganda), from the Caribbean and Cyprus. This is not to imply, however, that the Jewish, Chinese and Vietnamese communities are accordingly of any less importance. The

Commonwealth connection for the Jewish community dates back to 1656 when, in the days of the Protectorate, they were readmitted to the UK.

26. This point is systematically expounded in the work of James Fowler, among others. Faith is understood generically as a human universal, including but not limited to or identified with religion (Fowler 1981), cf. Smith (1979).

27. From within the British Humanist Association, this is the position which has been consistently maintained by its representatives on the Religious Education Council of England and Wales since its foundation in 1973, and also on such local SACREs as have chosen to include Humanists as members. Its advocates from the BHA Education Committee include David Bothwell, Harry Stopes-Roe and John White.

## Notes for chapter 11

1. Code: CE Anglican, NC Nonconformist, C Catholic, J Jewish, M Muslim, S Sikh, U unattached; 15 age; b boy, g girl.

## Notes for chapter 14

1. Contrary to the impression sometimes given, members of newly settled minority groups are not invariably more devout than the host population.

2. As illustration of 'occasional conformity', membership statistics of the Church of England reveal that approximately three-fifths of the total population of this country are baptised and one-fifth confirmed. See Church of England (1981).

3. Detailed examples of the content of young people's responses during interviews are given in the full research report: Martin and Pluck (1977).

4. See Hardy (1979) and Laski (1980). For related experiences in childhood, see Robinson (1977) and Paffard (1973).

5. Independently, the work of D. Elkind and R. Williams in North America, of A. Godin in Belgium, of K. Tamminen in Finland, and of G. Westling and S. Pettersson in Sweden has built on the same Piagetian base with similar results.

## Notes for chapter 16

1. Not to be confused with earlier developmental hypotheses such as G. Hall's 'ontogeny recapitulates phylogeny' or Gesell and Ilg's (1946, Gesell et al.'s 1956) 'age portraits'. The 'cognitive developmental' approach has stressed much more the interaction between subject and social context.

2. Kohlberg's cross-cultural data are limited in quantity, but evidence from Israel, Turkey and Taiwan encouraged him to advance the claim to have discovered this trans-cultural constant: cf. Kohlberg, (1967.)

3. A cultural relativism which accepts the principle that humankind is utterly conditioned by time and place has emerged comparatively recently in the West – the 'Midas touch' turns all to history – whereas existence in the Indian tradition has been perceived as impermanent for thousands of years.

4. It is a moot point whether the funding and publicity were counter-productive. Certainly they guaranteed momentum, whereas a comparable venture in the field of Moral Education in Oxford sponsored by the Farmington Trust was cut at the quick of its development.

5. The year of completion of Kohlberg's Chicago PhD thesis: 'The Development of Modes of Moral Thinking and Choice in the Years Ten to Sixteen'.

6. In the follow-up longitudinal study the 75 original boys became 50; the reported regression is predominantly related to changed social context.

7. It would appear that Stage 6 is now regarded as the preserve of select moral philosophers. Stage 4B is becoming the most commonplace goal instead.

8. Opting out of the S. Milgram 'volunteers for electric shock' experiment appeared to correlate with Stage 6 thinkers or Stage 2. Since Stage 6 is no longer considered realistic for most people, the emergent basis of predictive correlation suddenly disappears.

9. The question of validity of the notion of 'altruism' whether in human or animal kind is at the centre of major debate in sociobiology: cf. Dawkins (1976), Montagu (1980).

10. The Indian emphasis on ahimsa (non-violence) reaches 'extreme' expression in the Jains who may even be wary of quenching living flame or breathing in a micro-organism that unwittingly could be killed.

11. See Niebuhr (1932), and Tillich (1957), ch 13–15. The link between the traditional Christian notion of sin and the Hegel-Marx translation of it as 'alienation' is often overlooked.

12. See C. S. Lewis (1943) for the general point and for school texts: Bull (1971) and Parrinder (1973).

13. The point is most commonly made with reference to Theravada Buddhism; cf. N. Smart (1971), p. 366.

14. On the theological front he appeals elsewhere to David Tracy's *Blessed Rage for Order* and *the Analogical Imagination.*

15. Some parallels have been drawn between Kohlberg's casuistical analysis of subjects' statements and those of Rabbinic tradition on the one hand and Roman Catholic consistorial courts on the other.

16. The field of comparative ethics is currently being opened up; see *Journal of Religious* Ethics and more particularly Hindery (1978).

17. Power and Kohlberg (1980) op. cit., p. 356 for religion and morality in Indian traditions; cf. N. Smart (1958), ch. 7.

18. The term 'religiate' is coined to indicate that there is public evidence and experience to be understood irrespective of private belief on the part of the individual.

19. The constitution of the RE Council of England and Wales includes representatives of professional teacher associations and of the main parent religious communities, including the British Humanist Association.

20. This was built into the Schools Council (1977a) *Ground Plan for the Study of Religion*; by contrast, the Soviet system concentrates on induction into one particular ideology.

21. Arguably a Jonestown or an Iranian surprise takeover might better be anticipated or countered given effective RE provision in US state schools?

## Notes for chapter 19

1. This account is based upon a highly effective assembly in a primary school in North-West England in 1981 and the author expresses his gratitude to the school concerned.

2. Surveys which have investigated the frequency, timing, length, order and key ingredients of assemblies are available. See Jones (1969), Schools Council (1972), West Glamorgan LEA (1979); and Gates (1982b). See also the work of P. Souper (1972) of the Education Department, Southampton University, on the conduct of assemblies regionally and nationally.

3. This is reflected in the increasingly elaborate statement about the Act of Worship found in LEA Agreed Syllabuses See Williams (1957), commonly quoted in subsequent syllabuses. The irony of RE and school assemblies becoming more elaborate when society itself was, if anything, becoming less overtly involved with church-going is made much of in Cannon (1964).

4. Despite several attempts to discredit John Hull personally after the publication of this book, he was already establised as a respected teacher and writer in the field of RE; he is the editor of the *British Journal of Religious Education* (then called *Learning for Living*), and Senior Lecturer in Educational Studies at Birmingham University

5. See Dearden (1968), Schools Council (1972), Cole (1974), Webster (1974), ILEA (1978). The Durham Report (Church of England Commission 1970) presents the argument for continuing the act of worship for all pupils, by analogy with the attendance of a 'mixed' congregation on civic occasions. The particular weakness of this comparison is the degree of 'voluntariness' involved in the school occasion. See the comment of Edwin Cox (1970) and Ninian Smart (1970).

6. The problem of arriving at a curriculum rationale for moral education has seemed in principle to be less difficult than for RE. Thus Hirst (1965) is confident that public norms for agreeing what constitutes morality are

easily available. This stance and that of Peters (1960) has been largely shared by John Wilson, Richard Pring and others. Peter McPhail too, while less conceptual in emphasis, is confident that ME justifies itself in terms of the concerns which arise from interpersonal encounter – almost a social psychology version of natural law.

For RE, the need for critical justification has entailed demonstrating that its grounds in the curriculum do not depend primarily on legal requirement or ecclesiastical tradition, but on the nature of religion as a form of knowledge and the continuing interest of boys and girls in the fundamental questions and insights which, together, constitute the religious experience of mankind past and present. The work of Ninian Smart (1968b) has been especially important in this field.

A summary of some of the debate in curriculum philosophy is found in Chapter 2. The Schools Council *Groundplan* (1977a), provides a theoretical taxonomy for the subject and the Schools Council *Primary RE: Discovering an Approach* (1977b), sets out the potential for primary school RE Arguably, the lack of consensus in society generally on moral questions and the common roots of religion and morality in the heart of personal intention, belief and belonging bring the matter of the mutuality of RE and ME back into focus.

7. This is implicit in much of James (1968) and apparent in the more recent vogue in references to 'Moral Education Across the Curriculum'.

8. For instance, the Roman Catholic Voluntary Aided Church School is more deliberately concerned to introduce boys and girls to the full practice and beliefs of the parent community of faith than the equivalent Anglican school which is seen as contributing to *national* educational provision. The distinction is set out in *The Fourth R* (1970). In addition, the local catchment of a church school may well bring in children of other than believing Christian backgrounds. How the school treats this minority/majority is critical both morally and theologically.

9. The issues here are the very theological ones which are the present preoccupation of both the World Council of Churches and the Vatican in their substantial dialogue with other faiths. Responses as to what is appropriate in schools in England and Wales can be found in National Catholic Commission for Racial Justice (1975) and Manchester [CE] Diocesan Board of Education (1981)

10. See McPhail (1972), Appendix A.

11. Welsh Office *Education Survey, No. 3, Religious Education in the Secondary Schools of Wales*, HMSO, 1975.

12. The lack of stories from beyond white and Western Europe is at last being recognized in more recent content selections for anthologies for assemblies. See Hedges (1970), Butler (1975), Purton (1981).

13. Martin et al. (1976), also Britton (1970).

14. Esslin (1968).

15. See, for instance, Avon, Birmingham (1974) and ILEA. (1968)

# Chapter sources

# Bibliography

Ahmed, A. S. (1988) *Discovering Islam: Making Sense of Muslim History and Society.* London: Routledge & Kegan Paul.

Alder, C. (1971) 'Education' *in Religion.* London: Goldsmiths' College.

Allen, C. (2005) 'Justifying Islamophobia: A Post-9/11 Consideration of the European Union and the British Contexts', *The American Journal of Islamic Social Sciences* **21**(3), 1–23.

Allen, R. F. (1977). 'Supplying the missing dimension', in Piediscalzi, N. and Collie, W. E. (eds) *Teaching about Religion in Public Schools.* Niles, IL: Argus Communications.

Alves, C. (1968) *Religion and the Secondary School.* London: SCM Press.

——— (1972) *The Christian in Education.* London: SCM Press.

——— (1991) 'Just a matter of words? The religious education debates in the House of Lords', *British Journal of Religious Education,* **13**(3), 168–74.

Alves, C. and Stanley, M. (1972) *Exploring God's World.* London: Macmillan.

Anthony, S. (1971) *The Discovery of Death in Childhood and After.* London: Allen Lane.

Argyle, M. (1972) *Psychology of Interpersonal Behaviour* (2nd edn). Harmondsworth: Penguin.

Argyle, M. and Beit-Hallahmi, B. (1975) *Social Psychology of Religion.* London: Routledge & Kegan Paul.

Arnold, M. (1889) *Reports on Elementary Schools, 1852–82.* London: Macmillan.

Ayer, A. J. (1936) *Language, Truth and Logic.* London: Gollancz.

Bailey, E. (1986) *A Workbook of Popular Religion.* Dorchester: Partners Publications.

——— (1997) *Implicit Religion in Contemporary Society.* Kampen: Kokpharos.

Baird, R. D. (1971) *Category Formation and the History of Religions.* The Hague: Mouton.

——— (1992) *Essays in the History of Religions.* New York: Peter Lang.

Barr, D. L. and Collie, W. E. (1981) 'Religion in the schools: The continuing controversy', *Church & State,* March, 8–16.

Barr, J. (1993) *Biblical Faith and Natural Theology: Gifford Lectures for 1991.* Oxford: Clarendon Press.

Barrett, D. B. (ed.) (1982) *The World Christian Encyclopaedia.* Oxford: Oxford University Press.

Barrett, D. B. et al. (eds) (2001) *World Christian Encyclopedia. A comparative survey of churches and religions in the modern world* (2nd edn,) 2 vols. Oxford and New York: Oxford University Press.

Beard, R. M. (1969) *An Outline of Piaget's Developmental Psychology.* London:, Routledge.

Beier, U. (ed.) (1966) *Origins of Life and Death: African Creation Stories.* Oxford: Heinemann.

Ben-Itto, H. (2005) *The Protocols of the Elders of Zion: the Lie that Wouldn't Die.* London: Vallentine Mitchell.

Berger, B. and Berger, P. (1983) *The War over the Family.* London: Hutchinson.

Billington, R. (1966) 'Five pointers for the success of the "non-church"', *The Times,* 19 November.

Birmingham (1974) *Agreed Syllabus* and *Handbook* (revised in 1975). Education Department, City of Birmingham.

Birnie, I. H. (1967) *Encounter.* London: McGraw-Hill.

Bok, S. (1978) *Lying: Moral Choice in Public and Private Life.* Hassocks, Sussex: Harvester Press.

Bowden, J. (1969) 'The Bible, Dodging the Main Question', *Learning for Living* 8(5), 20–3

Bowker, J. (1978) *The Religious Imagination.* London: Oxford University Press.

——— (1997) *Oxford Dictionary of World Religions.* London: Oxford University Press.

Bradford (1974) *Guidelines to RE. in a Multi-Faith Community.* City of Bradford, Education Authority.

Braybrooke, M. (ed.) (1992) *Stepping Stones to a Global Ethic.* London: SCM Press.

Brennan, D. (1969) *A Guide to Audio-Visual Aids for RE.* London: Chapman.

Bridger, P. (1974) *West Indian Family in Britain* Oxford, REP, 1974, pp. 7–12.

Brierley, P. (1997) *UK Christian Handbook, 1998–9,* Vol. 2: *Religious Trends.* London: Christian Research.

British Council of Churches (1972) *Inter-Faith Dialogue in Education.* London BCC.

Britton, J. (1970) 'What's the use? A schematic account of language function', *Educational Review,* **23**(1).

——— (1972) *Language and Learning.* Harmondsworth: Penguin.

Brophy, B. (1967) *RE in State Schools.* London: Fabian Society.

Broudy, H. S. (1971) 'Sartre's Existentialism and Education', *Education Theory* **21**(2), Spring, pp. 155–77.

Brown, A. (ed.) (1986) *Festivals in World Religions.* London: Longman.

Brusselmans, C. (ed.) (1980) *Toward Moral and Religious Maturity.* Parsippany,: Silver Burdett.

Bull, N. (1971) *The Way of Wisdom* Series III,: *Rulers.* London: Longman.

Burston, W. H. and Green, C. W. (1972) *Handbook for History Teacher* (2nd edn). London: Methuen.

Butler, D. G. (1975) *Many Lights.* London: Geoffrey Chapman.

Cam, P. (ed.) (1993/4) *Thinking Stories 1 and 2.* London: Hale & Iremonger.

Cambridgeshire Agreed Syllabus Conference (1970) *Religious Education.* Cambridge LEA.

Campbell, C (1969) 'Humanism in Britain: the Formation of a Secular Value-Oriented Movement', in Martin, D. (ed.) *A Sociological Yearbook of Religion in Britain*. London. SCM Press.

Cannon, C. (1964) 'Influence of Religion on Education Policy, 1902–44', *British Journal of Education Studies* **12**(2).

Carter, S. L. (1993) *The Culture of Disbelief: How American Law and Politics Trivialise Religious Devotion*. New York: HarperCollins.

Cassirer, E. (1953) *Language and Myth*. New York: Dover Publications.

Catholic Commission for Racial Justice (1984) *Learning from Diversity*. London: Catholic Media Office.

Chadwick, P. (1994) *Schools of Reconciliation: Issues in Joint Roman Catholic–Anglican Education*. London: Cassell.

Chazan, B. (1980) 'Jewish education and moral development', in Munsey, B. *Moral Development, Moral Education and Kohlberg*. AL: Religious Education Press pp. 298–325.

Cheetham, R. (2004) *Collective Worship. Issues and Opportunities*. London, SPCK

Christian, W. A. (1964) *Meaning and Truth in Religion*. Princeton. Princeton, NJ: UP.

——— (1972) *Opposition of Religious Doctrines: A Study of Dialogue among Religions*. London: Macmillan.

——— (1987) *Doctrines of Religious Communities: A Philosophical Guide*. New Haven, CT: Yale University Press.

Christian Education Movement (1966) *A Bibliography for the Use of Teachers* (6th edn). London: CEM

——— (n.d.) *"Which and Why" Cards, Talk Abouts, Focus Wallcharts, Projects*. London: CEM.

——— (n.d.) *Focus on Service*. London: Annandale.

Church, J. (ed.) (1996) *Social Trends 27*. London: HMSO.

Church of England (1980) *A Kind of Believing: Report to General Synod*. London: Church Information Office.

——— (1981) *Statistical Supplement to the Church of England Yearbook*. London: Church Information Office.

——— Commission on Religious Education in Schools (1970) *The Fourth R: The Report of the Commission* … (The Durham Report). London: National Society/SPCK.

*Church of England Yearbook 1997*. London: Church House Publishing.

Clements, S. et al. (1962) *Reflections*. Oxford: University Press;

Cleverley, G. and Phillips, B. (1975) *Northbourne Tales of Belief and Understanding*. London: McGraw.

Colby, A., Kohlberg, L., Gibbs, J. and Lieberman, M. (1980) 'A Longitudinal Study of Moral Judgment,' (unpublished paper). Cambridge MA: Harvard University: Center for Moral Education.

Cole, W. O. (ed.) (1973) *Religion in the Multi-Faith School*. Leeds: Yorkshire Committee for Community Relations.

——— (1974) 'School Worship – a Reconsideration', *Learning for Living* **13**(2).

—— (ed.) (1977) *World Religions: a Handbook for Teachers* (2nd edn). London: Commission for Racial Equality.

Comper, P. (1994) 'Racism, parental choice and the law', in Halstead, J. M. (ed.) *Parental Choice and Education Principles*. London: Kogan Page.

Conn, W. E. (1981) 'Affectivity in Kohlberg and Fowler', *Religious Education*, **76**(1) 33–48.

Cook, E. (1969) *The Ordinary and the Fabulous*. London: Cambridge University Press.

Cotterill, J. Hills (1969) *Facing Life's Challenge*. London: Nelson.

Cox, E. (1970) 'What are the assumptions', *Learning for Living* **10**(1), 11–13.

Crick, B. (1998) *Education for Citizenship and the Teaching of Democracy in Schools. Final report of the Advisory Group on Citizenship*. London: QCA.

Cruickshank, M. (1963) *Church and State in English Education, 1870 to the Present Day*. London: Macmillan.

Davie, G. (1994) *Religion in Britain since 1945: Believing without Belonging*. Oxford: Basil Blackwell.

Davies, J. (ed.) (1993) *The Family: Is It Just Another Lifestyle Choice?* London: Institute of Economic Affairs Health and Welfare Unit.

Davies, N. (1999) *The Isles: A History*. London: Macmillan.

Dawkins, R. (1976) *The Selfish Gene*. Oxford: Oxford University Press.

—— (1993) 'Viruses of the mind', in Dahibom, Bo (ed.), *Dennett and his Critics: Demystifying Mind*. Oxford: Basil Blackwell. Available http:// www.physics.wisc.edu/-shalizi/Dawkins/virusesofthemind.html

—— (1997) *Climbing Mount Improbable*. Harmondsworth: Penguin.

Dearden, R. F. (1968) *Philosophy of Primary Education*. London: Routledge.

Debray, R. (2002) *L'enseignement du fait religieux dans l'école laïque. Rapport au ministre de l'éducation nationale*. Paris: Odile Jacob.

d'Entrèves, A. P. (1951) *Natural Law*. London: Hutchinson.

DES (Department of Education and Science) (1967) *Children and their Primary Schools* (The Plowden Report), Vol. 1. London: HMSO.

—— (1969) *Reports on Education 58*, September. London: TTMS.

—— (1985) *GCSE National Criteria: Religious Studies*. London: HMSO.

DfE (Department for Education) (1994) *Religious Education and Collective Worship*, Circular 1/94. London: DfE.

Dimbleby, J. (1994) *The Prince of Wales: A Biography*. London: Little, Brown.

Dolbeare, K. M. and Hammond, P. E. (1971) *School Prayer Decisions*. Chicago: Chicago University Press.

Duffy, E. (1992) *The Stripping of the Altars: Traditional Religion in England, 1400–1580*. New Haven, CT: Yale University Press.

Duke, M. H. and Whitton, E. (1977) *A Kind of Believing*. London: General Synod Board of Education.

Durkin, K. (1996) *Developmental Social Psychology*. Oxford: Blackwell.

Duska, R. and Whelan, M. (1977) *Moral Development: A Guide to Piaget Kohlberg*. Dublin: Gill & Macmillan.

Dykstra, C. (1981) *Vision and Character: A Christian Educator's Alternative to Kohlberg*. Ramsey: Paulist Press.

Educational Foundation for Visual Aids (1968), *Visual Aids: films, filmstrips and transparencies*, Part I, *RE* London.

Elias, J. L. (1982) 'Ideology and RE', *Lumen Vitae* **37** (4), 382–95.

Eliot, T. S. (1939) *The Idea of a Christian Society*. London: Faber.

Elkind, D. (1961) 'The child's conception of his religious denomination: 1 The Jewish child', *Journal of Genetic Psychology*, Provincetown, MA: USA.

——— (1962) 'The child's conception of his religious denomination: 2 The Catholic child', *Journal of Genetic Psychology*, Provincetown, MA: USA.

——— (1963) 'The child's conception of his religious denomination: 3 The Protestant child', *Journal of Genetic Psychology*, Provincetown, MA: USA.

——— (1964a) 'Age changes in the meaning of religious identity', *Review of Religious Research*, **6**(1), New York Religious Research Association, .

——— (1964b) 'The child's conception of his religious identity' *Lumen Vitae* **19**, Brussels, Lumen Vitae Press pp. 635–46.

——— (1964c) 'Piaget's semi-clinical interview and the study of spontaneous religion', *Journal for the Scientific Study of Religion* **4**, 40–7.

——— (1967) 'The Developmental Psychology of Religion', in Kidd, A. H. and Rivoire, J. L. *Perceptual Development in Children* (Chapter 8). London: University of London Press.

——— (1971) 'Development of religious understanding in children and adolescents', in Strommen, M. (ed.) *Research on Religious Development*. New York: Hawthorn Books.

Elkind, D. and Flavell, J. H. (1969) *Studies in Cognitive Development*. Oxford: Oxford University Press.

Elkind, D. Long, D. and Spilka, B. (1967) 'The child's conception of prayer', *Journal for the Scientific Study of Religion*, (6), Storrs, CT: University of Connecticut.

ERA (1988) *Education Reform Act*. London: HMSO. Downloadable from government website: http://www.opsi.gov.uk/acts/acts1988/Ukpga_19880040_en_1.htm#end

Esslin, M. (1968) *The Theatre of the Absurd*. Harmondsworth: Penguin.

Evans, C. (1973) *Cults of Unreason*. London: Harrap.

Evans, K. (1985) *The Development and Structure of the English Education System*. London: Hodder & Stoughton.

Evening, M. (1972) *Approaches to RE* London: Hodder.

Everington, J. (1996) 'A question of authenticity: the relationship between educators and practitioners in the representation of religious traditions', *British Journal of Religious Education* **18**(2), 69–77.

Fernhout, H. (1989) 'Moral education as grounded in faith', *Journal of Moral Education* **18**(3), 186–98.

Ferré, F. (1967a) *Basic Modern Philosophy of Religion*. New York: Scribner.

——— (1967b) *Theology for Christian Education*. Philadelphia, PA: Westminster.

Finel, J. (ed.) (1975) *World Religions for CSE or 16 Plus*. Brunner School, Shap Working Party.

Flannery, A. (ed.) (1981) *Vatican Council II: The Conciliar and Post-Conciliar Documents.* Chapter 64: Pastoral Constitution on Church in the Modern World. Leominster: Fowler Wright.

Fowler, J. W. (1981) *Stages of Faith: The Psychology of Human Development and the Quest for Meaning.* New York: Harper & Row.

Francis, L. (1981) *Christianity and the Child Today. A Research Perspective on the Situation in England.* Oxford: Farmington Institute for Christian Studies.

Fromm, E. (1942) *Fear of Freedom.* London: Routledge & Kegan Paul.

—— (1947) *Man for Himself: An enquiry into the Psychology of Ethics.* New York: Rinehart.

—— (1956) *The Sane Society.* London: Routledge & Kegan Paul.

—— (1967) *Psychoanalysis and Religion.* New York: Bantam.

Furth, H. G. (1970) *Piaget for Teachers.* Englewood Cliffs, NJ: Prentice-Hall.

Fynn (1974) *Mr God, This Is Anna.* London: Collins.

Galloway, A. D. (1975) 'Theology and Religious Studies – the Unity of Our Discipline', *Religious Studies* 11(2), 157–66.

Gates, B. E. (1975) 'The Politics of Religious Education', in Taylor, M. (ed.) *Progress and Problems in Moral Education.* Slough: National Foundation for Educational Research.

—— (1976) 'Religion in the Developing World of Children and Young People. Unpublished doctoral thesis, Lancaster University.

—— (ed.) (1982a) *RE Directory of England and Wales.* Lancaster' St Martin's RE Enquiry Service.

—— (1982b) *How They Assemble: a report on the act of worship in Lancashire Schools.* Lancashire: St Martin's College.

—— (1993) *Time for Religious Education and teachers to match. A digest of under-provision.* Lancaster: Religious Education Council.

—— (1995) 'Secular education and the logic of religion: shall we re-invent the wheel?', in Masefield, P. (ed.) *Aspects of Religion: Essays in Honour of Ninian Smart* (Toronto Studies in Religion, Vol. 18). New York: Peter Lang.

—— (2005a) 'Guest Editorial', *British Journal of Religious Education* 27(2), 99–102.

—— (2005b) 'Faith schools and colleges of education since 1800', in Gardner, R. et al. (eds) *Faith Schools: Consensus or conflict,* London: RoutledgeFalmer.

Gay, J. D. (ed.) (1998) *Collective Worship Reviewed.* Abingdon: Culham College Institute. downloadable at: http://www.culham.ac.uk/Res_conf/cw_reviewed

Gesell, A. and Ilg, F. L. (1946) *The Child from Five to Ten.* London, Hamish Hamilton

Gesell, A., Ilg, F. L. and Ames, L. B. (1956) *Youth. The Years from Ten to Sixteen.* London: Hamish Hamilton.

Gill, J. (2000a) 'The nature and justifiability of the Act of Collective Worship in schools'. unpublished PhD thesis, University of Plymouth.

———— (2000b) 'Approaches to Collective Worship in Multi-Faith Schools', in Leicester, M., Modgil, C. and Modgil, S. *Education, Culture and Values, V: Spiritual and Religious Education.* London: Falmer Press.

Godin, A. (1957) *Research in religious psychology,* Brussels Lumen Vitae Press.

———— (ed.) (1957–68) *Lumen Vitae* quarterly, Brussels: Lumen Vitae Press.

———— (1960) 'Magical mentality and the sacramental life in children', *Lumen and Vitae* **15**, Brussels: Lumen Vitae Press.

———— (1962) *Child and adult before God,* Brussels: Lumen Vitae Press.

———— (1968a) *From Cry to word: contributions to the psychology of prayer,* Brussels: Lumen Vitae Press.

———— (1968b) 'Genetic development of the symbolic function: meaning and limits of the work of R. Goldman', *Religious Education* **LX**(VIII) New York: Religious Education Association.

———— (1971) 'Some Developmental Tasks in Christian Education', in Strommen, M. (ed.) *Research on Religious Development.* New York: Hawthorn Books pp. 109–54.

Goldman, R. J. (1959) 'What is religious knowledge?', *National Froebel Education Bulletin* **117**, London: Froebel Education Institute.

———— (1963) 'Children's Spiritual Development', *Studies in Education: First Years in School,* London: Evans.

———— (1964) *Religious Thinking from Childhood to Adolescence.* London: Routledge & Kegan Paul.

———— (1965a) 'The Application of Piaget's schema of operational thinking to religious story data', *British Journal of Educational Psychology* **35**(2).

———— (1965b) *Readiness for Religion.* London: Routledge & Kegan Paul.

———— (1965–) *Symbols, Bread, Myself.* London: Hart-Davie's.

Gray, I. A. S. (1999) 'Religious Observance in Schools: A Scottish Perspective', *British Journal of Religious Education* **22**(1), 35–45.

Greeley, A. (1974) *Ecstasy: A Way of Knowing.* Englewood Cliffs, NJ: Prentice-Hall.

———— (1992) 'Religion in Britain, Ireland and the USA', in Jowell, R. et al. (eds) *British Social Attitudes: Social Attitudes,'* 11. Aldershot: Dartmouth pp. 51–79.

Green, R. M. (1978). *Religious Reason, The Rational and Moral Basis of Religious Belief.* New York: Oxford University Press.

———— (1988) *Religion and Moral Reason: A New Method for Comparative Study.* Oxford: Oxford University Press.

Greer, J. (1972) *A Questioning Generation.* Belfast: Church of Ireland Board of Education.

Grimmitt, M. (1973) *What Can I Do in Religious Education?* Great Wakering: Mayhew-McCrimmon.

Grosset, P. (1966) *Things that Matter.* London: Evans.

Hacker, G. et al. (1969) *Conflict 1 and 2.* London: Nelson.

Hampshire Agreed Syllabus Conference (1970) *Approaches to RE.* Hampshire LEA.

Hancock, A. and Robertson, R. A. (1965) *People Today*, 1. *Ourselves*, 2. *Our Society*. London: Longman.

Hand, M. (2006) *Is Religious Education Possible? A Philosophical Investigation*. London: Continuum.

Haq, S. (1980) 'Moral Education in Pakistan', *Journal of Moral Education* **9**(3), 156–65.

Hardy, A. (1979) *The Spiritual Nature of Man: A Study of Contemporary Religious Experience*. Oxford: Clarendon Press.

Hargreaves, D. (1990) 'The Future of Teacher Education', Hockerill Lecture, Hockerill Educational Foundation, Frinton-on-Sea.

—— (1994) *The Mosaic of Learning: School and Teachers for the Next Century*. London: Demos, Paper 8.

Hay, D. (1982) *Exploring Inner Space*. Harmondsworth: Penguin.

Hedges, S. (1970) *With One Voice*. Exeter: Religious Education Press.

Hemming, J. (1973) 'The continuing search', *London Educational Review* **2**(2), 61–9.

Hick, J. (1970) 'The Re-construction of Christian Belief for Today and Tomorrow: 2. Other World Religions', *Theology* **73**(603), pp. 399–405.

—— (ed.) (1974) *Truth and Dialogue: the Relationship between World Religions*. London: Sheldon Press.

Hilliard, F. H. (1961) *Teaching Children about World Religions*. London: Harrap.

—— (1964) 'Divinity Studies in Teacher Training', *Theology* **67**(532), October, pp. 438–42.

—— (1965) *How Men Worship*. London: Routledge & Kegan Paul.

Hindery, R. (1978) *Comparative Ethics in Hindu and Buddhist Tradition*. Delhi, Motilal Banarsidass.

Hinnells, J. R. (ed.) (1970) *Comparative Religion in Education*. Newcastle: Oriel Press.

Hinnells, J. R. and Sharpe, E. J. (eds) (1972) *Hinduism*. Newcastle: Oriel Press.

Hirst, P. H. (1965) 'Morals, Religion and the Maintained School', *British Journal of Educational Studies* **14**(1).

—— (1967) 'The Role of Religion in Public Education, in Sizer, T. R. (ed.) *Religion and Public Education* Boston, MA: Houghton Mifflin pp. 329–39.

—— (1972) 'Liberal Education and the Nature of Knowledge', in Dearden, R. F. et al. (eds) *Education and the Development of Reason* London: Routledge & Kegan Paul pp. 391–414.

Hirst, P. H. and Peters, R. S. (1970) *The Logic of Education*. London: Routledge.

Hocking, W. E. (1940) *Living Religions and a World Faith*. New York: Macmillan.

Hoggart, R. (1958) *Uses of Literacy*, Harmondsworth: Penguin. pp. 112–19

Holbrook, D. (1964) *The Secret Places*. London: Methuen.

Holm, J. (1969) 'Life Themes: What are They?', *Learning for Living* **9**(2), 15–18.

———— (1975) *Teaching Religion in School.* Oxford: Oxford University Press.

Holm, J. and Bowker, J. (eds) (1994) *Picturing God.* London: Pinter.

Hourani, G. F. (1980) 'Ethical presuppositions of the Qur'ān', *Muslim World.*

———— (1985) *Reason and Tradition in Islamic Ethics.* Cambridge: Cambridge University Press.

House of Lords (1971) Education in a Multi-racial Britain, *Hansard* 326:23, 15 December.

Howe, G. M. et al. (1963) *National Atlas of Disease and Mortality.* London: Nelson.

Hull, J. M. (1972) 'The Theology of Themes', *Scottish Journal of Theology* **25**(1), 20–31.

Hull, J. M. (1975a) 'Agreed Syllabuses, past, present and future', in Smart, N. and Horder, D. (eds) *New Movements in RE* London: Temple Smith pp. 97–119.

———— (1975b) *School Worship: An Obituary.* London: SCM Press.

———— (1989) *The Act Unpacked.* London: Christian Education Movement.

Huntington, S. P. (2004) *Who are we? America's Great Debate.* London: Simon & Schuster.

Hyde, K. E. (ed.) (1970) *Topic Books: The Senses 1 and 2; Neighbours 1 and 2.* London: Lutterworth Educational.

Inner London Agreed Syllabus Conference (1968) *Learning for Life.* London ILEA.

Inner London Education Authority (1978) *Assemblies in County Schools* London: County Hall.

Institute of Christian Education (1954) *Religious Education in Schools.* London: SPCK.

Isaacs, N. (1930) 'Children's *why* questions', in Isaacs, S. *Intellectual Growth of Young Children.* London: Routledge & Kegan Paul.

Jackson, R. (1997) *Religious Education: An Interpretative Approach.* London: Hodder & Stoughton.

———— (ed.), (2003) *International Perspectives on Citizenship. Education and Religious Diversity.* London: RoutledgeFalmer.

James, A. G. (1974) *Sikh children in Britain.* London: Oxford University Press.

James, C. (1968) *Young Lives at Stake.* London: Collins.

Jones, C. M. (1969) *Worship in the Secondary School.* Religious Education Press.

———— (1972) *RE in the Primary School.* London: Evans Methuen.

———— (1973) 'Religious or moral education?', *London Educational Review* **2**(1), 54–9.

Joy, D. M. (1980) 'Moral development: Evangelical perspectives', *Religious Education* **75**(2), 142–51.

Jurgensmeyer, M. (1993) *The New Cold War? Religious Nationalism Confronts the Secular State.* Berkeley, CA:, university of California Press.

Kalam, T. P. (1981) 'The Myth of Stages and Sequence in Moral and Religious Development', unpublished doctoral thesis, Lancaster University.

Katz, M. (2004) *Banares Muharram and the Coals of Karbala* (film). Madison, WI: University of Wisconsin Centre for South Asia.

Keiner, J. (1996) 'Opening up Jewish education to inspection: the impact of the Ofsted inspection system in England', *Education Policy Analysis Archives* **4**(5).

Kent, G. (1968) *Projects in the Primary School.* London: Batsford.

Kinniburgh, E. (1970) 'Theology and the Teacher of Religious Knowledge', *Scottish Journal of Theology* **23**(2), May, 183–90.

Klostermeier, K. (1969) *Hindu and Christian in Vrindaban.* London: SCM Press.

Kohlberg, L. (1967) 'Moral and Religious Education and the public schools: A developmental view', in Sizer, T. (ed.) *The Role of Religion in Public Education.* Boston, MA: Houghton-Mifflin.

—— (1971a) 'From is to ought: How to commit the naturalistic fallacy and get away with it in the study of moral development', in Mischel, T. (ed.) *Cognitive Development and Epistemology* New York: Academic Press, pp. 151–235.

—— (1971b) 'Stages of moral development as a basis for moral education', in Beck, C. M., Crittenden, B. S. and Sullivan, E. V. (eds) *Moral Education: Interdisciplinary Approaches.* Toronto: University Press, pp. 23–92.

—— (1974) 'Education moral development and faith', *Journal of Moral Education*, **4**, 5–16.

—— (1976) 'Moral stages and moralization: The cognitive developmental approach', in Lickona, T. (ed.) *Moral Development and Behaviour.* New York: Holt, Rinehart Winston, pp. 31–53.

—— (1980) 'Educating for a just society: An updated and revised statement', in Munsey, B. (ed.) *Moral Development, Moral Education and Kohlberg.* Birmingham AL: Religious Education Press, pp. 455–70.

Kohlberg, L. and Candee, D. (1984) 'The Relationship of Moral Judgement to Moral Action', in Kohlberg, L. *Psychology of Moral Development* (Chapter 7). New York: Harper & Row.

Kohlberg, L. Colby, A., Gibbs, J., Speicher-Dubin, B. and Power, C. (1980) *The Measurement of Moral Judgment.* Cambridge for Moral Education London: MA: Harvard Center.

Kohlberg, L. and Power, C. (1981) 'Moral development, religious thinking and the question of a seventh stage', in *Essays on Moral Development.* London: Harper & Row.

Konstant, D. (1966) *Syllabus for Catholic Primary Schools.* London: Burns & Oates.

—— (1967) *Secondary Schools.* London, Burns & Oates.

Kozol, J. (1972) *Free Schools.* New York: Bantam.

Krausz, E. (1971) *Ethnic Minorities in Britain.* London: MacGibbon & Kee.

Kronenburg, S. and Longley, P. (1972) *Discovering Religion Workcards.* Guildford: Lutterworth Educational.

Küng, H. (1991) *Global Responsibility: In Search of a New World Ethic.* London: SCM Press.

Küng, H. and Kuschel, K.-J. (1993) *A Global Ethic. The Declaration of the Parliament of the World's Religions*. London: SCM Press.

Kung, H. and Moltmann, J. (eds) (1990) 'The ethics of world religions and human rights', *Concilium*, Special Issue 1990/2. SCM Press.

Lancashire Agreed Syllabus Conference (1968) *Religion and Life*. Preston: Lancashire LEA.

Lance, D. (1967) *11–16. A Complete Course for RE at the Secondary School Level*. London: Darton, Longman & Todd.

Lane, D. (1972) *Politics and Society in the USSR*. London: Weidenfeld and Nicolson.

Langer, S. (1957) *Philosophy in a New Key: A Study in the Symbolism of Reason, Rite and Art*. Cambridge, MA: Harvard University Press.

Laski, M. (1961) *Ecstasy: a study of some secular and religious experiences*. London: Barrie & Rockliff.

―――― (1980) *Everyday Ecstasy*. London: Thames & Hudson.

Lealman, B. (1983) 'The last step of reason?', *Journal of Moral Education* **12**(2), 104–10.

Lee, R. S. (1965) *Your Growing Child and Religion*. Harmondsworth: Penguin.

Lerner, M. J. (1980) *The Belief in a Just World: A Fundamental Delusion*. New York: Plenum Press.

Lewis, C. S. (1943) 'Illustrations of the Tao', in *Abolition of Man*, Appendix. Oxford: Clarendon Press.

Lewis, E. (nd) *Children and Their Religion*. London: Sheed & Ward.

Lewis, P. (1994) *Islamic Britain: Religion, Politics and Identity among British Muslims*. London: I. B. Tauris.

Ling, T. (1973) 'Religion in England: Majorities and Minorities', *New Community* **2**(2), 117–24.

Little, D. (1993) 'The nature and basis of human rights', in Outka, G. and Reeder, J. P. Jr (eds) *Prospects for a Common Morality*. Princeton, NJ: Princeton University Press.

Little, L. C. (1968a) *Religion and Public Education in the News, 1957–67* Westminster: The author.

―――― (1968b) *Religion and Public Education: a Bibliography* (3rd edn). Pittsburg, PA: University Book Center.

―――― (1971) 'The Role of Religion in Public Education', in Strommen, M. P. (ed.) *Research on Religious Development* (Chapter 8). New York: Hawthorn.

Loukes, H. (1961) *Teenage Religion*. London: SCM Press.

―――― (1965) *New Ground in Christian Education*. London: SCM Press.

―――― (1968) 'Religious Education: the Death of a Subject', *Times Educational Supplement*, 12 April.

―――― (1973) *Teenage Morality*. London: SCM Press.

Luhmer, K. (1990) 'Moral education in Japan', *Journal of Moral Education* **19**(3), 172–81.

Lukes, S. (1985) *Marxism and Morality*. Oxford: Clarendon Press.

Lupton, H. (1970) *RE in the CSE*. CEM, Teachers' Dept Paper, Annandale.

Mabey, R. (ed.) (1970), *Connections: A Teachers' Guide.* Harmondsworth: Penguin.

Macmurray, J. (1935) *Reason and Emotion.* London: Faber.

McPhail, P. (1972) *Moral Education in the Secondary School.* London: Longman.

MacRae, D. (1964) 'The Crisis of Sociology', in Plumb, J. H. *Crisis in the Humanities.* Harmondsworth: Penguin.

Madge, V. (1965) *Children in search of meaning.* London: SCM Press.

—— (1971) *Introducing young children to Jesus.* London: SCM Press.

Manchester Diocesan Board of Education (1981) *Church School Education and Islam in Multi-faith Manchester.* Manchester CE Diocese.

Marratt, H. (1971) *The Recruitment, Employment and Training of Teachers of Religious Education.* London: British Council of Churches.

—— (1989) *Handbook on RE for Agreed Syllabus Conferences, SACREs and Schools.* St Martin's College Lancaster: Religious Education Council.

Marshall, S. (1963) *Experiment in Education.* Cambridge: Cambridge University Press.

Martell, B. (1972) 'Religion in the secondary school', *London Educational Review* 1(3), 52–60.

Martin, B. and Pluck, R. (1977) *Young People's Beliefs.* London: Church of England Board of Education, mimeo.

Martin, D. (1967) *A Sociology of English Religion.* London: SCM Press.

Martin, N. et al. (1976) *Writing and Learning Across the Curriculum 11–16.* London: Ward Lock.

Marty, M. E. and Scott Appleby, R. (eds) (1991–5) *Fundamentalism Project* (Vols 1–5). Chicago: Chicago University Press.

Maurer, A. (1966) 'Maturation of Concepts of Death', *British Journal of Medical Psychology* 39(1).

May, P. R. (1971) *Moral Education in School.* London: Methuen.

May, P. R. and Johnston, O. R. (1968) *Religion in Our Schools.* London: Hodder.

Mehta, G. (1980) *Karma Cola: Marketing the Mystic East.* London: Jonathan Cape.

Mernissi, F. (1996) *Rebellion's Women and Islamic Memory.* London: Zed Books.

Metcalf, B. (1983) 'The case of Pakistan.' in Merkl, P. H. and Smart, N. (eds) *Religion and Politics in the Modern World.* New York: New York University Press.

Michaelson, R. (1970) *Piety in the Public School: Trends and Issues in the Relationship between Religion and the Public School in the US.* New York: Macmillan.

Millar Report (1972) *Moral and Religious Education.* Edinburgh: HMSO.

Miller, H. L. (1966) 'The Preparation for Teaching Religion in the Public School' Athens, OH: Ohio State University PhD.

Mischey, E. J. (1976) 'Faith Development and Its Relationship to Moral Reasoning and Identity Status in Young Adults' unpublished PhD thesis, Toronto University.

Mogford, B. (1968) 'Ideas on Primary Education', *Ideas* 6, 1–5.

Montagu, A. (ed.) (1980) *Sociobiology Examined.* London: Oxford University Press.

Moran, G. (1971) *Design for Religion*. New York: Search Press.

Morrish, I. (1973) *The Background of Immigrant Children*. London: Allen & Unwin.

Mukherjee, H. (1983) 'Moral education in a plural society', *Journal of Moral Education* **12**(2), 125–30.

Mumford, C. (1979) *Young Children and RE*. Leeds: Leeds University.

Munsey, B. (1980) *Moral Development, Moral Education and Kohlberg*. Birmingham, AL: Religious Education Press.

Murray, D. (1985) *Worlds Apart: Segregated Schools in Northern Ireland*. Belfast: Appletree Press.

National Association of Head Teachers (1994) *Survey on RE and Collective Worship: A Policy Statement*. London: NAHT.

National Catholic Commission for Racial Justice (1975) *Where Creed and Colour Matter: A Survey of Black Children in Catholic Schools*. London: Catholic Information Office.

National Swedish Board of Education (1971) in May Newsletter: *School Research*. Stockholm.

Nationwide Initiative in Evangelism (1980) *Prospects for the Eighties*. London: Bible Society.

Naylor, N. (1971) 'An analysis of courses in Religion in Colleges of Education with critical comments', in Religious Studies Section *Bulletin No. 2*, (June) A.T.C.D.E., 1–17.

Newson, J. and Newson, E. (1968) *Four Years Old in an Urban Community*. London: Allen & Unwin.

Niebuhr, R. (1932) *Moral Man, Immoral Society*. New York: Scribner.

Nielsen, N. C. (1993) *Fundamentalism, Myths and World Religions*. Albany: State of New York University Press

Northamptonshire Agreed Syllabus Conference (1968), *Fullness of Life: an Exploration of Christian Faith for Primary Schools* and *Life and Worship* (Senior section), Northants LEA.

O'Connor, D. J. (1957) *Introduction to the Philosophy of Education*. London: Routledge.

Ogden, S. (1967) 'The Strange Witness of Unbelief', in *The Reality of God* (Chapter 4). London: SCM.

Ogletree, T. W. (1966) *Death of God Controversy*. London SCM Press.

O'Keeffe, B. (1986) *Faith and Culture and the Dual System: A Comparative Study of Church and County Schools*. Brighton: Falmer Press.

O'Leary, D. (ed.) (1983) *RE and Young Adult*. Slough: St Paul Publications.

Oliner, S. P. and Oliner P. M. (1988) *The Altruistic Personality. Rescuers of Jews in Nazi Europe*. New York: Macmillan.

Ontario Department of Education (1971) *World Religions*. Toronto.

Opie, I. and Opie, P. (1959) *Lore and Language of School Children*. Oxford: Oxford University Press.

Oser, F. (1980) 'Stages of religious judgment', in Brusselmans, C. *Toward Moral and Religious Maturity*. Pansippany, Silver Burdett pp. 277–315.

Ouseley, H. (2001) *Community Pride, not Prejudice. Making Diversity Work in Bradford.* Bradford: Bradford Vision.

Paffard, M. (1973) *Inglorious Wordsworths: a study of some transcendental experiences in childhood and adolescence.* London: Hodder.

Parrinder, E. G. (1973) *Themes for Living: Man and God.* London: Hulton.

Parrinder, G. (1975) 'Religious Studies in Great Britain', *Religion* (IHAR 13th Congress Issue), 1–11.

Partington G. (1984) '(Im)moral education in South Australia', *Journal of Moral Education* **13**(2), 90–100.

—— (1990) 'Moral education in some English-speaking societies: antinomian and fundamentalist challenges', *Journal of Moral Education* **19**(3), 182–91.

Pearce, B. (ed.) (1997) *The Quest for Common Values: Report of a Seminar.* London: Inter Faith Network UK.

Peatling, J. H. (1973) 'The Incidence of Concrete and Abstract Religious Thinking in the Interpretation of Three Bible Studies', unpublished PhD Thesis, New York University.

—— (1977) 'On Beyond Goldman: Religious Thinking and the 1970s', in *Learning for Living* **16**(3), 99–108.

Peck, R. F. et al. (1960) *The Psychology of Character Development.* New York: Wiley.

Peel, E. A. (1972) *Nature of Adolescent Judgement.* London: Staples.

Peters, R. S. (1960) *Ethics and Education.* Routledge & Kegan Paul.

Phenix, P. (1958) *Philosophy of Education.* New York: Holt, Rinehart & Winston.

—— (1959) *Religious Concerns in Contemporary Education; A Study of Reciprocal Relations.* New York: Columbia University Press.

—— (1964) *Realms of Meaning.* New York: McGraw-Hill.

—— (1966) *Education and Worship of God.* Philadelphia: Westminster.

Piaget, J. (1926) *The language and thought of the child.* London: Routledge.

—— (1929) *The child's conception of the world.* London: Routledge.

—— (1952) *The child's conception of number.* London: Routledge.

Piaget, J. and Weil, A. (1951) 'The development of the idea of the homeland and of relations with other countries', *International Social Science Bulletin* **3**, 561–71.

Pieterse, J. N. (2004) *Globalization and Culture. Global Mélange.* Lanham, NJ: Rowan & Littlefield.

Pirner, M. (2006) 'Popular Media Culture – Common Ground for Religious Education in a World or Religious Diversity?' Paper presented at Nuremberg Forum IX.

Power, C. (1979) 'The Moral Atmosphere of a Just Community High School' doctoral dissertation, Harvard Graduate School.

Power, F. C. and Kohlberg, L. (1980) 'Religion, morality and ego development', in Brusselmans, C. (ed.) *Towards Moral and Religious Maturity.* Parsippany, Silver Burdett, pp. 343–12.

Purton, R. (1981) *Festivals and Celebration.* Oxford: Blackwell.

QCA and DfES (Department for Education and Skills) (2004) *Religious Education. The non-statutory national framework.* London: Qualifications and Curriculum Authority. Available to download from:http://www.qca.org.uk/9817.html

Rainbow, J. D. C. (ed.) (1975) 'The Lancashire Religious Education Survey', *Learning for Living* **14**(5), 170–86, 193.

Ramji, R. (2005) 'From Navy Seals to The Siege: Getting to Know the Muslim Terrorist, Hollywood Style', *Journal of Religion and Film* **9**(2).

Ramsey, I. T. (1971) 'Education in a Multi-Racial Britain', *Hansard: House of Lords Official Report,* 326:23.

Reimer, E. (1971) *School is Dead.* Harmondsworth: Penguin.

Religious Education Council of England and Wales (REC) (1996) *Collective Worship in Schools.* Abingdon: Culham College Institute.

———— (1972) *Frontiers of Enquiry, 4. The Gods.* London: Granada.

Richardson, R. (ed.) (2000) *The Parekh Report: The Future of* London: Profile Books.

Richmond, J. (1970) *Theology and Metaphysics.* London: SCM Press.

Richmond, W. K. (1973) *Free School.* London: Methuen.

Riesman, D. (1961) *The Lonely Crowd,* 'Preface' (3rd edn). New Haven, CT: Yale University Press.

Robinson, E. (1972a) 'I called it "It"', *Faith and Freedom,* Manchester College, Oxford.

———— (1972b) 'How does a child experience religion', *Times Educational Supplement,* 15 December.

———— (1977) *The Original Vision.* Oxford: Religious Experience Research Unit.

Robinson, J. A. T. (1965) *New Reformation.* London: SCM Press.

Robson, G. (1997) 'Religious education, government policy and professional practice, 1988–95', *British Journal of Religious Education* **19**(1) 13–23.

Rodhe, S. (1971) in Parrinder, G. (ed.) *Teaching about Religions.* London: Harrap, pp. 77–98.

Rosen, C. (1967) 'All in the day's work', in Britton, J. (ed.) *Talking and writing.* London: Methuen.

Rosenzweig, L. (1977) 'Towards universal justice: Some implications of L. Kohlberg's research for Jewish identity', *Religious Education* **72**, November–December.

———— (1980) 'Kohlberg in the classroom: Moral education models', in Munsey, B. (ed.) *Moral Development, Moral Education and Kohlberg.* Birmingham AL: Religious Education Press, pp. 359–80.

Ruddock, J. (1972) *Cambridge Journal of Education.* **22**.

Runnymede Trust (1997) *Islamophobia.* London: Runnymede Trust.

Russell, K. and Tooke, J. (1967) *Learning to Give.* Oxford: Pergamon.

Sacks, J. (1994) *Will We Have Jewish Grandchildren? Jewish Continuity and How to Achieve It.* London: Valentine Mitchell.

Schacht, J. and Bosworth, C. E. (1979) *The Legacy of Islam* (2nd edn). London: Oxford University Press.

Schools Council (1967) *Examination Bulletin 17. CSE Trial Exams: RK* London: HMSO.

—— (1971) *Working Paper 36: Religious Education in the Secondary School.* London: Evans Methuen.

—— (1972) *Working Paper 44: Religious Education in Primary Schools.* London: Longman.

—— (1977a) *Groundplan for the Study of Religion.* London: Schools Council.

—— (1977b) *Primary RE: Discovering an Approach.* London: Macmillan Education.

—— Integrated Studies (1972) *Teachers Guide Unit 2 and 3.* Oxford: Oxford University Press.

—— Writing Research Unit (1974) *Development of Writing Ability, 11–18.* London: Macmillan.

School Curriculum and Assessment Authority (SCAA) (1994) *Model Syllabuses for Religious Education,* 2 vols: *Model 1: Living Faiths Today; Model 2: Questions and Teaching.* London: SCAA.

Scottish Executive Education Department (2005) *Circular 1/2005 Provision of Religious Observance in Scottish Schools,* published electronically at http://www.scotland.gov.uk/Publications/2005/03/20778/53820

Shap Working Party, (1972a) *World Religions: Aids for Teachers.* London: Community Relations Commission.

—— (1972b) 'World Religions in Education: Islam', *Learning for Living.* **11**(3).

—— (2007) *Calendar of Religious Festivals,* obtainable via Shap website: http://www.shap.org.

Sharpe, E. J. (1972) 'Christian Attitudes to Non-Christian Religions', in *World Religions: Aids for Teachers.* London: Community Relations Commission.

Sheffield University Institute of Education (1961) *RI in Secondary Schools: A Summary and a Syllabus.* London: Nelson.

Shulik, R. (1977) 'Faith Development, Moral Development, and Old Age' PhD dissertation, Chicago University.

Shulik, R. and Kohlberg, L. (1980) 'The Aging Person as Philosopher: Development in Adult Years' unpublished paper, Harvard Moral Education Center.

Siegel, P. N. (1986) *The Meek and the Militant: Religion and Power Across the World.* London: Zed Books.

Skinner, B. F. (1948) 'Superstition in the Pigeon', *Journal of Experimental Psychology* **38**, 168–72.

Smart, N. (1958) *Reasons and Faiths.* London: Routledge & Kegan Paul.

—— (1968a). *The Yogi and the Devotee.* London: Allen & Unwin.

—— (1968b) *Secular Education and the Logic of Religion.* London: Faber.

—— (1969a) *Religious Experience of Mankind,* London: Fontana.

—— (1969b) 'Comparative Study of Religion in Schools' in Macy C, (ed.), *Let's Teach Them Right.* London: Pemberton, pp. 61–9.

—— (1970a) 'What is truth in RE?', *Learning for Living* **10**(1), 13–15.

—— (1970b) 'Religion as a Subject', *Church Quarterly Review* **23**, 227–33.

—— (1970c) 'The Structure of the Comparative Study of Religion', in Hinnells, J. R. (ed.) *Comparative Religion in Education* Newcastle: Oriel, pp. 20–31.

—— (1971) *The Phenomenon of Religion.* London: Macmillan.

—— (1972) *Guardian*, 29 August.

—— (1973a) *The Phenomenology of Religion.* London: Macmillan.

—— (1973b) *The Science of Religion and the Sociology of Knowledge: Some Methodological Questions.* Princeton, NJ: Princeton University Press.

—— (1975) 'The Exploration of Religion and Education', *Oxford Review of Education* **1**(2), 99–105.

—— (1983) *Worldviews: Crosscultural Explorations of Human Beliefs.* New York: Scribners.

—— (1989) *The World's Religions: Old Traditions and Modern Transformations.* Cambridge: Cambridge University Press.

—— (1996) *Dimensions of the Sacred: An Anatomy of the World's Beliefs.* London: HarperCollins.

—— (1999) *World Philosophies.* London: Routledge.

Smart, N. and Horder, D. (eds) (1975) *New Movements in Religious Education*, London: Temple Smith.

Smart, R. C. and Smart N. (1967) *Children: Development and Relationships.* New York: Macmillan.

Smith, D. E. (1963) *India as a Secular State.* Princeton, NJ: Princeton University Press.

—— (1971) *Religion, Politics and Social Change in the Third World.* New York: Free Press.

Smith, J. W. D. (1936) *Psychology and religion in early childhood* (revised edn. 1953) London: SCM Press.

Smith, K. N. (1969) *Themes.* London: Macmillan.

Smith, R. U. (ed.) (1972) *Religion and the Public School Curriculum.* New York: Religious Education Association.

Smith, W. C. (1962) *The Meaning and End of Religion* New York, Macmillan.

—— (1979) *Faith and Belief.* Princeton, NJ: Princeton University Press.

Smurl, F. (1972) *Religious Ethics: A Systems Approach.* NJ: Englewood Cliffs Prentice-Hall.

Souper, P. C. (1972) *The spiritual Dimension of Education.* Southampton: University Press.

Spiro, M. E. (1966) 'Religion: Problems of Definition and Explanation', in Banton, M. (ed.) *Anthropological Approaches to the Study of Religion*, London: Tavistock Publications, pp. 85–126.

—— (1982) *Buddhism and Society.* Berkeley: California University Press.

Stephens, D. (ed.) (1991) *RE, Attainment and National Curriculum*, Lancaster: Religious Education Council of England and Wales.

Stopford, R. (1966) 'Christian Education and Christian Unity', in Wedderspoon, A. (ed.) *RE 1944–84*, London, Allen & Unwin pp. 11–29.

Streng, F. J. (1973) *Ways of Being Religious.* Englewood Cliffs, NJ: Prentice-Hall.

Swann, M. (1985) *Education for All. London:* HMSO.

Tansey, P. J. and Unwin, D. (1969a) *Simulation and Gaming in Education.* London: Methuen.

——— (1969b) 'Simulation, the Games Explosion', *Social Education* **33**(2), 175–99.

Taylor, J. (1976) *'The Half Way' Generation.* Slough: NFER.

Taylor, J. L. and Walford, R. (1972) *Simulation in the Classroom:* Part 3. Harmondsworth: Penguin.

Taylor, M. J. (1965) *Religious and Moral Education.* New York: Center for Applied Research in Education.

Thatcher, M. (1990) 'What the Prime Minister said', *Times Educational Supplement,* 20 April.

Thompson, P. (2003) *Whatever happened to Religious Education?* Cambridge: Lutterworth.

Tibawi, A. L. (1972) *Muslim Education: Its Tradition and Modernisation.* London: Luzac.

Tillich, P. (1957) *Systematic Theology* (Vol. 2), London: Nisbet.

——— (1959) 'Theology of Education', in *Theology of Culture.* Oxford: Oxford University Press.

——— (1963a) *Systematic Theology* (Vol. 3). London: Nisbet.

——— (1963b) *Christianity and the Encounter of the World Religions.* New York: Columbia University Press.

——— (1963c) *Morality and Beyond.* New York: Harper & Row.

——— (1966) *The Future of Religions.* New York: Harper & Row.

Titmuss, R. (1970) *The Gift Relationship: From Human Blood to Social Policy.* London: Allen & Unwin.

Towler, R. (1974) *Homo Religiosus.* London: Constable

Townsend, H. E. R. and Brittan, E. M. (1973) *Multi-racial education: need and innovation.* London: Evans/Methuen Educational.

Tracy, D. (1975) *Blessed Rage for Order.* New York: Seabury Press.

——— (1981) *The Analogical Imagination.* New York: Crossroad.

Trevelyan, G. M. (1944) *English Social History.* London: Longman.

Turiel, E. (2003) 'Resistance and Subversion in Everyday Life', *Journal of Moral Education,* **32**(2), 115–30.

United Nations (2001) *Crossing the Divide: Dialogue among Civilisations* South Orange, NJ: Seton Hall University.

Vaux, R. de (1961) *Ancient Israel. Life and Institutions.* London: Darton, Longman & Todd.

Vidler, A. (1964) 'The Future of Divinity', in Plumb, J. H. (ed.) *Crisis in the Humanities.* Harmondsworth: Penguin, pp. 82–95.

Waddington, R. (1984) *Future in Partnership.* London: National Society.

Wainright, A. (1968) 'RE in the English Examination System', in Moray House College of Education *Curriculum and Examinations in R.E.* Edinburgh: Oliver & Boyd.

Wallwork, E. (1980) 'Morality, religion and Kohlberg's theory', in Munsey, B. (ed.) *Moral Development, Moral Education, and Kohlberg.* Birmingham AL: Religious Education Press, pp. 269–97.

Warshaw, T. (1964) 'Studying the Bible in Public School', *English Journal,* 53(2).

Webster, D. (1974) 'School Worship – The Way Ahead?', *Learning for Living* 14(2).

Webster, J. (1962) 'Teaching the Gospel', *Learning for Living* 2(1).

Weller, P. (ed.) (1997) *Religions in the UK: A Multifaith Directory* (2nd edn). Derby: University of Derby and Inter Faith Network.

———— (2001) *Religions in the UK: A Multi-Faith Directory* (3rd edn). Derby, University of Derby: Multi-Faith Centre.

Welsh Office (1975) *Education Survey, No. 3, Religious Education in the Secondary Schools of Wales.* Cardiff: HMSO.

West Glamorgan LEA (1979) *County Survey of RE* Swansea.

West Riding of Yorkshire County Council Education Department (1966) *West Riding Agreed Syllabus: Suggestions for Religious Education.* Wakefield.

Wheldon, H. (1972) *Observer,* 19 March.

Whitney, J. R. (1972) 'Religion in Public Schools: Some Pluralist Arguments for Religious Studies in the Public School Curriculum', *Bulletin,* Council on Study of Religion 3(2), 15–20.

Williams, J. G. (1957) *Worship and the Modern Child.* London: SPCK.

Williams, N. (1969) 'Children's moral thought. Part 1: Categories of moral thought', *Moral Education'* 1(1); 'Part II: Towards a theory of moral development', *Moral Education* 1(2).

Williams, N. and Williams, S. (1970) *The Moral Development of Children.* London: Macmillan.

Williams, R. (1961) *The Long Revolution.* London: Chatto & Windus.

———— (1971) 'A Theory of God-concept Readiness', *Religious Education.* LXVI(1), New York: Religious Education Association,

Wilson, B. (1966) *Religion in Secular Society.* London: Watts.

Wilson, J. et al. (1968), *Introduction to Moral Education,* Harmondsworth: Penguin.

Wilson, J. (1971) *Education in Religion and the Emotions.* London: Heinemann.

———— (1972) *Practical Methods of Moral Education.* London: Heinemann.

Wright, D. (1972) 'A Review of Empirical Studies in the Psychology of Religion', *ARE Bulletin,* Extended Supplement 1.

# Subject Index

# Name Index